ALSO BY AMERICA'S TEST KITCHEN

PRAISE FOR AMERICA'S TEST KITCHEN

"A mood board for one's food board is served up in this excellent guide . . . This has instant classic written all over it."
Publishers Weekly (starred review) on *Boards: Stylish Spreads for Casual Gatherings*

"In this latest offering from the fertile minds at America's Test Kitchen the recipes focus on savory baked goods. Pizzas, flatbreads, crackers, and stuffed breads all shine here . . . Introductory essays for each recipe give background information and tips for making things come out perfectly."
Booklist (starred review) on *The Savory Baker*

"Reassuringly hefty and comprehensive, *The Complete Autumn and Winter Cookbook* by America's Test Kitchen has you covered with a seemingly endless array of seasonal fare . . . This overstuffed compendium is guaranteed to warm you from the inside out."
NPR on *The Complete Autumn and Winter Cookbook*

Selected as the Cookbook Award Winner of 2021 in the General Category
International Association of Culinary Professionals (IACP) on *Meat Illustrated*

Selected as the Cookbook Award Winner of 2021 in the Single Subject Category
International Association of Culinary Professionals (IACP) on *Foolproof Fish*

"The book's depth, breadth, and practicality makes it a must-have for seafood lovers."
Publishers Weekly (starred review) on *Foolproof Fish*

"Another flawless entry in the America's Test Kitchen canon, *Bowls* guides readers of all culinary skill levels in composing one-bowl meals from a variety of cuisines."
BuzzFeed Books on *Bowls*

"*The Perfect Cookie* . . . is, in a word, perfect. This is an important and substantial cookbook . . . If you love cookies, but have been a tad shy to bake on your own, all your fears will be dissipated. This is one book you can use for years with magnificently happy results."
Huffpost on *The Perfect Cookie*

Selected as the Cookbook Award Winner of 2019 in the Health and Special Diet category
International Association of Culinary Professionals (IACP) on *The Complete Diabetes Cookbook*

"If you're one of the 30 million Americans with diabetes, *The Complete Diabetes Cookbook* by America's Test Kitchen belongs on your kitchen shelf."
Parade.com on *The Complete Diabetes Cookbook*

"True to its name, this smart and endlessly enlightening cookbook is about as definitive as it's possible to get in the modern vegetarian realm."
Men's Journal on *The Complete Vegetarian Cookbook*

"The book offers an impressive education for curious cake makers, new and experienced alike. A summation of 25 years of cake making at ATK, there are cakes for every taste."
The Wall Street Journal on *The Perfect Cake*

MODERN
BISTRO

Home Cooking Inspired
by French Classics

AMERICA'S TEST KITCHEN

Library of Congress Cataloging-in-Publication Data has been applied for

ISBN 978-1-948703-46-8

AMERICA'S TEST KITCHEN
21 Drydock Avenue, Boston, MA 02210

Printed in Canada
10 9 8 7 6 5 4 3 2 1

Distributed by Penguin Random House
Publisher Services
Tel: 800.733.3000

Pictured on front cover Pan-Roasted Filets Mignons with Garlic-Herb Butter (page 144), Potato Galette (page 250), Bibb and Frisée Salad with Radicchio and Hazelnuts (page 64), Roasted King Trumpet Mushrooms (page 240)

Pictured on back cover Galettes Complètes (page 264), Bistro Burgers with Pâté, Figs, and Watercress (page 134), White Chocolate Mousse with Raspberry Sauce (page 305)

Editorial Director, Books **Adam Kowit**

Executive Food Editor **Dan Zuccarello**

Deputy Food Editors **Leah Colins and Stephanie Pixley**

Executive Managing Editor **Debra Hudak**

Book Editor **Kaumudi Marathé**

Test Cooks **Sāsha Coleman, Olivia Counter, Jacqueline Gochenouer, Eric Haessler, and Hisham Hassan**

Assistant Editor **Emily Rahravan**

Editorial Support **Valerie Cimino, Katrina Munichiello, April Poole, and Rachel Schowalter**

Library Intern **Hannah Appleby-Wineberg**

Design Director, Books **Lindsey Timko Chandler**

Associate Art Director **Molly Gillespie**

Photography Director **Julie Bozzo Cote**

Senior Photography Producer **Meredith Mulcahy**

Senior Staff Photographers **Steve Klise and Daniel J. van Ackere**

Staff Photographer **Kevin White**

Additional Photography **Carl Tremblay and Joseph Keller**

Food Styling **Joy Howard, Sheila Jarnes, Catrine Kelty, Chantal Lambeth, Gina McCreadie, Kendra McNight, Ashley Moore, Christie Morrison, Marie Piraino, Elle Simone Scott, Kendra Smith, and Sally Staub**

Project Manager, Creative Operations **Katie Kimmerer**

Senior Print Production Speciaist **Lauren Robbins**

Production and Imaging Coordinator **Amanda Yong**

Production and Imaging Specialists **Tricia Neumyer and Dennis Noble**

Copy Editor **Cheryl Redmond**

Proofreader **Vicki Rowland**

Indexer **Elizabeth Parson**

Chief Creative Officer **Jack Bishop**

Executive Editorial Directors **Julia Collin Davison and Bridget Lancaster**

contents

WELCOME TO AMERICA'S TEST KITCHEN

This book has been tested, written, and edited by the folks at America's Test Kitchen, where curious cooks become confident cooks. Located in Boston's Seaport District in the historic Innovation and Design Building, it features 15,000 square feet of kitchen space including multiple photography and video studios. It is the home of *Cook's Illustrated* magazine and *Cook's Country* magazine and is the workday destination for more than 60 test cooks, editors, and cookware specialists. Our mission is to empower and inspire confidence, community, and creativity in the kitchen.

We start the process of testing a recipe with a complete lack of preconceptions, which means that we accept no claim, no technique, and no recipe at face value. We simply assemble as many variations as possible, test a half-dozen of the most promising, and taste the results blind. We then construct our own recipe and continue to test it, varying ingredients, techniques, and cooking times until we reach a consensus. As we like to say in the test kitchen, "We make the mistakes so you don't have to." The result, we hope, is the best version of a particular recipe, but we realize that only you can be the final judge of our success (or failure). We use the same rigorous approach when we test equipment and taste ingredients.

All of this would not be possible without a belief that good cooking, much like good music, is based on a foundation of objective technique. Some people like spicy foods and others don't, but there is a right way to sauté, there is a best way to cook a pot roast, and there are measurable scientific principles involved in producing perfectly beaten, stable egg whites. Our ultimate goal is to investigate the fundamental principles of cooking to give you the techniques, tools, and ingredients you need to become a better cook. It is as simple as that.

To see what goes on behind the scenes at America's Test Kitchen, check out our social media channels for kitchen snapshots, exclusive content, video tips, and much more. You can watch us work (in our actual test kitchen) by tuning in to *America's Test Kitchen* or *Cook's Country* on public television or on our websites. Listen to *Proof, Mystery Recipe*, and *The Walk-In* (AmericasTestKitchen.com/podcasts), to hear engaging, complex stories about people and food. Want to hone your cooking skills or finally learn how to bake—with an America's Test Kitchen test cook? Enroll in one of our online cooking classes. And you can engage the next generation of home cooks with kid-tested recipes from America's Test Kitchen Kids.

Our community of home recipe testers provides valuable feedback on recipes under development by ensuring that they are foolproof. You can help us investigate the how and why behind successful recipes from your home kitchen. (Sign up at AmericasTestKitchen.com/recipe_testing.)

However you choose to visit us, we welcome you into our kitchen, where you can stand by our side as we test our way to the best recipes in America.

facebook.com/AmericasTestKitchen
instagram.com/TestKitchen
youtube.com/AmericasTestKitchen
tiktok.com/@TestKitchen
twitter.com/TestKitchen
pinterest.com/TestKitchen

AmericasTestKitchen.com
CooksIllustrated.com
CooksCountry.com
OnlineCookingSchool.com
AmericasTestKitchen.com/kids

getting started

cooking that's coming home again:
an introduction to the bistro

The roots of bistro cooking come from a time when families in Paris brought renters into their homes, offering them room and board, and cooking meals for them, making the simple dishes familiar to them. Bistros then evolved into small neighborhood restaurants in Paris, often run by a husband and wife, one of whom cooked while the other managed front–of–house. Locals frequented these restaurants, assured of delicious, affordable fare (not haute cuisine), a good glass of wine, a welcoming host, and friendly fellow diners.

Hearty, flavorful, and satisfying, bistro fare is often spoken of as warmly as family and friends are. Food writer Patricia Wells describes the bistro as "a way of life," a representation of conviviality; people enjoying each other's company over shared food. The wine served is considered good but not expensive or rare. In fact, going to a bistro might feel like you are going to a dear friend's home for drinks and dinner.

By the time bistros made it across the pond to the United States, French bistro food—French onion soup, coq au vin, sole meunière, steak frites—had become iconic cooking thanks to the efforts of Julia Child, James Beard, Jacques Pépin, and others. Today, eating at a bistro stateside means you will find a mix of flavors on the menu, from French standards to American classics like burgers or mac and cheese. Often there are also Italian pasta dishes and food from other cuisines, like Moroccan tagines, all connected to each other by their heartiness and simplicity. Indeed, since bistro food stems from French family cooking, known as la cuisine française traditionnelle, wherever it comes from today, it is generous, simple, and replicable.

The recipes here represent our homage to the bistro, the iconic hangout of French origin. We've tested many French recipes over the years, so we decided to assemble an exciting collection for you to cook through. There is simple weeknight fare like Salade Niçoise (page 66) and Walk Away Ratatouille (page 210) and fun projects to try when you have time, like Gnocchi à la Parisienne with Pistou (page 214) or Authentic Baguettes at Home (page 294). There are classic hearty bistro dishes like Carbonnade à la Flamande (page 150) and Cassoulet (page 161) that your family will love, and of course, tempting desserts such as Profiteroles with Chocolate Sauce (page 306) or silken Grand Marnier Soufflé that will wow your guests. Since chefs are always tweaking their menus, using interesting global ingredients from harissa and gochujang to soy sauce and miso inventively, we offer our tweaks too, from Chive-Lemon-Miso Compound Butter (page 15) to serve with steak and chicken to Braised Lamb Shanks with Bell Peppers and Harissa (page 158) and Pink Pickled Turnips to serve on a Charcuterie Board (page 43) or with our Creamy Cauliflower Soup with Hawaij (page 82).

This collection will show you how to braise, sear, sauté, and confit in true French bistro style, with the scientific underpinnings of these techniques. We confit much more than duck, using the technique to successfully preserve turkey thighs as well as fennel, and we take the kneading out of bread making by using a long hydration instead.

If you want to host an oyster bar, a fondue evening, or a cocktail party with a charcuterie board, these recipes will get you there. And what would a bistro meal be without the right drink? Our apéritif recipes can accompany your brunch or appetizers, and we also suggest wine pairings for your main courses.

So we'll help you make your table that delicious place where everyone wants to linger. The joie de vivre is on you.

what goes into bistro food?

Today, we have the freedom to buy most fresh produce year-round, but many bistro classics were derived from a need to use what was available and in season and, in the days before refrigeration, to preserve ingredients for as long as possible. By cooking what was seasonal, the French used ingredients in their prime, whether it was mâche (lamb's lettuce) growing wild in a field, asparagus in the springtime, celery root and lentils in the less-abundant fall, or seafood caught that very day.

If not to be used immediately, ingredients were preserved. Summer herbs were dried and made into a blend employed the rest of the year to flavor food. We know one of these blends as herbes de Provence, which brought forth the aromas of summer in the dead of winter. Duck was confited and put away for later use; fruits were turned into jam or preserves. Pâté and rillettes preserved chicken and meat; smoking had the same effect on fish.

Using and preserving ingredients happened in other ways too: modest bits of meats were cooked with spices and herbs, and leftovers were creatively converted into something new. When people grew their own food or had to spend hard-earned money to buy it at the weekly market, nothing could be thrown out. If a rooster or hen got old, it was butchered and made into coq au vin using handy red or white wine, or it found itself in a stockpot being cooked into stock or broth. Potatoes left over after dinner were sautéed with onions and garnished with parsley the next day, a dish that became famous as potatoes Lyonnaise. If bits of beef needed using up, in the South of France they became a stew called daube Provençale, which derived its flavors from slow cooking as well as from mushrooms, garlic, and local ingredients such as briny niçoise olives, bright tomatoes, floral orange zest, fresh thyme, and bay leaves. The trick was to make it all taste irresistibly good.

bistro ingredients 101

ANCHOVIES

The French love to use these little fish in sauces, stews, and dressings. Their distinctly salty, pungent profile mellows in the food they are cooked with and adds a deeply savory quality that amplifies the flavor of the other ingredients without making the dish taste fishy.

BLACK PEPPER

Ground black pepper, one of the world's most ubiquitous and well-loved spices, holds a place of honor next to salt on restaurant tables and at kitchen work-stations, thanks to its balanced heat and earthiness. It's long been an important part of French cuisine and appears in bistro recipes like steak au poivre, which bears its name. All true peppercorns are harvested from *Piper nigrum*, a vining plant native to the Indian state of Kerala on the Malabar coast. Peppercorns have been cultivated and used in Indian cooking since 2000 BCE and heavily traded throughout Europe and Asia since 100 CE.

CAPERS

Capers are the edible flower buds of the caper bush, pickled and used as a seasoning. If a bud is not harvested, it forms a purple flower. After it wilts, the stigma that's left behind grows into a fruit called a caperberry. The French like salty, lightly acidic capers in sauces and salads, and they can be stirred whole into dishes or sprinkled over a finished dish as garnish.

DUCK FAT

Fatty acids give fat its particular flavor profile, but in unrefined animal fat, when these acids are exposed to heat, they oxidize to form new flavor compounds that improve flavor and add complexity. In refined oils like olive oil, many volatile fatty acids and aroma compounds have been stripped away to make a neutral tasting fat. We like the rich taste of duck fat in our Carbonnade à la Flamande (page 150) and Duck Fat–Roasted Potatoes (page 253).

HERBES DE PROVENCE

An aromatic blend from the south of France, herbes de Provence may be the one most commonly associated with French food. It combines dried lavender flowers with rosemary, sage, thyme, marjoram, and fennel, and sometimes chervil, basil, tarragon, or savory. A natural partner for poultry and pork, herbes de Provence is worth trying in an herb butter to brush under turkey or chicken skin before roasting the bird. You can use a readymade blend, of course (smell to ensure it is still fragrant and potent), or make your own (page 21).

LARDONS

These thick batons of bacon are used by French cooks in dishes including salade lyonnaise, coq au vin, and boeuf bourguignon. Lardons are often sliced from ventreche, an unsmoked, salt-cured rolled style of bacon. Since ventreche isn't readily available in the United States, we chose the best substitute: pancetta.

DIJON MUSTARD

Dijon mustard is not the only mustard made in France, but it is certainly the best known. Named after the Burgundy town of Dijon, the center of mustard making in France in the Middle Ages, prepared mustard simply consists of mustard seeds, white wine or wine vinegar, water, and salt. Creamy or grainy, with more body than conventional yellow mustard, Dijon packs a wallop of clean, nose-tingling heat. The French use it in everything from vinaigrettes and dips to pan sauces and glazes for roasted meats, fish, and vegetables.

OLIVES

France is known for several varieties of olive, like picholine, a torpedo-shaped green olive; Nyons, a black olive also known as Tanche, from the town of Nyons; and the most famous, niçoise, from Nice. In our recipes, niçoise olives star in Salade Niçoise (page 66) and you will find olives as a counterpoint to rich cheese and hearty meats on charcuterie and cheese boards.

RED AND WHITE WINE VINEGARS

As vinegars go, red and white wine varieties are utility players, especially in France. Neither is as distinct in flavor as Spain's sherry vinegar or Italy's balsamico, but that's exactly what makes them valuable pantry staples; a good version of either can deliver a jolt of clean acidity and balanced fruity sweetness to just about any dish. The advantage of white wine vinegar is that it doesn't impart color to dishes, so we use its crisp acidity to brighten pan sauces for chicken and fish.

SAFFRON

Sometimes known as "red gold," saffron is the world's most expensive spice. The delicate stigmas of *Crocus sativus* flowers must be harvested by hand in a painstaking process, which is one of the reasons for the spice's costliness. Luckily, a little saffron goes a long way, adding a distinct reddish-gold color, notes of honey and grass, and a slight hint of bitterness to dishes like Bouillabaisse (page 196) or Saffron Rouille (page 18).

VADOUVAN

The English colonized India but the French had colonized parts of the subcontinent long before they arrived. One of the things the French took back to France from India was a blend of ground spices they called vadouvan. We offer a recipe for it (page 245) and a dish to use it in: Sautéed Radishes with Vadouvan and Almonds (page 244).

twelve bistro techniques to master

Apart from giving us a profusion of recipes, French cuisine has given us techniques like cooking en cocotte, sautéing, confit, and flambéing. Here are some you will master with the recipes in this book:

Fold a Tender Omelet
Use a pan that's the right size; stir and tilt to form curds; set the egg; then fold and ease your omelet (page 260) onto a plate.

Dress a Salad Right
Whisk a vinaigrette, make warm dressings, or dress ingredients separately for some salads (Salade Niçoise, page 66) so components are well coated but stay vibrant.

Simmer Complex Soups and Stews
Cook it low and slow, whether it's bouillabaisse, beef bourguignon, or Coq au Vin (page 104), to flavor meat and add rich depth.

Sear a Perfect Bistro Steak
Sear steaks slowly to get a good sear on both sides. After cooking, make sure the meat rests to allow juices to redistribute so it is juicy-tender.

Put a Burnished Crust on Sole Meunière and Other Seafood
Salt, rest, then wipe seafood dry before searing it in a hot pan for the golden brown color you love.

Roast Crisp-Skinned Chicken, and Duck, Too
Butterfly chicken so it cooks and crisps evenly. Salt and refrigerate duck before roasting and give the thighs a head start on cooking.

Make a Confit of It
Preserve duck thighs in duck fat (Duck Confit, page 124). Then try our Turkey Thigh Confit with Citrus Mustard Sauce (page 128) and Fennel Confit (page 236), too.

Double-Fry for the Crispiest Frites
Deep-fry your french fries, tossed in cornstarch, before cooking your steak. Then fry the potatoes again for crisp, crunchy fries that are tender inside.

Master Butter & Egg Sauces
Whisk together a silky butter sauce (Beurre Blanc, page 192) using a whisk, but go modern with a blender to make egg sauces like hollandaise and mayonnaise quickly.

Whip Airy Soufflés
Make sure to use an equal number of whites and yolks for savory cheese or sweet Grand Marnier souf-flés to get the right rise and richness.

Shuck Oysters for your Own Raw Bar
Use the right tool, an oyster knife. Learn the best way to crush ice, too.

Unmold a Caramelized Tarte Tatin
Cool the tarte for 20 to 30 minutes so you can flip it out safely onto a plate.

kitchen tools

All kitchen tasks go better when you use well-designed equipment. Some you need repeatedly, others you might consider having on hand for making baguettes, piping pâte a choux, and so on. Here are some of our faves.

CUTTING

A good chef's knife (**Victorinox Swiss Army Fibrox Pro 8-Inch Chef's Knife**) is indispensable for precision work such as mincing a shallot and heavy-duty jobs such as breaking down a butternut squash. When we need control, a paring knife (**Victorinox Swiss Army Fibrox Pro 3¼" Spear Point Paring Knife**) is more maneuverable and hugs curves better. We use it for scoring chicken skin, piercing boiled potatoes to gauge doneness, coring tomatoes, and peeling fruits and vegetables. A mandoline allows us to slice fruit and vegetables more precisely, consistently, quickly, and thinly than a chef's knife. Some mandolines also have julienning attachments. We use our **Super Benriner Mandoline Slicer** or the **OXO Good Grips Chef's Mandoline Slicer 2.0** to thinly slice celery for Bibb and Frisée Salad with Grapes and Celery (page 64). Though we like a vegetable peeler to shave carrots for our Carrot and Smoked Salmon Salad (page 72), a mandoline works, too.

WHISKING, KNEADING, MIXING

Traditionally, whisks were used in France to whip cream, whisk eggs, make a vinaigrette or sauce. We use them for whisking butter into Beurre Blanc (page 192) and making stovetop custards. But to make perfect mayonnaise, purée soups such as Creamy Cauliflower Soup with Hawaij (page 82), and more, we turn to our winning blender, the **Vitamix 5200**. For a less expensive option, we like the **Breville Fresh and Furious**. We use a stand mixer to whip egg whites into stiff peaks for omelets and soufflés. And our food processor makes kitchen tasks faster and easier, whether it's chopping vegetables, kneading bread dough, making bread crumbs, or grinding beef for our Grind-Your-Own Sirloin Burger Blend (page 133).

COOKING

Apart from the traditional cooking vessels in our kitchens, we like having ramekins (**Le Creuset Stackable Ramekin**) and a soufflé dish (**HIC 64 Ounce Soufflé**) handy to use for soufflés, pots de crèmes, and crème brûlées. We love our winning 8-inch nonstick skillet, the **OXO Good Grips Hard Anodized Pro Nonstick 8-inch Fry**, for instance, for making, folding, and releasing omelets onto a plate beautifully, like our Omelet with Cheddar and Chives (page 258).

BAKING

These tools are essential: a rolling pin (**J.K. Adams Plain Maple Rolling Dowel**) to roll out dough for tarts; pie plates for Quiche Lorraine (page 274) and Potato Galette (page 250); a loaf pan for No-Knead Brioche Sandwich Loaf (page 292); and baking sheets for Fennel, Olive, and Goat Cheese Tart (page 38). Also handy are a pastry brush (**Ateco 1.5" Flat Stainless Steel Ferrule Pastry Brush, BPA-free**) and a pastry bag fitted with the appropriate-size tip, the most efficient tool for piping uniformly sized mounds of dough for Gougères (page 31) and filling Profiteroles (page 306) with cream. And if you want to try making baguettes, buy a good **couche**. We like **San Francisco Baking Institute's Linen Couche, 18" Wide**.

SEAFOOD

If you like cooking seafood, having two good fish spatulas is essential, and nonstick is best. We like the **Matfer Bourgeat Exoglass Pelton Spatula**. Have clean dish cloths handy to use while debearding mussels or shucking oysters. Use a wide, lipped platter for serving oysters on ice and make sure to have plenty of crushed ice on hand (for more on crushing ice, turn to page 49). Now all you need is an oyster knife. Regular knives are unsuitable because they're too sharp and flexible; the thick, dull blades of oyster knives function as levers to pry shells apart without cutting into them. A slightly upturned tip, like in our winner **R. Murphy New Haven Oyster Knife with Stainless Steel Blade**, is helpful when inserting the point into the oyster hinge, and it's able to slice oyster muscle without damaging the meat.

MISCELLANEA

A kitchen is filled with miscellaneous tools that are important for cooking. For this book, we share three: a mallet, a meat pounder, and a thermometer. A smooth mallet is useful for pitting niçoise olives for Chicken Provençal with Saffron, Orange, and Basil (page 114) and crushing ice to make a bed for Oysters on the Half Shell (page 48). We use a meat pounder (**Norpro Grip EZ Meat Pounder**) to flatten boneless pieces of meat or poultry into evenly thin cutlets like those for Chicken Paillard (page 102), so that they can cook through quickly and consistently. And a good thermometer takes the guesswork out of cooking, telling you exactly what's going on inside your food whether you are deep-frying or making custard. Old dial-faced thermometers are slow and imprecise: Digital is the only way to go and **ThermoWorks Thermapen ONE** remains our go-to.

last but not least:
wine & cheese

WINE IN YOUR GLASS

Wine is often used in French cooking (Wine in the Kitchen, page 154) and also serves as a drink at mealtime. At a bistro, you will likely find Chablis, from the northernmost region of Burgundy; Beaujolais; and wines from the Loire Valley, such as Cabernet Franc, on the menu. These are great food wines with moderate alcohol, acidity, and minerality. But you don't have to drink only French wines with bistro food, you can enjoy wines such as an American Pinot Noir or an Italian Soave, too.

Here are some tips to help you decide what to drink or serve:

Remember not to buy low-quality wines for cooking. A good rule of thumb is to cook with wines you would like to drink, but not very expensive ones. If you are cooking with a certain wine for a dish, say Burgundy for beef bourguignon, you could pair your meal with that wine. In fact, if you are not using the entire bottle for a recipe, measure out what you need and sip the rest as you cook!

If what you plan to eat is fatty, it will pair well with tannic wines—imagine Steak Frites with Cabernet Sauvignon or Bordeaux with Filet Mignon. Fatty foods also work very well with high-acid wines, which is why Champagne is so great with fried treats. Wine is also the perfect accompaniment for oysters; try a sparkling wine for a celebratory sip.

If your food is salty, high-acid wines like Chablis or Muscadet make an excellent pairing as do off-dry wines like a Halbtrocken Riesling.

The saying goes, "What grows together, goes together." Often this is true, so if you are making a bouillabaisse from Provence, you might serve a hearty Provencal rosé like Bandol, which can hold up to the stew's intense flavors.

Forget the red with meat, white with fish rule. Drink the wine you like with the food you like; just choose a wine that will complement what you're serving. For instance, if you want to serve a red wine with your fish, try a lighter-bodied red like a Gamay.

If you're serving something sweet, pair it with an acidic wine, and vice versa. Try a Sancerre or a Muscat with dessert. Or buy an Italian Vermentino, which is high-acid and also fruit-forward.

You don't have to break the bank to buy good wine. Look for a shop curated by someone who cares about wine. Don't be afraid to tell the staff what you are planning to serve and ask for their suggestions.

If you have time, bring home some of their recommended wines and taste them before your next dinner party. That way, you'll know what you like. If you don't want to be disappointed, don't serve a wine to your guests that you haven't tasted.

And of course, before you serve red wine, open the bottle and let the wine breathe. Pouring it into a carafe is a great way to let it breathe, too.

FRENCH CHEESE ON YOUR PLATE

The cheese you buy from France may have a certification of authenticity and a label of quality (like the ones given to wines, butter, and other agricultural products) granted by the French government. They indicate a tradition and quality worth recognizing. There are thought to be over 1,600 cheeses produced in France, but only about 50 of them have this certification. Legend has it that the start of certification, sometimes called Appellation d'Origine Contrôlée (AOC), dates back to the 15th century when the production of Roquefort cheese began to be regulated by the French government.

1 Fresh Cheeses

The most well-known fresh cheese may be Boursin. Neither it, nor other fresh cheeses, are cooked or aged, and they have no rind. While Boursin is industrially produced, every region of France boasts its own farm-produced fresh cheeses.

2 Soft Cheeses

Apart from Brie (lush, buttery), Camembert (soft, creamy), and Époisses (runny; pungent), soft cheeses include Munster (yes, it is French!), and Pont-l'Évêque. These cheeses are unpressed, have a soft rind, and are delectable with baguettes or crudités.

3 Semi-Soft Cheeses

Cheeses such as Raclette, Morbier, and Reblochon (page 218) are defined by their moisture content. Soft but not runny, they have a buttery taste and texture. Mild flavored, they can be salty, too. Brie and Camembert are sometimes also classified as semi-soft cheeses.

4 Firm/Hard Cheeses

The terms "firm" and "hard" are often used interchangeably for cheese. If you consider a cheese like Parmesan hard, then the term "firm" makes sense for cheeses like Gruyère (Swiss) and Comté (French), both used for fondue, while "hard" describes Mimolette, a snacking cheese.

5 Blue Cheeses

There are many blue cheeses made around France, but the most well-known may be soft, crumbly, salty Roquefort; the cow's milk cheese, Saint-Augur from Auvergne; and a goat's milk cheese called Bleu de Chèvre.

chapter one

butter, sauces & seasonings

———————

CULTURED BUTTER

makes: about 2 cups butter and about 2 cups buttermilk

total time: 45 minutes, plus 24 hours to 1 week resting

With the help of friendly bacteria, you can make rich, tangy butter that's a lot more interesting than store-bought sticks. All it takes is cream, some starter culture like buttermilk, and time. The flavor is so fabulous you'll want to make it again and again. You'll also get buttermilk out of the process, to use in your biscuits and pancakes. The tangy, complex-tasting cultured butter can make even a simple baguette taste special, but it's especially good mixed with chives for our Baguette with Radishes, Butter, and Herbs (page 24). We prefer the taste of butter made with pasteurized cream as opposed to ultrapasteurized cream. The ideal temperature range for churning butter is 55 to 60 degrees; colder and the fat is too firm and will stick to the sides of the food processor bowl; warmer and the fat is liquid instead of solid, leading to greasy butter. In step 2, chill the cream in the refrigerator or over an ice bath. For the most complex, tangy flavor, we recommend aging the cream for a week. At that point, the cream may smell quite pungent, but most of what you smell resides in the liquid that gets separated out, leaving the butter surprisingly mellow. This recipe requires cheesecloth.

    4   cups pasteurized heavy cream
    2   tablespoons buttermilk
    ¼   teaspoon table salt (optional)

1   Combine cream and buttermilk in clean lidded container. Cover container and let sit at room temperature until mixture smells tangy and buttery and thickens to sour cream–like consistency, at least 24 hours or up to 1 week.

2   Chill cream mixture to 55 to 60 degrees.

3   Process cream mixture in food processor until mixture turns from grainy whipped cream to lumps of butter splashing in liquid, 1 to 3 minutes. Stop processor immediately.

4   Fill medium bowl halfway with ice and water. Line fine-mesh strainer with triple layer of cheesecloth, leaving few inches of cloth hanging over sides of strainer, and set over large bowl. Drain butter mixture in prepared strainer (buttermilk will collect in bowl). Lift cheesecloth by edges and twist and squeeze tightly over strainer to press out more buttermilk (stop when butter starts to squeeze through cheesecloth). Transfer cheesecloth-wrapped butter to ice bath until firm around exterior, about 2 minutes. Transfer buttermilk to airtight container.

5   Remove butter from cheesecloth and transfer to now-empty bowl. Stir and press with wooden spoon (metal utensil will conduct heat from your hands and make butter soft) to force out additional buttermilk from butter, 1 to 2 minutes. Drain buttermilk from bowl, add to buttermilk container, and refrigerate until ready to use. Knead salt, if using, into butter with wooden spoon. Transfer butter to second airtight container and refrigerate until ready to use. (Butter can be refrigerated for up to 2 months.)

Butter Culture

Around the world, butter made in the traditional way starts by mixing a starter culture, buttermilk or yogurt, into cream. Live bacteria from the buttermilk start to work in the cream, fermenting some of the lactose sugar into lactic acid, which gives it a distinctive tanginess and thickens it slightly. After a day, the cultured cream is ready to go into the churn. Historically, culturing wasn't something you did to make your butter better. It was just what happened. If you were a farmer with a cow or two, it's likely you needed a few days' worth of cow's milk to amass enough cream for a batch of butter. As your bucket of cream sat around, waiting in vain for refrigeration to be invented, wild bacteria naturally found their way into it and soured it a bit, which jump-started the butter-making process.

COMPOUND BUTTER

makes: about ½ cup

total time: 10 minutes, plus 10 minutes resting

Use storebought butter or homemade Cultured Butter (page 14) to make this aromatic butter.

Whip 8 tablespoons softened unsalted butter in bowl with fork until light and fluffy. Mix in one of the following ingredient combinations and season with salt and pepper to taste. Cover in plastic wrap and let rest so flavors blend, about 10 minutes, or roll into log and refrigerate. (Butter can be refrigerated in airtight container for up to 4 days or frozen, wrapped tightly in plastic wrap, for up to 2 months.)

ingredient combinations

CHIVE-LEMON MISO

¼ cup white miso

2 teaspoons grated lemon zest plus 4 teaspoons juice

¼ teaspoon pepper

¼ cup minced fresh chives

PARSLEY-CAPER

¼ cup minced fresh parsley

4 teaspoons capers, rinsed and minced

PARSLEY-LEMON

¼ cup minced fresh parsley

4 teaspoons grated lemon zest

TARRAGON-LIME

¼ cup minced scallion

2 tablespoons minced fresh tarragon

4 teaspoons lime juice

rolling compound butter into a log

1. Use spatula to place butter-herb mixture on piece of plastic wrap. Roll into log.

2. Twist ends of plastic wrap around cylinder of herb-butter mixture and refrigerate or freeze.

3. Slice unwrapped refrigerated or frozen cylinder of herb-butter mixture into even pieces to use.

CRÈME FRAÎCHE

makes: about 1 cup

total time: 10 minutes, plus 12 hours setting

This dairy product, whose name means "fresh cream" in French, is actually a kind of soured cream. Crème fraîche is made by adding cultures to heavy cream that has as much as 45 percent butterfat and fermenting it until it achieves a lush, fluid consistency with subtle tang and complex, nutty notes. In France, the bacteria present in unpasteurized cream naturally thicken and ferment the dairy. Crème fraîche's high fat content means that, unlike sour cream, it won't curdle when exposed to high temperatures. You can substitute it in equal amounts in almost any application calling for heavy cream, and when whipped, it holds air as well as whipped cream does. We use it to add creaminess in soups, top smoked salmon, and dollop on fruit or desserts such as Gâteau Breton with Apricot Filling (page 312).

- 1 cup pasteurized heavy cream (avoid ultra-pasteurized)
- 2 tablespoons buttermilk

Stir together cream and buttermilk. Cover and place in warm location (75 to 80 degrees is ideal; lower temperatures will lengthen fermentation time) until thickened but still pourable, 12 to 24 hours. Store crème fraîche in a sealed container in the refrigerator for up to 1 month.

MAKE-AHEAD HOMEMADE MAYONNAISE

makes: about 1½ cups

total time: 15 minutes

The custardy richness and delicate tang of homemade mayonnaise lights up anything it touches. We make this French condiment for use in sandwiches, on burgers, and in bistro fare such as Apple-Fennel Rémoulade (page 61). Making a batch takes minutes, most of the work can be done in a food processor, and there's a good chance you have all the ingredients on hand. Pitfalls? Homemade mayonnaise is prone to "breaking," meaning that the oil and water fail to emulsify and remain a runny, greasy mess instead of forming a thick, creamy spread. And, unlike commercial mayonnaise that's made with pasteurized eggs, homemade versions are typically prepared with unpasteurized raw eggs. But ours can be stored for one month because it's made with pasteurized egg yolks, achieved using a simple microwave method that heats the yolks to 160 degrees. Mixing the yolks with water and lemon juice keeps the egg base fluid even though it has been heated. Immediately whisking oil into that base cools it and prevents it from overthickening. At the same time, whisking breaks the oil into tiny droplets, the critical starting point for any mayo. Since the oil is a major part of this recipe, use a freshly opened bottle for the best results. This recipe was designed to be made in a food processor; we don't recommend substituting other appliances.

- 3 tablespoons water
- 2 large egg yolks
- 4 teaspoons lemon juice
- 1½ cups vegetable oil, divided
- ¾ teaspoon table salt
- ½ teaspoon Dijon mustard
- ¼ teaspoon sugar

1 Gently stir water, egg yolks, and lemon juice in bowl until no streaks of yolk remain. Microwave, stirring gently every 10 seconds, until mixture thickens slightly and registers 160 to 165 degrees, 1 to 2 minutes. Immediately add ¼ cup oil, salt, mustard, and sugar; whisk to combine. (Tiny droplets of oil will float to top of mixture.)

2 Strain mixture through fine-mesh strainer into bowl of food processor. With processor running, slowly drizzle in remaining 1¼ cups oil in thin stream, about 2 minutes. Scrape bottom and sides of bowl and process 5 seconds longer. Transfer to airtight container and refrigerate for up to 1 month.

the most reliable way to make mayo

One of the biggest deterrents to making mayonnaise is that it can fail to form an emulsion, creating a greasy, runny mess. Here is our solution.

1. Whisk In Some Oil
Incorporating the first ¼ cup of oil by hand reliably establishes a base emulsion.

2. Process Remaining Oil
Slowly incorporating the rest of the oil using a food processor breaks the oil into tiny droplets that stay well emulsified.

AÏOLI

makes: about 1½ cups

total time: 10 minutes

The word 'aïoli' is derived from the French word 'ail', meaning garlic, and 'oli' which is Provençal for oil. Aïoli, a garlicky mayonnaise, traditionally makes use of raw, minced garlic, from which it proudly gets its defining flavor. It is by tradition the centerpiece of a modest supper served with cooked vegetables, potatoes, and steamed fish. When properly made, aïoli is delightfully smooth and simple since it consists of only a few ingredients (olive oil, garlic, egg yolk, and lemon juice) and it makes a delicious sauce for the fries in Steak Frites (page 142). Using a whole egg makes our aïoli recipe extra-foolproof, ensuring that the volume of ingredients in the processor is large enough for the blades to catch. For a well-seasoned, flavorful (but not distracting or overpowering) sauce, we add a relatively small amount of peppery, fruity extra-virgin olive oil to the more neutral-tasting vegetable oil. Do not, however, substitute olive oil for the vegetable oil; the aïoli will turn out bitter.

1 large egg

4 teaspoons lemon juice

1½ teaspoons Dijon mustard

1 garlic clove, minced

¾ teaspoon table salt

¼ teaspoon sugar

Pinch cayenne pepper

1½ cups vegetable oil

2 tablespoons extra-virgin olive oil

Process egg, lemon juice, mustard, garlic, salt, sugar, and cayenne in food processor until combined, about 5 seconds. With processor running, slowly drizzle in vegetable oil until emulsified and mixture is thick, about 2 minutes. Scrape down sides of bowl with rubber spatula and continue to process 5 seconds longer. Transfer to airtight container and whisk in olive oil. Cover and refrigerate until ready to use. (Aïoli can be refrigerated for up to 1 week.)

SAFFRON ROUILLE

makes: about 1 cup

total time: 30 minutes

Rouille is a kind of mayonnaise often made with eggs, garlic, and saffron. It is believed to have gotten its name from the color that saffron brings to it because the word "rouille" means "rust" in French and the sauce is indeed rusty orange in color. Bread-thickened rouille is often used in bouillabaisse, as in our Chicken Bouillabaisse with Saffron Rouille (page 116). The egg yolk in this recipe is not cooked. If you prefer, 2 tablespoons Egg Beaters may be substituted. For an accurate measurement of boiling water, bring a kettle of water to a boil and then measure out the desired amount.

- 3 tablespoons boiling water, plus extra cold water as needed
- ¼ teaspoon saffron threads, crumbled
- 1 (3-inch) piece baguette, crusts removed, torn into 1-inch pieces (1 cup)
- 4 teaspoons lemon juice
- 1 large egg yolk
- 2 teaspoons Dijon mustard
- 1 garlic clove, minced
- ¼ teaspoon cayenne pepper
- ½ cup vegetable oil
- ½ cup extra-virgin olive oil

1   Combine boiling water and saffron in medium bowl and let steep for 5 minutes. Stir in baguette and lemon juice and let soak for 5 minutes; transfer to blender. Add egg yolk, mustard, garlic, and cayenne and process until uniform paste forms, about 1 minute, scraping down sides of blender jar as needed.

2   With blender running, slowly add vegetable oil and olive oil and process until sauce is emulsified, about 2 minutes. Adjust consistency with extra cold water as needed. Season with salt and pepper to taste. (Rouille can be refrigerated for up to 3 days.)

RED PEPPER ROUILLE

makes: about 1 cup

total time: 45 minutes

Another rouille version, popularized by Julia Child, uses red bell pepper to add body and color to the sauce instead of eggs and saffron. We like it for a variety of soups and stews. Cooking times vary, depending on the broiler, so watch the pepper carefully as it roasts. This rouille does not hold well, so make it on the day that you are planning to serve it.

- 1 large red bell pepper, stemmed, seeded, ribs removed, and cut to lie flat
- 2 ounces country-style French bread, trimmed of crust and cut into large cubes (2 cups)
- 2 garlic cloves, minced
- ⅛ teaspoon cayenne pepper
- ½ cup extra-virgin olive oil

1   Adjust oven rack 3 inches from broiler element and heat broiler. (If necessary, set overturned rimmed baking sheet on oven rack to elevate baking sheet.) Line baking sheet with aluminum foil.

2   Place bell pepper on prepared sheet and broil until skin is charred and puffed but flesh is still firm, 5 to 7 minutes, rotating sheet halfway through cooking. Transfer bell pepper to bowl, cover with foil, and let steam until skin peels off easily, 10 to 15 minutes. Peel and discard skin. Cut bell pepper into large pieces.

3   Process bread cubes, garlic, cayenne, and bell pepper in food processor until smooth, about 20 seconds. With processor running, slowly drizzle in oil; process until rouille has thick, mayonnaise-like consistency. Season with salt to taste.

FOOLPROOF HOLLANDAISE

makes: about 1¼ cups

total time: 10 minutes

Creamy, lemony hollandaise is a versatile and impressive way to elevate more than just brunch. The silky sauce makes an elegant, classic accompaniment to luxurious beef steaks or slices of holiday-worthy roasts, and can be used as a dip for poached shrimp, dolloped on roasted poultry, or drizzled over roasted asparagus. Hollandaise is notoriously finicky and prone to breaking because it requires butter to be emulsified into egg yolks. A stable hollandaise can be achieved the old-fashioned way with a double boiler, slow cooking, and constant monitoring, but we found the best way to make it foolproof was to use the blender. Slowly adding hot, melted butter (it needs to be 180 degrees to cook the eggs properly) into a mixture of egg yolks, lemon juice, and cayenne while the blender is running successfully creates a thick and creamy emulsion.

- 3 large egg yolks
- 2 tablespoons lemon juice
- ¼ teaspoon table salt
  - Pinch cayenne pepper, plus extra for seasoning
- 16 tablespoons unsalted butter, melted and hot (180 degrees)

Process egg yolks, lemon juice, salt, and cayenne in blender until frothy, about 10 seconds, scraping bottom and sides of blender jar as needed. With blender running, slowly add hot melted butter and process until hollandaise is emulsified, about 2 minutes. Adjust consistency with hot water as needed until sauce drips slowly from spoon. Season with salt and extra cayenne to taste. Serve immediately.

variation

FOOLPROOF SAFFRON HOLLANDAISE

Add ⅛ teaspoon crumbled saffron threads to blender with egg yolks.

MINT PERSILLADE

makes: about 1½ cups

total time: 20 minutes

Persillade, a French parsley ("persil" in French) sauce, gets a minty take here.

- 2½ cups fresh mint leaves
- 2½ cups fresh parsley leaves
- 6 garlic cloves, peeled
- 6 anchovy fillets, rinsed and patted dry
- 2 teaspoons grated lemon zest plus 2½ tablespoons juice
- ½ teaspoon table salt
- ⅛ teaspoon pepper
- ¾ cup extra-virgin olive oil

1 Pulse mint, parsley, garlic, anchovies, lemon zest, salt, and pepper in food processor until finely chopped, 15 to 20 pulses. Add lemon juice and pulse briefly to combine.

2 Transfer mixture to medium bowl and slowly whisk in oil until incorporated. Cover and let sit at room temperature for at least 1 hour to allow flavors to meld. Season with salt and pepper to taste. (Sauce can be refrigerated for up to 2 days. Bring to room temperature and whisk to recombine before serving.)

CHERMOULA

makes: about 1½ cups

total time: 10 minutes, plus 1 hour resting

This cilantro-garlic dressing makes a flavorful accompaniment to fish, chicken, and our Cauliflower Salad with Moroccan Chermoula (page 74).

2¼ cups fresh cilantro leaves

8 garlic cloves, minced

1½ teaspoons ground cumin

1½ teaspoons paprika

½ teaspoon cayenne pepper

½ teaspoon table salt

6 tablespoons lemon juice (2 lemons)

¾ cup extra-virgin olive oil

1 Pulse cilantro, garlic, cumin, paprika, cayenne, and salt in food processor until coarsely chopped, about 10 pulses. Add lemon juice and pulse briefly to combine.

2 Transfer mixture to medium bowl and slowly whisk in oil until incorporated. Cover and let sit at room temperature for at least 1 hour to allow flavors to meld. Season with salt and pepper to taste. (Sauce can be refrigerated for up to 2 days. Bring to room temperature and whisk to recombine before serving.)

GREEN ZHOUG

makes: about ½ cup

total time: 15 minutes

Zhoug is an Israeli hot sauce that can be either red or green. Our vibrant green version is made with fresh herbs, chiles, and spices. We use it to garnish our Creamy Cauliflower Soup with Hawaij (page 82) and also like it with fish or drizzled on soups or sandwiches.

6 tablespoons extra-virgin olive oil

½ teaspoon ground coriander

¼ teaspoon ground cumin

¼ teaspoon ground cardamom

¼ teaspoon table salt

Pinch ground cloves

¾ cup fresh cilantro leaves

½ cup fresh parsley leaves

2 green Thai chiles, stemmed and chopped

2 garlic cloves, minced

1 Microwave oil, coriander, cumin, cardamom, salt, and cloves in covered bowl until fragrant, about 30 seconds; let cool to room temperature.

2 Pulse oil-spice mixture, cilantro, parsley, chiles, and garlic in food processor until coarse paste forms, about 15 pulses, scraping down sides of bowl as needed. (Zhoug can be refrigerated for up to 4 days.)

CARAMELIZED ONION JAM

makes: about 1 cup

total time: 1 hour

We like the savory sweetness and rich color of caramelized onion jam atop our French Onion Burgers (page 132) but its flavor and thick, spreadable texture make it a delicious addition to any burger or sandwich.

- 3 tablespoons extra-virgin olive oil
- 1¼ pounds onions, halved and sliced thin
- 1 bay leaf
- ½ teaspoon minced fresh rosemary
- ½ teaspoon table salt
- ¼ teaspoon pepper
- 2 garlic cloves, peeled and smashed
- ¼ cup balsamic vinegar
- ¼ cup water
- 2 tablespoons sugar

1 Heat oil in Dutch oven over medium-high heat until shimmering. Add onions, bay leaf, rosemary, salt, and pepper. Cover and cook, stirring occasionally, until onions have softened, about 10 minutes.

2 Stir in garlic. Reduce heat to medium-low and cook, uncovered, scraping up any browned bits, until onions are golden brown, about 15 minutes.

3 Stir in vinegar, water, and sugar, scraping up any browned bits. Increase heat to medium-high and simmer until mixture is thickened and rubber spatula or wooden spoon leaves distinct trail when dragged across bottom of pot, about 2 minutes.

4 Discard bay leaf. Transfer onion mixture to food processor and pulse to jam-like consistency, about 5 pulses. Transfer onion jam to airtight container and let cool to room temperature. (Onion jam can be refrigerated for up to 4 days.)

HERBES DE PROVENCE

makes: about 2½ tablespoons

total time: 5 minutes

This French-inspired mix of dried herbs, which commonly includes rosemary, marjoram, thyme, lavender, and fennel (see more on page 5) lends a balanced, aromatic flavor to anything from poultry or pork to roasted potatoes. Most supermarkets sell this herb blend. If you want to make your own, here's our formula. If you can't find dried lavender, feel free to omit it altogether.

- 2 teaspoons dried marjoram
- 2 teaspoons dried thyme
- 1 teaspoon dried basil
- 1 teaspoon dried rosemary, crumbled
- 1 teaspoon dried sage
- ¼ teaspoon dried lavender (optional)
- ⅛ teaspoon ground fennel

Combine all ingredients in bowl. Store at room temperature in airtight container for up to 1 year.

chapter two

snacks & small plates

———————

COCKTAILS & RECIPE EXTRAS

BAGUETTE WITH RADISHES, BUTTER, AND HERBS

serves: 8 to 12

total time: 20 minutes

10 tablespoons European-style unsalted butter or Cultured Butter (page 14), softened

6 tablespoons minced fresh chives, divided

¼ teaspoon table salt

¼ teaspoon pepper

1 teaspoon lemon juice

1 teaspoon extra-virgin olive oil

1 cup coarsely chopped fresh parsley

1 (18-inch) baguette, halved lengthwise

8 ounces radishes, trimmed and sliced thin

Flake sea salt

why this recipe works   This French snack is rustic and chic. The fact that it is also supereasy makes it perfect for a spur-of-the-moment cocktail evening. Crusty baguette, farm-fresh radishes, and butter are a time-tested combination. We halve a baguette lengthwise and lay down just enough butter on top to coat both halves. We shingle thinly sliced radishes in a fish-scale pattern on the sliced, buttered bread. Easter egg and watermelon radishes are especially pretty. To complement their pepperiness, we top the baguette with a parsley salad, which also creates visual contrast and welcome brightness. And to finish, a generous sprinkle of sea salt. The success of this recipe depends on high-quality ingredients, including fresh baguette, good butter, and in-season radishes. We love this made with either European-style unsalted butter or Cultured Butter.

1   Combine butter, ¼ cup chives, salt, and pepper in bowl. Whisk remaining 2 tablespoons chives, lemon juice, and oil in second bowl. Add parsley and toss to coat. Season with salt and pepper to taste.

2   Spread butter mixture over cut sides of baguette. Shingle radishes evenly over butter and top with parsley salad. Sprinkle with flake sea salt to taste.

3   Cut baguette crosswise into 12 pieces. Serve.

LILLET TONIQUE

makes: 1 cocktail

total time: 5 minutes

Low-alcohol cocktails like Lillet Tonique have long been enjoyed in Europe during the predinner hour. Lillet Tonique was also popular at New York City parties in the 1970s, and low-alcohol drinks like it are rising in popularity again. This cocktail uses Lillet Blanc, a fortified wine from France that's aromatized with citrus and herbs. Lillet Blanc is similar to vermouth in that its alcohol content is greater than that of wine but less than that of a liqueur or spirit. Its formula dates back to the 1870s and originally contained quinine, the ingredient that makes tonic water bitter and is used to ward off malaria. Quinine was removed in the 1980s, making the current iteration of Lillet lighter and more citrus-forward. Traditionally Lillet is served on its own over ice as an aperitif. To make a cocktail with sharpness to complement our appetizers, we added the quinine back in, with tonic water. We garnish it with a lemon slice, to enhance the wine's citrus notes.

3 ounces Lillet Blanc

3 ounces tonic water, chilled

Lemon slice

Fill chilled wine glass halfway with ice. Add Lillet and tonic water and stir to combine using bar spoon. Using spoon, gently lift Lillet mixture from bottom of glass to top to combine. Top with additional ice and garnish with lemon slice. Serve.

GRUYÈRE, MUSTARD, AND CARAWAY CHEESE COINS

serves: 10 to 12 (makes 80 coins)

total time: 40 minutes, plus 1 hour chilling, 30 minutes cooling time

why this recipe works   Try this simple cheesy cracker with a glass of wine or munch it as a snack. Nutty Gruyère and whole-grain mustard give it French flair, and the food processor helps to combine the dry ingredients and the shredded cheese, keeping our cheese coins tender by limiting the handling of the dough. Adding a little cornstarch with the flour further ensures that the coins bake up flaky and buttery. We process the dry ingredients, add mustard and process again until the dough comes together. We roll the dough into logs, refrigerate them until firm, then slice them into thin coins before baking until lightly golden and perfectly crisp. If you like, serve these crackers with a dip or Baked Brie with Honeyed Apricots (page 28).

- 8 ounces Gruyère, shredded (2 cups)
- 1½ cups (7½ ounces) all-purpose flour
- 1 tablespoon cornstarch
- 1 teaspoon caraway seeds
- ½ teaspoon table salt
- ¼ teaspoon cayenne pepper
- ¼ teaspoon paprika
- 8 tablespoons unsalted butter, cut into 8 pieces and chilled
- ¼ cup whole-grain mustard

1   Process Gruyère, flour, cornstarch, caraway, salt, cayenne, and paprika in food processor until combined, about 30 seconds. Scatter butter pieces over top and process until mixture resembles wet sand, about 20 seconds. Add mustard and process until dough forms ball, about 10 seconds. Transfer dough to counter and divide in half. Roll each half into 10-inch log, wrap in plastic wrap, and refrigerate until firm, at least 1 hour.

2   Adjust oven racks to upper-middle and lower-middle positions and heat oven to 350 degrees. Line 2 rimmed baking sheets with parchment paper. Unwrap logs and slice into ¼-inch-thick coins, giving dough quarter turn after each slice to keep log round. Place coins on prepared sheets, spaced ½ inch apart.

3   Bake until light golden around edges, 22 to 28 minutes, switching and rotating sheets halfway through baking. Let coins cool completely on sheets before serving.

BAKED BRIE WITH HONEYED APRICOTS

serves: 8 to 10

total time: 30 minutes

¼ cup chopped dried apricots

¼ cup honey, divided

1 teaspoon minced fresh rosemary

¼ teaspoon table salt

¼ teaspoon pepper

2 (8-ounce) wheels firm Brie cheese, rind removed, cheese cut into 1-inch pieces

1 tablespoon minced fresh chives

why this recipe works   Baked Brie topped with jam or fruit is popular for good reason. When the cheese is warmed, it becomes rich and gooey, and pairing it with sweet fruit brings out the savory notes in the cheese. For sweet and creamy flavor in every bite, we reengineer the traditional whole wheel of baked Brie by trimming off the rind (which doesn't melt that well) and cutting the cheese into cubes. This allows our honey-apricot mixture to be evenly distributed throughout this deconstructed version of the dish, not just spooned on top. We bake the cheese in a cast-iron skillet: Since cast iron holds on to heat so well, it keeps the cheese in the ideal luscious, fluid state for serving, too. An extra drizzle of honey and some minced chives at the finish reinforce the sweet-savory flavor profile. Be sure to use a firm, fairly unripe Brie for this recipe. Serve with baguette, crackers, or Melba toast.

1   Adjust oven rack to middle position and heat oven to 400 degrees. Microwave apricots, 2 tablespoons honey, rosemary, salt, and pepper in medium bowl until apricots are softened and mixture is fragrant, about 1 minute, stirring halfway through microwaving. Add Brie and toss to combine.

2   Transfer mixture to 10-inch cast-iron skillet and bake until cheese is melted, 10 to 15 minutes. Drizzle with remaining 2 tablespoons honey and sprinkle with chives. Serve.

GOUGÈRES

serves: 10–12 (makes 24 puffs)

total time: 1¼ hours

2 large eggs plus 1 large white

¼ teaspoon table salt

½ cup water

2 tablespoons unsalted butter,
cut into 4 pieces

Pinch cayenne pepper

½ cup (2½ ounces) all-purpose flour

4 ounces Gruyère cheese, shredded
(1 cup)

Smooth Tops, Unburnt Bottoms

Smooth Puffs
Use the back of a spoon lightly coated
with vegetable oil spray to smooth
away any creases and large peaks on
each mound of dough.

No Burnt Bottoms
Bake gougères on the upper rack to
mitigate the bottoms' exposure to
heat. Or place one rimmed baking
sheet into another, to create a thin air
gap between sheets that keeps the top
sheet cooler. If you don't have two
sheets, create multiple tiny air gaps by
lining your baking sheet with crinkled
foil before covering it with parchment.

why this recipe works   Made from choux paste enriched with
cheese, gougères hail from Burgundy and are an ideal nibble to pair
with a glass of red wine. A perfect gougère has a caramel-colored,
crisp exterior that yields to a tender, slighty moist interior. An extra
egg white in the batter ups the protein for more structure, resulting
in an airier puff, and the water creates more steam for increased
height. The puffs can be made in advance and recrisped. Use a
Gruyère aged for about one year. Doubled baking sheets prevent
overbrowning the undersides of the puffs. In step 4, the dough
can be piped using a pastry bag fitted with a ½-inch plain tip.

1   Adjust oven rack to upper-middle position and heat oven to
425 degrees. Line rimmed baking sheet with parchment paper and
set in second rimmed baking sheet. In 2-cup liquid measuring cup,
beat eggs and white and salt until well combined. (You should
have about ½ cup egg mixture. Discard excess.) Set aside.

2   Heat water, butter, and cayenne in small saucepan over medium
heat. When mixture begins to simmer, reduce heat to low and
immediately stir in flour using wooden spoon. Cook, stirring constantly, using smearing motion, until mixture is very thick, forms
ball, and pulls away from sides of saucepan, about 30 seconds.

3   Immediately transfer mixture to food processor and process
with feed tube open for 5 seconds to cool slightly. With processor
running, gradually add reserved egg mixture in steady stream,
then scrape down sides of bowl and add Gruyère. Process until
paste is very glossy and flecked with coarse cornmeal–size pieces
of cheese, 30 to 40 seconds. (If not using immediately, transfer
paste to bowl, press sheet of greased parchment directly on
surface, and store at room temperature for up to 2 hours.)

4   Scoop 1 level tablespoon of dough. Using second small spoon,
scrape dough onto prepared sheet into 1½-inch-wide, 1-inch-tall
mound. Repeat, spacing mounds 1 to 1¼ inches apart. (You should
have 24 mounds.) Using back of spoon lightly coated with vegetable
oil spray, smooth away any creases and large peaks on each mound.

5   Bake until gougères are puffed and upper two-thirds of each
are light golden brown (bottom third will still be pale), 14 to
20 minutes. Turn off oven; leave gougères in oven until uniformly
golden brown, 10 to 15 minutes (do not open oven for at least
8 minutes). Transfer gougères to wire rack and let cool for
15 minutes. Serve warm. (Cooled gougères can be stored in airtight container at room temperature for up to 24 hours or frozen
in zipper-lock bag for up to 1 month. To serve, crisp gougères in
300-degree oven for about 7 minutes.)

GOCHUJANG AND CHEDDAR PINWHEELS

serves: 6 to 8 (makes 18 pinwheels)

total time: 40 minutes,
plus 1 hour chilling

1 (9½ by 9-inch) sheet puff
  pastry, thawed

2 tablespoons gochujang paste

2 ounces sharp cheddar cheese,
  shredded (½ cup)

3 tablespoons minced fresh
  chives, divided

1 tablespoon sesame seeds

1 large egg beaten with 1 teaspoon water

why this recipe works At your next cocktail party, these gorgeous bites will deliver oomph: The spicy, sweet, umami savoriness of Korean gochujang (chile paste) combines with the flakiness of puff pastry, the creamy sharpness of cheddar, and the crunch of chives and sesame seeds for a morsel that guests will find irresistible. Sliced into thin rounds and baked, these two-bite swirls are crispy and cheesy, bursting with heat, nuttiness, and a hint of sweetness. Be sure to use gochujang paste, which comes in a tub, instead of gochujang sauce, which comes in a bottle and has a different consistency. Convenient store-bought puff pastry works wonderfully for these quick pinwheels. To thaw frozen puff pastry, let it sit either in the refrigerator for 24 hours or on the counter for 30 minutes to 1 hour.

1 Dust counter lightly with flour. Unfold puff pastry and roll into 10-inch square. Spread gochujang paste evenly over entire surface of pastry, leaving ½-inch border along top edge. Sprinkle evenly with cheddar, 2 tablespoons chives, and sesame seeds. Gently roll rolling pin over toppings to press into pastry.

2 Starting at edge of pastry closest to you, roll into tight log and pinch seam to seal. Wrap in plastic wrap and refrigerate until firm, about 1 hour. (Rolled pastry log can be refrigerated for up to 2 days before slicing and baking.)

3 Adjust oven rack to middle position and heat oven to 400 degrees. Line rimmed baking sheet with parchment paper and set in second rimmed baking sheet. Using sharp serrated or slicing knife, trim ends of log, then slice into ½-inch-thick rounds (you should have 18 rounds) and space them about 1 inch apart on prepared sheet.

4 Brush pastries with egg wash and bake until golden brown and crispy, 14 to 16 minutes, rotating sheet halfway through baking. Transfer pinwheels to wire rack, sprinkle with remaining 1 tablespoon chives, and let cool for 5 minutes. Serve warm or at room temperature.

FRENCH KISS

makes: 1 cocktail

total time: 5 minutes

The simple, refreshing cocktail made with equal parts sweet and dry vermouth makes a delicate, understated partner to our deeply flavorful bites. The French Kiss is often made with champagne and the sweetness of St. Germain or Chambord. We like the simplicity of a drink that stars just vermouth and allows the food to shine.

1½ **ounces sweet vermouth**

1½ **ounces dry vermouth**

Lemon twist

Add vermouths to mixing glass, then fill three-quarters full with ice. Stir until mixture is just combined and chilled, about 15 seconds. Strain cocktail into chilled old-fashioned glass half-filled with ice or containing 1 large ice cube. Garnish with lemon twist and serve.

PISSALADIÈRE

serves: 4 to 6 (makes two
14 by 8-inch tarts)

total time: 2¾ hours, plus
24 hours chilling

dough

- 3 cups (16½ ounces) bread flour
- 2 teaspoons sugar
- ½ teaspoon instant or rapid-rise yeast
- 1⅓ cups ice water
- 1 tablespoon extra-virgin olive oil
- 1½ teaspoons table salt

toppings

- ¼ cup extra-virgin olive oil, divided
- 2 pounds onions, halved and sliced ¼ inch thick
- 1 teaspoon packed brown sugar
- ½ teaspoon table salt
- 1 tablespoon water
- ½ cup pitted niçoise olives, chopped coarse, divided
- 8 anchovy fillets, rinsed, patted dry, and chopped coarse, divided plus 12 fillets for garnish, divided (optional)
- 2 teaspoons minced fresh thyme, divided
- 1 teaspoon fennel seeds, divided
- ½ teaspoon pepper, divided
- 2 tablespoons minced fresh parsley, divided

why this recipe works   Often eaten as an appetizer or a light supper with a salad, pissaladière is a pizza-like Provençal tart. It features salty black olives and anchovies on a backdrop of sweet caramelized onions and earthy fresh thyme on a wheaty crust that is part chewy pizza and part crunchy cracker. The tart is easy to prepare, provided each ingredient is handled carefully. We make the dough in a food processor and knead it just enough so that it has the structure to stand up to the toppings. To keep our crust thin and prevent it from bubbling, we poke it all over with the tines of a fork. Starting the onions covered and then uncovering them caramelizes and browns them perfectly, with no burning. A bit of water stirred in at the end of cooking keeps them from clumping when spread over the crust. To protect the black olives and thyme from burning in the oven, we spread them on the dough first and then cover them with the onions. Finally, we chop the anchovies to keep them from overpowering the other flavors. If you don't have a baking stone, bake the tarts on an overturned and preheated rimmed baking sheet set on the lowest oven rack. If desired, let the dough rise in the refrigerator for 8 to 16 hours in step 2; let the refrigerated dough soften at room temperature for 30 minutes before using.

1 **for the dough**   Pulse flour, sugar, and yeast in food processor until combined, about 5 pulses. With processor running, slowly add ice water and process until dough is just combined and no dry flour remains, about 10 seconds. Let dough rest for 10 minutes.

2   Add oil and salt to dough and process until dough forms satiny, sticky ball that clears sides of bowl, 30 to 60 seconds. Transfer dough to lightly floured counter and knead by hand to form smooth, round ball, about 30 seconds. Place dough seam side down in lightly greased large bowl or container, cover tightly with plastic wrap, and refrigerate for at least 24 hours or up to 3 days.

3 **for the toppings**   Heat 2 tablespoons oil in 12-inch nonstick skillet over medium heat until shimmering. Stir in onions, sugar, and salt. Cover and cook, stirring occasionally, until onions are softened and have released their juice, about 10 minutes. Remove lid and continue to cook, stirring often, until onions are golden brown, 10 to 15 minutes. Transfer onions to bowl, stir in water, and let cool completely before using.

4   One hour before baking, adjust oven rack 4 inches from broiler element, set baking stone on rack, and heat oven to 500 degrees. Press down on dough to deflate. Transfer dough to clean counter, divide in half, and cover loosely with greased plastic. Pat 1 piece of dough into 4-inch round (keep remaining piece covered). Working around circumference of dough, fold edges toward center until ball forms.

5   Flip ball seam side down and, using your cupped hands, drag in small circles on counter until dough feels taut and round and all seams are secured on underside. (If dough sticks to your hands, lightly dust top of dough with flour.) Repeat with remaining piece of dough. Space dough balls 3 inches apart, cover loosely with greased plastic, and let rest for 1 hour.

6   Heat broiler for 10 minutes. Meanwhile, generously coat 1 dough ball with flour and place on well-floured counter. Press and roll into 14 by 8-inch oval. Transfer oval to well-floured pizza peel and reshape as needed. (If dough resists stretching, let it relax for 10 to 20 minutes before trying to stretch it again.) Using fork, poke entire surface of oval 10 to 15 times.

7   Brush dough oval with 1 tablespoon oil, then sprinkle evenly with ¼ cup olives, half of chopped anchovies, 1 teaspoon thyme, ½ teaspoon fennel seeds, and ¼ teaspoon pepper, leaving ½-inch border around edge. Arrange half of onions on top, followed by 6 whole anchovies, if using.

8   Slide flatbread carefully onto baking stone and return oven to 500 degrees. Bake until bottom crust is evenly browned and edges are crisp, 13 to 15 minutes, rotating flatbread halfway through baking. Transfer flatbread to wire rack and let cool for 5 minutes. Sprinkle with 1 tablespoon parsley.

9   Heat broiler for 10 minutes. Repeat with remaining dough, oil, and toppings, returning oven to 500 degrees when flatbread is placed on stone. Slice and serve.

SOCCA WITH SAUTÉED ONIONS AND ROSEMARY

serves: 4 to 6 (makes four 10-inch pancakes)

total time: 1¼ hours

socca

1½ cups water

1⅓ cups (6 ounces) chickpea flour

¼ cup extra-virgin olive oil, divided, plus extra for drizzling

1 teaspoon table salt

¼ teaspoon ground cumin

sautéed onions

2 tablespoons extra-virgin olive oil

2 cups thinly sliced onions

½ teaspoon table salt

1 teaspoon chopped fresh rosemary

why this recipe works These thin, crisp, nutty-tasting chickpea pancakes are beloved in Nice and throughout the French Riviera, where they are a popular snack alongside a glass of chilled rosé. Socca is commonly made by pouring a thin layer of batter into a pan and putting it in a ripping-hot wood–fired oven till it gets browned and crisp. To enjoy the flatbread at home, we cook it like a crêpe in a nonstick skillet on the stove. Swirling the batter in the pan makes for even, golden socca. The snack is excellent with just a drizzle of extra-virgin olive oil and a sprinkling of flaked sea salt, but we add a topping of sautéed onions and rosemary. Chickpea flour is also sold as garbanzo flour; we don't recommend using besan or gram flour here. It's best to use a scale to weigh the flour for this recipe.

1 **for the socca** Adjust oven rack to middle position and heat oven to 200 degrees. Set wire rack in rimmed baking sheet and place in oven. Whisk water, flour, 4 teaspoons oil, salt, and cumin in bowl until no lumps remain. Let batter rest while preparing onions, at least 10 minutes. (Batter will thicken as it sits.)

2 **for the sautéed onions** Heat oil in 10-inch nonstick skillet over medium-high heat until just smoking. Add onions and salt and cook until onions start to brown around edges but still have some texture, 7 to 10 minutes. Add rosemary and cook until fragrant, about 1 minute. Transfer onion mixture to bowl; set aside. Wipe skillet clean with paper towels.

3 Heat 2 teaspoons oil in now-empty skillet over medium-high heat until just smoking. Lift skillet off heat and pour ½ cup batter into far side of skillet; swirl gently in clockwise direction until batter evenly covers bottom of skillet.

4 Return skillet to heat and cook socca, without moving it, until well browned and crisp around bottom edge, 3 to 4 minutes (you can peek at underside of socca by loosening it from side of skillet with heatproof spatula).

5 Flip socca with heatproof spatula and cook until second side is just cooked, about 1 minute. Transfer socca, browned side up, to prepared wire rack in oven. Repeat 3 more times, using 2 teaspoons oil and ½ cup batter per batch.

6 Transfer socca to cutting board and cut each into 8 wedges. Top with sautéed onions, drizzle with extra oil, sprinkle with flake sea salt, and serve.

FENNEL, OLIVE, AND GOAT CHEESE TARTS

serves: 4 (makes two tarts)

total time: 45 minutes

1 (9½ by 9-inch) sheet puff pastry, thawed and halved

1 large fennel bulb, stalks discarded, bulb halved, cored, and sliced thin

3 tablespoons extra-virgin olive oil, divided

3 garlic cloves, minced

½ cup pitted oil-cured black olives, chopped

1 teaspoon grated lemon zest plus 1 tablespoon juice

8 ounces goat cheese, softened

5 tablespoons chopped fresh basil, divided

¼ teaspoon pepper

why this recipe works These elegant rectangular tarts are so beautiful and satisfying, you'll want to make them for your next party. And they are so easy to prepare, you'll be making them again and again. We use store-bought puff pastry for the crust and parbake it so it can puff up nicely. Fresh anise-flavored fennel, which we precook in the microwave, combined with oil-cured olives, tangy goat cheese, thinned with olive oil and brightened with fresh basil, make a creamy, aromatic filling that contrasts nicely with the rich, flaky pastry. To keep the filling from falling out of the shell, we cut a border around the edges of the baked crusts and lightly press down on the centers to make neat beds for the filling. Just 5 minutes more in the oven heats the filling through and browns the crusts beautifully. To thaw frozen puff pastry, let it sit either in the refrigerator for 24 hours or on the counter for 30 minutes to 1 hour.

1   Adjust oven rack to middle position and heat oven to 425 degrees. Arrange puff pastry halves spaced evenly on parchment paper–lined rimmed baking sheet and poke pastry all over with fork. Bake pastry until puffed and golden brown, about 15 minutes, rotating sheet halfway through baking.

2   Meanwhile, microwave fennel, 1 tablespoon oil, and garlic in covered large bowl, stirring occasionally, until softened and fragrant, 5 to 7 minutes. Drain fennel mixture and return to now-empty bowl. Stir in olives and lemon juice and season with salt and pepper to taste. Combine goat cheese, ¼ cup basil, pepper, lemon zest, and remaining 2 tablespoons oil in separate bowl.

3   Using tip of paring knife, cut ½-inch-wide border around top edge of each pastry, then press centers down with your fingertips. Spread goat cheese mixture evenly over center of pastry shells, then spoon fennel mixture over top. Bake tarts until cheese is heated through and crust is deep golden brown, 5 to 7 minutes. Let tart cool on sheet for 5 minutes, then sprinkle with remaining 1 tablespoon basil. Slice and serve.

pork rillettes
(page 44)

pink pickled
turnips
(page 43)

marinated olives
(page 43)

chicken liver pâté
(page 42)

Charcuterie Board

Here are some tips to help you set out a sumptuous, inviting charcuterie board for your next party.

Buy Some

Spend on quality meat. Buy cold cuts (charcuterie) like prosciutto and Iberico ham, adding smoked salmon if you wish. Buy rustic bread or baguettes to slice and serve with the meat. Hearty rye or pumpernickel cocktail bread slices offer welcome variety. Keep bread covered to prevent it from drying out.

Make Some

Prepare some food at home, like our easy Chicken Liver Pâté that tastes like a lot of effort went into making it. If you have time, cook a project recipe like Pork Rillettes too.

Add Cheese

Serve cheese with charcuterie to create satisfying mouthfuls. Put out at least 2 cheeses (1 soft and 1 firm) to accommodate varied tastes. Choose cheeses from different parts of the world, French Camembert, Danish blue, and English cheddar, or cheeses with varied textures, like goat cheese, Manchego, and Mimolette (for more on French cheese, see page 11).

Now Some Color, Please

Complete your board by adding color and texture: Home-made or store-bought pickled olives, fresh or pickled vegetables, grapes or sliced melon, peaches, persimmons, and dried fruit such as apricots, dates, and cranberries, and your favorite nuts. You can add compound butters (page 15), cream cheese, and condiments like Dijon mustard, too.

Et Voilà, It's Party Time

When your guests arrive, welcome them with a cocktail, and let them dig in.

CHICKEN LIVER PÂTÉ

makes: about 2 cups

total time: 30 minutes, plus 6 hours cooling

Pâté, a purée of chicken livers, butter, and aromatics has a mellow flavor and a velvety texture that seems to melt on the tongue. To avoid the telltale chalky taste of overcooked livers, cook them until just rosy in the center. The exposed surface of pâté tends to oxidize quickly, discoloring and developing a slight metallic taste. Pressing plastic wrap flush against the surface of the pâté minimizes this effect. Any remaining discoloration can be easily scraped away before serving. Since livers, like all organ meats, are highly perishable, this pâté is best eaten soon after it is made.

- 8 tablespoons unsalted butter
- 3 large shallots, sliced
- 1 tablespoon minced fresh thyme
- ¼ teaspoon table salt
- 1 pound chicken livers, rinsed and patted dry, fat and connective tissue removed
- ¾ cup dry vermouth
- 2 teaspoons brandy

1 Melt butter in 12-inch skillet over medium-high heat. Add shallots, thyme, and salt and cook until shallots are lightly browned, about 5 minutes. Add chicken livers and cook, stirring constantly, about 1 minute. Add vermouth and simmer until livers are cooked but still have rosy interiors, 4 to 6 minutes.

2 Using slotted spoon, transfer livers to food processor, leaving liquid in skillet. Continue to simmer liquid over medium-high heat until slightly syrupy, about 2 minutes, then add to processor.

3 Add brandy to processor and process mixture until very smooth, about 2 minutes, stopping to scrape down sides of bowl as needed. Season with salt and pepper to taste, then transfer to bowl and smooth top. Press plastic wrap flush against surface of pâté and refrigerate until firm, at least 6 hours or up to 2 days. Let soften at room temperature for 30 minutes before serving.

MARINATED OLIVES

makes: about 2 cups

total time: 30 minutes, plus 4 hours marinating

Olives bring color and tart salty flavor to a charcuterie or cheese board. You can buy a wide variety of prepared olive products, but you can also easily make your own marinated olives with a lot more flavor and freshness. Make sure to bring the mixture to room temperature before serving or the oil will look cloudy and congealed.

 1 cup brine-cured green olives with pits
 1 cup brine-cured black olives with pits
 ¾ cup extra-virgin olive oil
 1 shallot, minced
 2 teaspoons grated lemon zest
 2 teaspoons minced fresh thyme
 2 teaspoons minced fresh oregano
 1 garlic clove, minced
 ½ teaspoon red pepper flakes
 ½ teaspoon table salt

Pat olives dry with paper towels. Toss with oil, shallot, lemon zest, thyme, oregano, garlic, pepper flakes, and salt in bowl. Cover and refrigerate for at least 4 hours or up to 4 days. Let sit at room temperature for at least 30 minutes before serving.

PINK PICKLED TURNIPS

makes: 4 cups

total time: 1 hour, plus 2 days pickling

This traditional Middle Eastern condiment adds color and tanginess to our charcuterie board. Turnips seasoned with garlic, allspice, and black peppercorns get a vibrant fuchsia hue from beets in the brine. They need to be refrigerated for two days to allow the brine to fully penetrate and pickle the vegetables. These pickles cannot be processed for long-term storage.

 1¼ cups white wine vinegar
 1¼ cups water
 2½ tablespoons sugar
 1½ tablespoons kosher salt
 3   garlic cloves, smashed and peeled
 ¾   teaspoon whole allspice berries
 ¾   teaspoon black peppercorns
 1   pound turnips, peeled and cut into 2 by ½-inch sticks
 1   small beet, trimmed, peeled, and cut into 1-inch pieces

1   Bring vinegar, water, sugar, salt, garlic, allspice, and peppercorns to boil in medium saucepan over medium-high heat. Cover, remove from heat, and let steep for 10 minutes. Strain brine through fine-mesh strainer, then return to saucepan.

2   Place two 1-pint jars in bowl and place under hot running water until heated through, 1 to 2 minutes; shake dry. Pack turnips vertically into hot jars with beet pieces evenly distributed throughout.

3   Return brine to brief boil. Using funnel and ladle, pour hot brine over vegetables to cover. Let jars cool to room temperature, cover with lids, and refrigerate for at least 2 days before serving. (Pickled turnips can be refrigerated for up to 1 month; turnips will soften over time.)

PORK RILLETTES

makes: 3 cups

total time: 5 hours

Rillettes (pronounced ree-yehts) are a meaty, rich, satisfying treat. Meat is braised till tender and easily shreddable, then beaten with fat to make the spread. The time spent is well worth it; you'll love the luscious hybrid of whipped pâté and Southern-style pulled pork, with fresh aromatic herbs thrown in. Rillettes are good for two weeks in the refrigerator, which lets you enjoy them in various ways: on a charcuterie board; in a sandwich; or as an afterschool snack on crackers, with tart cornichons or dill pickles.

- 5 teaspoons minced fresh thyme, divided
- 2 teaspoons kosher salt
- 2 teaspoons pepper
- 2 pounds boneless pork butt roast, pulled apart at seams, trimmed, and cut into 1-inch pieces
- 2 tablespoons unsalted butter, divided, plus 16 tablespoons melted and cooled, divided
- 1 onion, chopped
- 2 celery ribs, chopped
- 1 cup dry white wine
- 2 cups chicken broth
- 2 bay leaves
- 2 shallots, minced
- 2 tablespoons minced fresh chives
- 2 tablespoons minced fresh parsley

1 Combine 1 tablespoon thyme, salt, and pepper in large bowl. Add pork and toss to coat. Cover and refrigerate for 12 to 24 hours.

2 Adjust oven rack to lower-middle position and heat oven to 325 degrees. Melt 1 tablespoon butter in Dutch oven over medium heat. Add onion and celery and cook until softened and lightly browned, 5 to 7 minutes. Stir in wine, bring to simmer, and cook until almost completely evaporated, 6 to 8 minutes. Stir in broth and bring to simmer.

3 Pat pork dry with paper towels. Add pork and bay leaves to Dutch oven and return to simmer. Cover, transfer pot to oven, and cook until pork is tender and falls apart when prodded with fork, about 2 hours. Transfer pork to large plate and let cool to room temperature, about 30 minutes. Strain braising liquid through fine-mesh strainer into fat separator. Measure out and reserve ¼ cup of liquid from fat separator; discard remaining liquid and fat.

4 Meanwhile, melt 1 tablespoon butter in 10-inch skillet over medium heat. Add shallots and cook until softened, about 5 minutes. Stir in remaining 2 teaspoons thyme and cook until fragrant, about 30 seconds. Let cool to room temperature.

5 Using stand mixer fitted with paddle, mix cooled pork, 1 tablespoon reserved braising liquid, cooled shallot mixture, 8 tablespoons melted butter, chives, and parsley on low speed until meat shreds and mixture is cohesive, 1 to 2 minutes, adding remaining reserved braising liquid as needed. Season with salt and pepper to taste.

6 Spoon rillettes into four 8-ounce ramekins and smooth tops. Refrigerate until completely chilled and set, about 1 hour. Top chilled ramekins evenly with remaining 8 tablespoons melted butter to seal and return to refrigerator to set, about 1 hour. Bring to room temperature and stir in butter cap before serving. Sealed pork rillettes can be wrapped tightly and refrigerated for up to 2 weeks.

ANCHOÏADE

makes: about 1½ cups

total time: 45 minutes

¾ cup whole blanched almonds

20 anchovy fillets (1½ ounces), rinsed, patted dry, and minced

2 tablespoons raisins

2 tablespoons lemon juice, plus extra for seasoning

1 garlic clove, minced

1 teaspoon Dijon mustard

¼ teaspoon pepper

⅛ teaspoon table salt

¼ cup extra-virgin olive oil, plus extra for serving

1 tablespoon minced fresh chives, divided

why this recipe works   Bold anchovies aren't just for elegantly adorning dishes or for contributing brininess in small amounts. A Provençal favorite, anchoïade is a potently flavorful mixture of nutty anchovies (a lot of them), olive oil, and garlic that can be spread on toast or used as a dip. To make a smooth, anchovy-rich paste, we start by creating a creamy, neutral-flavored base with almonds. When boiled and puréed, the nuts take on a smooth consistency that helps keep our dip cohesive and provides richness without greasiness. We add the anchovy fillets to the softened almonds, along with raisins for subtle sweetness. Dijon mustard, garlic, and lemon juice round out the flavors. Because extra-virgin olive oil can become bitter if overprocessed, we wait until the dip is mostly smooth before slowly drizzling in the oil. Fresh chives and a final drizzle of olive oil are all this dip needs for a refined presentation to match its sophisticated anchovy flavor. Serve with slices of plain or toasted baguette or raw vegetables.

1   Bring 4 cups water to boil in medium saucepan over medium-high heat. Add almonds and cook until softened, about 20 minutes. Drain and rinse well.

2   Process drained almonds, anchovies, ¼ cup water, raisins, lemon juice, garlic, mustard, pepper, and salt in food processor to mostly smooth paste, about 2 minutes, scraping down sides of bowl as needed. With processor running, slowly add oil and process to smooth puree, about 2 minutes.

3   Transfer mixture to bowl, stir in 2 teaspoons chives, and season with salt and extra lemon juice to taste. (Dip can be refrigerated for up to 2 days; bring to room temperature before serving.) Sprinkle with remaining 1 teaspoon chives and drizzle with extra oil before serving.

OYSTERS ON THE HALF SHELL

serves: 2 or 3

total time: 15 minutes

3   pounds crushed ice

12   oysters, well scrubbed

How to Have Your Oyster...

SIP some of the liquor. It's OK to pour off some and also OK if some spills during shucking. SLURP the whole oyster into your mouth. CHEW it well so that you really get to taste it.

why this recipe works   There's nothing fancier than hosting an oyster raw bar shindig. But if you're unsure about how to shuck oysters (page 50) or unsure about how to serve them at home, we've got you covered. To serve oysters on the half shell the way they'd be served in a restaurant or raw bar, the first step is to crush ice by hand (page 49). You will also need an oyster knife and a large, deep, chilled serving platter. The ice chills the oysters and condiments and keeps the oysters securely nestled on the platter so that they don't tip. If you're serving the oysters with accompaniments, embed the serving bowl in the ice before filling it.

Arrange ice in even layer on chilled serving platter. Shuck 1 oyster and discard top shell; place oyster on ice, being careful not to spill much liquid. Repeat with remaining oysters.

LIME-AND-SOY-MARINATED SCALLIONS

serves: 8 (makes about ½ cup)

total time: 20 minutes

3   tablespoons lime juice (2 limes)
   2 scallions, sliced thin

1   tablespoon water

1   tablespoon soy sauce

½   teaspoon sugar

Stir all ingredients together and refrigerate for at least 15 minutes or up to 24 hours before serving.

RED WINE VINEGAR MIGNONETTE GRANITÉ

serves: 8 (makes about ⅔ cup)

total time: 10 minutes, plus 1 hour freezing

We froze that tart-sweet mignonette you enjoy on oysters and made it into a topping of flavorful ice flakes. For a traditional mignonette, skip the freezing and scraping steps; simply refrigerate the mixed ingredients for at least 30 minutes or up to two days, and serve chilled.

½   cup red wine vinegar

3   tablespoons water

2   teaspoons finely grated shallot

¾   teaspoon sugar

1   teaspoon coarsely ground pepper

In shallow bowl, stir together vinegar, water, shallot, and sugar. Freeze until fully frozen, at least 1 hour or up to 2 days. One hour before serving, place small serving bowl in freezer. To serve, scrape frozen mixture with fork to create ice crystals. Stir in pepper. Transfer to chilled serving bowl; serve or cover and freeze until ready to use.

The Best Way to Crush Ice Is by Hand

The best approach to crushing ice is the old-fashioned way: by hand. Fill a heavy-duty 1-gallon zipper-lock freezer bag about three-quarters full with ice cubes and press out as much air as possible before sealing. Wrap the bag tightly with a large dish towel. Then simply strike the wrapped bag with a mallet, skillet, or rolling pin to break the ice to the desired size. Don't use a pin made of softwood or one with ball bearings, as it could be damaged by the ice. You will need about 5 pounds to create a 1½-inch-thick layer of ice a rimmed baking sheet. This will keep about twenty-four 2½- to 3-inch oysters cold for about 30 minutes. If you're using a smaller platter, store extra ice in a colander set in a bowl in the fridge. Use this stash to refresh your oyster platter as needed.

how to shuck oysters

With an oyster knife, dish towel, and some practice, you'll be able to shuck safely and confidently.

1. Fold dish towel several times into thin, tight roll. Grip towel in fist of hand that will be holding oyster, wrapping 1 end over your thumb and tucking it between your thumb and forefinger.

2. Using your protected thumb, hold oyster in place with hinge facing away from thumb. Insert tip of oyster knife into hinge of oyster.

3. Work tip of knife into hinge using twisting motion. When shells begin to separate, twist knife to pop hinge.

4. Run knife along top shell, scraping abductor muscle from shell to release oyster. Slide knife under oyster to scrape abductor muscle from bottom shell.

How to Shop

There are five species of commercially cultivated oysters farmed in North American waters: Eastern, Pacific, European flat (also known as Belon), Kumamoto, and Olympia.

In Person

Specimens should be heavy for their size (a sign of freshness) and shut tight (or close up when you touch them).

Online

Oysters are increasingly available online directly from farmers, and they tolerate shipping exceptionally well because they can survive out of water for days as long as they're kept fridge-cold. Here are a few of our favorite purveyors and the oysters they offer.:

- Bon Secour Fisheries (Eastern)
- Real Oyster Cult (Eastern, Pacific)
- Taylor Shellfish Farms (Pacific, Kumamoto)

How to Store

Depending on the variety and freshness, oysters keep anywhere from a few days to a week as long as they're refrigerated. (Online sources often specify shelf life.) Keep them in a bowl covered with a damp towel, remoistening it as needed to prevent the oysters from drying out. Do not store oysters directly on or underneath ice; they will die in fresh water. (It's OK to place them on ice for serving.)

ROASTED OYSTERS ON THE HALF SHELL WITH MUSTARD BUTTER

serves: 4 to 6

total time: 55 minutes

Roasting is a great option if you're nervous about shucking or eating raw oysters, or simply want a new way to serve them on the half shell. Warming them in a hot oven makes them easier to shuck, and placing them on crumpled aluminum foil steadies the oysters so they don't tip over. Dolloped with mustard butter after shucking and returned to the oven to cook through, the oysters emerge plump, tender, and dressed with a punchy sauce. You need an oyster knife and a large serving platter for this recipe. Use oysters that are 2½ to 3 inches long so they cook evenly.

- 5 tablespoons unsalted butter, softened
- 3 tablespoons minced fresh parsley, divided
- 1 tablespoon whole-grain mustard
- 24 oysters, 2½ to 3 inches long, well scrubbed

    Lemon wedges

1   Adjust oven rack to middle position and heat oven to 450 degrees. Stir butter, 2 tablespoons parsley, and mustard in bowl until well combined. Gently crumple and uncrumple two 24-inch lengths of aluminum foil. Place 1 piece in 18 by 13-inch rimmed baking sheet and second piece on large serving platter; cover foil on platter with dish towel for presentation, if desired. Nestle oysters, cupped side down, into foil on prepared sheet and bake until oysters open slightly, about 5 minutes. (It's OK to eat oysters that don't open.) Let oysters rest until cool enough to handle, about 5 minutes.

2   Shuck 1 oyster and discard top shell. Return oyster to foil, being careful not to spill much liquid. Repeat with remaining oysters.

A Few Good Reasons to Try Oysters

Stunningly Diverse

Like wine grapes, each oyster possesses a certain inherent shape, flavor characteristics, and innumerable delightful nuances determined by exactly where and how it's been farmed. Even bivalves of the same species raised in neighboring bays can look and taste distinctly different.

Environmentally Friendly

Everything oysters need to grow occurs naturally in their habitat, which sets them apart from other seafood cultivated via aquaculture. Plus, oysters are filter feeders that strain out excess nitrogen and microparticles as they pump water through their bodies, purifying the habitat for marine life around them.

Safe to Eat

Nearly 98 percent of oysters we eat come from aquaculture, an industry scrupulously regulated by federal and state agencies.

Can Be Great Year-Round

All oysters are plump and flavorful from late fall through spring, but triploids—oysters developed by scientists to have three sets of chromosomes instead of two (diploids)—are just as good in summer months. Being sterile, they retain all their stored food instead of giving it up to spawn, which depletes their mass.

3   Distribute mustard butter evenly among oysters, about ¾ teaspoon per oyster. Bake until thickest part of largest oyster registers 160 to 165 degrees, 5 to 8 minutes. Let rest for 5 minutes. Using tongs, carefully transfer oysters to prepared platter, nestling them into foil or towel to hold them level. Sprinkle remaining 1 tablespoon parsley over oysters. Serve, passing lemon wedges separately.

SALT COD FRITTERS

serves: 6 to 8 (makes 24 fritters)

total time: 1 hour, plus
24 hours soaking

1   **pound salt cod, checked for bones and rinsed thoroughly**

12   **ounces russet potatoes, peeled and cut into 1-inch pieces**

6   **garlic cloves, smashed and peeled**

½   **cup heavy cream**

2   **tablespoons minced fresh chives**

1   **large egg, lightly beaten**

2   **teaspoons grated lemon zest, plus lemon wedges for serving**

¼   **teaspoon table salt**

⅛   **teaspoon pepper**

⅛   **teaspoon baking powder**

1   **quart peanut or vegetable oil, for frying**

why this recipe works   Salt cod fritters are a perfect bite to share with friends over drinks and conversation. Easy to pop in your mouth, these small supercrisp deep-fried nuggets have a satisfying creamy, briny filling. Cod was once dried and salted to preserve it. Today it's desirable that way because it becomes tender, buttery, and meaty and has a firm, steak-like texture that we love in these fritters. Unlike croquetas, which are bound by béchamel or have an outer layer of bread crumbs, fritters are typically made with a base of potato and egg, aromatics (we use garlic and chives), and liquid (water, milk, or cream). Here, russet potatoes provide texture but their mild flavor doesn't interfere with the filling; an egg gives body and structure; heavy cream adds a rich contrast to the brininess; and baking powder keeps this mixture light through frying. Look for salt cod in fish markets and well-stocked supermarkets. It is shelf-stable and typically packaged in a wooden box or plastic bag. Be sure to change the water when soaking the salt cod as directed in step 1, or the fritters will taste unpalatably salty.

1   Submerge salt cod in large bowl of cold water and refrigerate until cod is soft enough to break apart easily with your fingers, about 24 hours, changing water twice during soaking.

2   Drain cod, transfer to large saucepan along with potatoes and garlic, and cover with water by 2 inches. Bring to boil, then reduce heat to medium and simmer until potatoes are tender, 15 to 20 minutes.

3   Drain cod mixture in colander, then transfer to large bowl. Using potato masher, mash until mixture is mostly smooth. Stir in cream, chives, egg, lemon zest, salt, pepper, and baking powder until well incorporated. (Mixture can be refrigerated in airtight container for up to 2 days. Let sit at room temperature for 30 minutes before frying.)

4   Line serving platter with triple layer of paper towels. Pinch off and roll cod mixture into 24 balls (about 2 tablespoons each) and arrange on large plate. Add oil to large Dutch oven until it measures about ¾ inch deep and heat over medium-high heat to 375 degrees. Add half of fritters to oil and cook until golden all over, about 6 minutes, stirring to prevent sticking. Adjust burner, if necessary, to maintain oil temperature between 350 and 375 degrees. Using wire skimmer or slotted spoon, transfer fritters to prepared platter. Return oil to 375 degrees and repeat with remaining balls. Season with salt to taste. Serve immediately with lemon wedges.

BROILED SHRIMP COCKTAIL WITH CREAMY TARRAGON SAUCE

serves: 12

total time: 30 minutes, plus 30 minutes chilling

why this recipe works   We created a modern shrimp cocktail for sharing. Instead of leaving shrimp plain, we flavor them with fragrant coriander, salt, sugar, and cayenne. Next, we broil them in place of the standard poaching method. The sugar in the spice rub caramelizes quickly under the broiler, adding a nice sear to the shrimp and enhancing their sweetness. Instead of a predictable ketchup-based sauce, we serve the shrimp with mayonnaise, freshened with tarragon. Dry the shrimp thoroughly before cooking. You can substitute dill, basil, cilantro, or mint for the tarragon. We prefer to use jumbo shrimp here, but extra-large shrimp (21 to 25 per pound) can be substituted; if using smaller shrimp, reduce the broiling time by about 2 minutes.

creamy tarragon sauce

- 1 cup mayonnaise
- ¼ cup lemon juice (2 lemons)
- 3 scallions, minced
- 3 tablespoons minced fresh tarragon
- ½ teaspoon table salt
- ¼ teaspoon pepper

shrimp

- 1 teaspoon table salt
- 1 teaspoon ground coriander
- ½ teaspoon pepper
- ½ teaspoon sugar
- ⅛ teaspoon cayenne pepper
- 3 pounds jumbo shrimp (16 to 20 per pound), peeled and deveined
- 3 tablespoons extra-virgin olive oil

1   **for the creamy tarragon sauce**   Stir all ingredients together in serving bowl. Cover and refrigerate until flavors have blended, at least 30 minutes or up to 24 hours.

2   **for the shrimp**   Adjust oven rack 3 inches from broiler element and heat broiler. (If necessary, set upside-down rimmed baking sheet on oven rack to get closer to broiler element.) Combine salt, coriander, pepper, sugar, and cayenne in large bowl. Pat shrimp dry with paper towels, add to bowl and toss with oil and spice mixture.

3   Spread half of shrimp in single layer on rimmed baking sheet Broil shrimp until opaque and edges begin to brown, about 6 minutes. Transfer shrimp to serving platter and cover to keep warm. Repeat with remaining shrimp; transfer to platter. Serve with sauce.

chapter three
salads & soups

————

RECIPE EXTRAS

HERB SALAD

serves: 4 to 6

total time: 10 minutes

3 tablespoons extra-virgin olive oil

¼ teaspoon grated lemon zest plus
1 tablespoon juice

¼ teaspoon kosher salt

2 cups fresh parsley leaves

2 cups mixed tender herb leaves

why this recipe works   To transform herbs from extra (garnish) to star (salad), we toss them with a dressing and eat them as a salad; with appetizers, with mains like Roasted Salmon with Orange Beurre Blanc and Steak Frites, or in the French way, before dessert as a palate cleanser. A simple dressing of lemon juice and olive oil perfectly complements the aromatic herbs. We classify most herbs as hearty or delicate, which refers to their texture and the strength or volatility of their flavor compounds. In general, volatile flavor compounds in hearty herbs like rosemary, thyme, oregano, sage, and marjoram are somewhat more heat-stable so they are used in cooking. Delicate herbs such as basil, parsley, cilantro, dill, mint, chives, and tarragon are delicious raw and we suggest any combination—say, dill, chives, chervil, and tarragon—for this salad. Herbs like cilantro and Italian basil also make great additions. Though this is a great way to use up herbs left over from a batch you bought for another recipe, make sure they are still vibrant and high-quality. Wash and dry them thoroughly (excess liquid can wilt the leaves or dilute the dressing) and dress them lightly. To introduce more dynamic color, texture, and bulk, add up to ½ cup of thinly sliced vegetables, like radishes, shallots, fennel, or celery.

Add oil, lemon zest and juice, and salt to large bowl. Season with pepper to taste, and whisk to thoroughly combine. Add parsley and herb leaves and toss until evenly coated with dressing. Season with salt to taste. Serve immediately.

APPLE-FENNEL RÉMOULADE

serves: 6 to 8

total time: 15 minutes

¼ cup mayonnaise

2 tablespoons whole-grain mustard

2 tablespoons lemon juice

2 tablespoons capers, rinsed, plus
   1 tablespoon brine

4 celery ribs, sliced thin on bias

1 fennel bulb, 1 tablespoon fronds
   minced, stalks discarded, bulb halved,
   cored, and sliced thin crosswise

1 apple, cored and cut into
   2-inch-long matchsticks

why this recipe works   Rémoulade has been made in France since at least the 17th century. The name of this mayonnaise, often flavored with anchovies, pickles, and capers, comes from the Italian "remolata" (or "gremolata"). Typically used in France as a seafood dipping sauce, it also famously appears in julienned celery root salad (céleri rémoulade), a popular bistro dish. We gave it a twist by tossing rémoulade with very thinly sliced ribs of celery instead of celeriac, adding fennel and an apple cut into matchsticks. The crunchy, sweet–tart, anise–tinged salad pairs nicely with chicken and seafood. While any apple variety works, we recommend a crisp-sweet variety such as Fuji, Gala, or Honeycrisp. We prefer to use our Make-Ahead Homemade Mayonnaise (page 16), but any store-bought mayonnaise will work in this recipe.

Whisk mayonnaise, mustard, lemon juice, and caper brine together in large bowl. Add celery, fennel bulb, apple, and capers and toss to combine. Season with salt and pepper to taste. Top with fennel fronds and serve.

CREOLE POTATO SALAD

serves: 8

total time: 35 minutes, plus
30 minutes cooling + 1 hour
refrigerating time

potato salad

- 3 pounds Yukon Gold potatoes, peeled and cut into ¾-inch chunks
- ¼ cup white wine vinegar, divided

  Table salt for cooking potatoes
- 3 hard-cooked large eggs, chopped
- 1 celery rib, chopped fine
- ½ green bell pepper, chopped fine
- 2 tablespoons minced fresh parsley

rémoulade

- 1¼ cups mayonnaise
- ⅓ cup cornichons, drained and chopped
- 4 scallions, sliced thin
- 1 tablespoon prepared horseradish
- 2 teaspoons spicy brown mustard
- 2 teaspoons ketchup
- 2 teaspoons lemon juice
- 2 garlic cloves, minced
- 1 teaspoon paprika
- ¾ teaspoon Worcestershire sauce
- ½ teaspoon sugar
- ½ teaspoon table salt
- ½ teaspoon pepper
- ¼ teaspoon cayenne pepper

why this recipe works   French cuisine has influenced cooking the world over but in the US, that may be most true in Louisiana's Cajun and Creole cooking traditions, of which gumbo and jambalaya are famous examples. There are countless other dishes, techniques, and sauces that still bear French names in Louisiana but have been adapted to the local palate. One is rémoulade. In France, rémoulade is made of mayonnaise mixed with Dijon mustard, capers, anchovies, and chopped gherkins. We use it in Apple–Fennel Rémoulade (page 61), without the anchovies. In Louisiana, rémoulade is spicy and assertive, made with Creole mustard, hot sauce, Worcestershire sauce, lemon juice, and sometimes horseradish. For this bistro salad, we toss Louisiana rémoulade with cooked potatoes for a dish with impressive depth, a looser texture (thanks to the additional liquids), and some heat. Ketchup adds sweetness and, with the paprika, contributes the pinkish hue traditionally associated with the sauce. Scallions and parsley bring welcome freshness. To keep the potatoes firm, we add vinegar to the cooking water; the acid in the vinegar slows down the release of starch molecules, helping the potatoes hold their shape. You can use dill pickles in place of the cornichons. We prefer to use our Make-Ahead Homemade Mayonnaise (page 16), but any store-bought mayonnaise will work in this recipe.

1   for the potato salad   Combine potatoes, 8 cups water, 2 tablespoons vinegar, and 1 tablespoon salt in Dutch oven and bring to boil over high heat. Reduce heat to medium and simmer until potatoes are just tender, 14 to 17 minutes.

2   Drain potatoes thoroughly in colander, then transfer to large bowl. Drizzle remaining 2 tablespoons vinegar over hot potatoes and toss gently to coat. Let potatoes cool at room temperature for 30 minutes; then refrigerate until cool, about 30 minutes longer, stirring halfway through chilling.

3   for the rémoulade   Whisk all ingredients in bowl until combined.

4   Add eggs, celery, bell pepper, parsley, and rémoulade to chilled potatoes and fold gently to combine. Season with salt and pepper to taste. Cover and refrigerate to let flavors blend, about 30 minutes. Serve. (Salad can be covered and refrigerated for up to 2 days.)

BIBB AND FRISÉE SALAD WITH GRAPES AND CELERY

serves: 4

total time: 25 minutes

why this recipe works   This fresh, colorful salad makes a light accompaniment to any meal and is infinitely variable: Just change the fruits and nuts you add. We pair light, frilly, slightly bitter frisée with soft, buttery, mild Bibb lettuce for a variety of flavors, and contrast the greens with thinly sliced celery and the sweet, juicy pop of seedless red grapes. Blue cheese gives a hint of richness as does champagne vinegar in our vinaigrette. You can substitute green seedless grapes for the red, if desired. Use a mandoline to thinly slice the celery.

dressing

- 1 tablespoon champagne vinegar
- 1½ teaspoons very finely minced shallot
- ½ teaspoon mayonnaise
- ½ teaspoon Dijon mustard
- ⅛ teaspoon table salt
- 3 tablespoons extra-virgin olive oil

salad

- 1 head Bibb lettuce, torn into bite-size pieces (7 cups)
- 1 small head frisée, torn into bite-size pieces (3 cups)
- 6 ounces seedless red grapes, halved (1 cup)
- 1 celery rib, sliced thin
- 3 ounces blue cheese, crumbled (¾ cup), divided

1   **for the dressing**   Whisk vinegar, shallot, mayonnaise, mustard, and salt in medium bowl until no lumps of mayonnaise remain. Whisking constantly, slowly drizzle in oil until emulsified. Season with pepper to taste.

2   **for the salad**   Place lettuce, frisée, grapes, celery, and half of blue cheese in large bowl. Toss to combine. Drizzle with dressing and toss until greens are evenly coated. Season with salt to taste. Sprinkle with remaining blue cheese. Serve immediately.

variation

BIBB AND FRISÉE SALAD WITH RADICCHIO AND HAZELNUTS

Omit grapes. Place 1½ ounces (1 cup) of radicchio leaves, torn into bite-size pieces, and 2 tablespoons toasted hazelnuts in bowl with lettuce and frisée. Drizzle with dressing and season as directed in step 2.

SALADE NIÇOISE

serves: 6

total time: 40 minutes

dressing

- ½ cup lemon juice (3 lemons)
- 1 shallot, minced
- 2 tablespoons finely chopped fresh basil, parsley, or dill
- 1 tablespoon minced fresh thyme or rosemary
- 2 teaspoons minced fresh oregano
- 1 teaspoon Dijon mustard
- ¾ cup extra-virgin olive oil

salad

- 1¼ pounds small red potatoes, unpeeled, quartered

  Table salt for cooking vegetables
- 2 tablespoons dry vermouth
- 2 heads Boston or Bibb lettuce (1 pound), torn into bite-size pieces
- 12 ounces olive oil–packed tuna, drained
- 3 small tomatoes, cored and cut into eighths
- 1 small red onion, sliced very thin
- 8 ounces green beans, trimmed and halved crosswise
- 6 Easy-Peel Hard-Cooked Eggs (page 67), quartered
- ¼ cup pitted Niçoise olives
- 10–12 anchovy fillets, rinsed (optional)
- 2 tablespoons capers, rinsed (optional)

why this recipe works   Salade niçoise originated as a working man's dish in the city of Nice, France. Served composed or tossed, it was a satisfying dish for fishermen after a hard day's work. The ingredients were local and easily available, and provided a satisfying meal, a feast for the eyes, nose, and tastebuds. Traditional recipes are made with one fish—tuna or anchovies—and ripe tomatoes, hard-cooked eggs, spring onions, and local olives on greens. Some regional versions include small fava beans, mesclun, cucumber, and radishes too. Boiled potatoes and green beans are a later addition to the dish. For our version, we wanted to combine well-dressed, well-seasoned components that complement, not crowd, one another. We pair fruity extra-virgin olive oil with lemon juice for the dressing, then add fresh herbs, shallot, and Dijon mustard. Apart from the tuna, we use vine-ripened tomatoes, Boston lettuce, and low-starch Red Bliss potatoes, which hold their shape. We season and dress each component of the salad individually so their colors and shapes stay intact. Prepare all the vegetables before you begin cooking the potatoes. For even cooking, use small red potatoes measuring 1 to 2 inches in diameter. Compose the salad on your largest serving platter and leave some space between the mounds of potatoes, tomatoes and onion, and green beans so that leaves of lettuce peek through.

1   **for the dressing**   Whisk lemon juice, shallot, basil, thyme, oregano, and mustard together in medium bowl. Whisking constantly, slowly drizzle in oil until emulsified. Season with salt and pepper to taste. Set aside. (Dressing can be refrigerated up to 24 hours; whisk to recombine before using.)

2   **for the salad**   Bring potatoes and 4 quarts cold water to boil in Dutch oven or stockpot over high heat. Add 1 table-spoon salt and cook until potatoes are tender when poked with paring knife, 5 to 8 minutes. Using slotted spoon, gently transfer potatoes to medium bowl (do not discard boiling water). Toss warm potatoes with vermouth and season with salt and pepper to taste; let sit for 1 minute. Toss in ¼ cup dressing; set aside.

3   While potatoes cook, toss lettuce with ¼ cup dressing in largebowl until coated. Arrange bed of lettuce on very large flat platter. Place tuna in now-empty bowl and break up with fork. Add ½ cup dressing and stir to combine; mound tuna in center of lettuce. Toss tomatoes and onion with 3 tablespoons dressing in now-empty bowl and season with salt and pepper to taste. Arrange tomato mixture in mound at edge of lettuce bed. Arrange potatoes in separate mound at opposite edge of lettuce bed.

4   Return water to boil; add green beans and 1 tablespoon salt. Cook until crisp-tender, 3 to 5 minutes. Meanwhile, fill large bowl halfway with ice and water. Drain green beans; transfer to ice bath; and let sit until just cool, about 30 seconds. Dry green beans well on triple layer of paper towels. Toss green beans with 3 tablespoons dressing in now-empty bowl and season with salt and pepper to taste. Arrange in separate mound at edge of lettuce bed.

5   Arrange eggs; olives; and anchovies, if using, in separate mounds at edge of lettuce bed. Drizzle eggs with remaining 2 tablespoons dressing; sprinkle salad with capers, if using. Serve immediately.

EASY-PEEL HARD-COOKED EGGS

makes: 2 to 6 eggs

total time: 35 minutes

Be sure to use large eggs that have no cracks and are cold from the refrigerator.

2-6 large eggs

1   Bring 1 inch water to rolling boil in medium saucepan over high heat. Place eggs in steamer basket. Transfer basket to saucepan. Cover, reduce heat to medium-low, and cook eggs for 13 minutes.

2   When eggs are almost finished cooking, combine 2 cups ice cubes and 2 cups cold water in medium bowl. Using tongs or spoon, transfer eggs to ice bath; let sit for 15 minutes. Peel before serving. (Eggs can be refrigerated in their shells in airtight container for up to 5 days.)

SALADE LYONNAISE

serves: 4

total time: 45 minutes

1 (½-inch-thick) slice pancetta (about 5 ounces)

2 tablespoons extra-virgin olive oil

1 tablespoon minced shallot

2 tablespoons red wine vinegar

4 teaspoons Dijon mustard

1 head frisée (6 ounces), torn into bite-size pieces

5 ounces chicory or escarole, torn into bite-size pieces (5 cups)

1 recipe Perfect Poached Eggs (page 69)

why this recipe works   There's a reason salade lyonnaise has long been iconic, beyond its namesake city of Lyon. The combination of bitter greens, salty bacon, rich poached egg, and punchy vinaigrette makes a happy marriage of flavors. The pungent greens stand up to the tart vinaigrette and are sturdy enough to hold up under the weight of the egg. Thick batons of bacon, known in France as lardons, retain meaty chew even when browned and crisped. Rather than American bacon, we call for pancetta in our recipe since it is unsmoked, salt cured, and rolled just like traditionally used ventreche (also known as French pancetta). The vinaigrette, whisked together in the warm pan used to brown the bacon, has just enough acidity to balance the pork's richness and the egg's flowing yolk and tender white, while gently tenderizing the frisée. Poached eggs deliver runny yolks that easily meld into the salad. Order a ½-inch-thick slice of pancetta at the deli counter; presliced or diced pancetta is likely to dry out or become tough. If you can't find chicory or escarole, dandelion greens are a good substitute. If using escarole, strip away the first four or five outer leaves and reserve them for another use. Serve with croutons or add crusty bread for a light lunch or dinner.

1   Cut pancetta crosswise into thirds, then cut each third crosswise into ¼-inch-wide pieces. Combine pancetta and 2 cups water in 10-inch nonstick or carbon-steel skillet and bring to boil over medium-high heat. Boil for 5 minutes, then drain. Return pancetta to now-empty skillet. Add oil and cook over medium-low heat, stirring occasionally, until lightly browned but still chewy, 4 to 6 minutes.

2   Pour off all but 2 tablespoons fat from skillet, leaving pancetta in skillet. Add shallot and cook, stirring frequently, until slightly softened, about 30 seconds. Off heat, add vinegar and mustard and stir to combine.

3   Drizzle vinaigrette over frisée in large bowl and toss thoroughly to coat. Add chicory and toss again. Season with salt and pepper to taste. Divide salad among individual plates. Gently place 1 egg on top of each salad, then season with salt and pepper to taste. Serve immediately.

PERFECT POACHED EGGS

makes: 4 eggs

total time: 24 minutes

Use the freshest eggs possible for this recipe.

- **4 large eggs**
- **1 tablespoon distilled white vinegar for poaching**
- **1 teaspoon table salt for poaching**

1 Bring 6 cups water to boil in Dutch oven over high heat. Meanwhile, crack eggs, one at a time, into colander. Let stand until loose, watery whites drain away from eggs, 20 to 30 seconds. Gently transfer eggs to 2-cup liquid measuring cup.

2 Add vinegar and salt to boiling water. Remove pot from heat. With lip of measuring cup just above surface of water, gently tip eggs into water, one at a time, leaving space between them. Cover pot and let sit until whites closest to yolks are just set and opaque, about 3 minutes. If after 3 minutes whites are not set, let sit in water, checking every 30 seconds, until whites are set.

3 Using slotted spoon, carefully lift and drain each egg over Dutch oven. Season with salt and pepper to taste, and serve.

CRISPY LENTIL AND HERB SALAD

serves: 4

total time: 45 minutes, plus 1 hour soaking

1 teaspoon table salt for brining

½ cup dried lentilles du Puy, picked over and rinsed

⅓ cup vegetable oil for frying

½ teaspoon ground cumin

¼ teaspoon plus pinch table salt, divided

1 cup plain Greek yogurt

3 tablespoons extra-virgin olive oil, divided

1 teaspoon grated lemon zest plus 1 teaspoon juice

1 garlic clove, minced

½ cup fresh parsley leaves

½ cup torn fresh dill

½ cup fresh cilantro leaves

¼ cup dried cherries, chopped

Pomegranate molasses

Pitas, warmed

why this recipe works The most well-known French lentils might just be lentilles du Puy from the Auvergne region. They get their distinctive peppery flavor from the volcanic soil they grow in. We wanted to use lentilles du Puy in a salad, preparing them in a manner not often used for lentils: deep-frying. This would make the lentils crisp and help them hold their shape but we found we needed to salt-soak the lentils before frying so they could get tender but not burn. Instead of tossing the fried lentils with a dressing, we use yogurt as an anchor, spreading it on a platter and topping it with a lightly dressed blend of fresh herbs tossed with the crunchy lentils and pieces of sweet dried cherries. Pita is ideal for scooping everything up in one perfect bite. You can use brown lentils instead of the lentilles du Puy. Be sure to use a large saucepan to fry the lentils, as the oil mixture will bubble and steam.

1 Dissolve 1 teaspoon salt in 1 quart water in bowl. Add lentils and let sit at room temperature for at least 1 hour or up to 24 hours. Drain well and pat dry with paper towels.

2 Heat vegetable oil in large saucepan over medium heat until shimmering. Add lentils and cook, stirring constantly, until crispy and golden in spots, 8 to 12 minutes (oil should bubble vigorously throughout; adjust heat as needed). Carefully drain lentils in fine-mesh strainer set over bowl, then transfer lentils to paper towel–lined plate. Discard oil. Sprinkle with cumin and ¼ teaspoon salt and toss to combine; set aside. (Cooled lentils can be stored in airtight container at room temperature for up to 24 hours.)

3 Whisk yogurt, 2 tablespoons olive oil, lemon zest and juice, and garlic together in bowl and season with salt and pepper to taste. Spread yogurt mixture over serving platter. Toss parsley, dill, cilantro, remaining pinch salt, and remaining 1 tablespoon olive oil together in bowl, then gently stir in lentils and cherries and arrange on top of yogurt mixture, leaving 1-inch border. Drizzle with pomegranate molasses. Serve with pitas.

CARROT
AND SMOKED
SALMON SALAD

serves: 4 to 6

total time: 50 minutes, plus
45 minutes marinating

2 pounds carrots with greens attached,
  divided, ¼ cup greens chopped

5 tablespoons cider vinegar, divided

1 tablespoon sugar

⅛ teaspoon plus ¾ teaspoon table
  salt, divided

¼ cup extra-virgin olive oil, divided

¼ teaspoon pepper

1 red grapefruit

2 tablespoons chopped fresh dill

2 teaspoons Dijon mustard

2 heads Belgian endive (4 ounces each),
  halved, cored, and sliced ½ inch thick

8 ounces smoked salmon

why this recipe works   What could be more delightful to dig into than this stunning salad that uses all parts of a fresh carrot, prepped three ways, and silky, rich smoked salmon, which is the same lovely shade of orange? We use carrots with their greens attached because they taste sweeter than bagged carrots, and the feathery greens are fresh and slightly bitter like parsley. We pickle some of the carrots, shaved into ribbons, for a sweet and punchy bite, and roast the remaining carrots, keeping the baking sheet close to the heat source for good browning. Tossing the roasted carrots with a Dijon-dill vinaigrette while slightly warm allows them to absorb a lot of flavor. Finally, raw endive brings a welcome crisp bitterness while grapefruit adds sweet-tart flavor. To finish, we chop up the carrot greens and toss them into the salad for a bistro–worthy dish that will impress your guests. Parsley can be substituted for the carrot greens. You should have about 1½ pounds of carrots after trimming the carrot greens.

1   Adjust oven rack to lowest position and heat oven to 450 degrees. Peel and shave 4 ounces carrots into thin ribbons with vegetable peeler; set aside. Peel and slice remaining carrots on bias ¼ inch thick; set aside.

2   Microwave ¼ cup vinegar, sugar, and ⅛ teaspoon salt in medium bowl until simmering, 1 to 2 minutes. Add shaved carrots and stir to combine. Let sit, stirring occasionally, for 45 minutes. (Drained pickled carrots can be refrigerated for up to 5 days.)

3   Toss sliced carrots, 1 tablespoon oil, pepper, and ½ teaspoon salt together in bowl to coat. Spread carrots in single layer on rimmed baking sheet, cut side down. Roast until tender and bottoms are well browned, 15 to 25 minutes. Let cool slightly, about 15 minutes.

4   Meanwhile, cut away peel and pith from grapefruit. Quarter grapefruit, then slice crosswise into ¼-inch-thick pieces.

5   Whisk dill, mustard, remaining 1 tablespoon vinegar, and remaining ¼ teaspoon salt together in large bowl. Whisking constantly, slowly drizzle in remaining 3 tablespoons oil until emulsified. Add endive, carrot greens, roasted carrots, pickled carrots, and grapefruit and toss to combine; season with salt and pepper to taste. Arrange salmon around edge of serving platter, then transfer salad to center of platter. Serve.

CAULIFLOWER SALAD WITH MOROCCAN CHERMOULA

serves: 4 to 6

total time: 50 minutes

1 head cauliflower (2 pounds), cored and cut into 2-inch florets

2 tablespoons extra-virgin olive oil

½ teaspoon table salt

¼ teaspoon pepper

½ red onion, sliced ¼ inch thick

1 cup shredded carrot

½ cup raisins

2 tablespoons chopped fresh cilantro

1 recipe Chermoula (page 20)

2 tablespoons sliced almonds, toasted

why this recipe works As more North African migrants move to France, many bistros are influenced by their cuisines. Chermoula is a traditional Moroccan marinade made with hefty amounts of cilantro, lemon, and garlic that packs a big punch of summer flavors. You might see this dressing used as a marinade for meat and fish, but here we make it the flavor highlight for a salad where cauliflower is the canvas. We focus first on the cooking method of the cauliflower. Roasting adds deep flavor to the cauliflower and balances the bright chermoula. To keep the cauliflower from overbrowning on the exterior before the interior is cooked, we start it covered and let it steam until barely tender. Then we remove the foil, add sliced onions, and return the pan to the oven to let both the onions and the cauliflower caramelize. Adding the onions to the same pan once the cauliflower is uncovered eases their preparation and ensures that they finish cooking at the same time. To highlight the natural sweetness of the cooked vegetables, we add shredded carrot and raisins, two traditional North African ingredients. Use the large holes of a box grater to shred the carrot.

1 Adjust oven rack to lowest position and heat oven to 475 degrees. Toss cauliflower with oil and sprinkle with salt and pepper. Arrange cauliflower in single layer on parchment paper–lined rimmed baking sheet. Cover tightly with aluminum foil and roast until softened, 5 to 7 minutes. Remove foil and spread onion evenly on sheet. Roast until vegetables are tender, cauliflower is deep golden brown, and onion slices are charred at edges, 10 to 15 minutes, stirring halfway through roasting. Let cool slightly, about 5 minutes.

2 Gently toss cauliflower-onion mixture, carrot, raisins, and cilantro with chermoula until coated. Transfer to serving platter and sprinkle with almonds. Serve warm or at room temperature.

WILTED SPINACH AND SHRIMP SALAD WITH BACON-PECAN VINAIGRETTE

serves: 4

total time: 30 minutes

2 heads Belgian endive (8 ounces), halved, cored, and cut into ½-inch strips

10 ounces (10 cups) baby spinach

6 tablespoons red wine vinegar

2 tablespoons whole-grain mustard

1½ teaspoons sugar

½ teaspoon table salt, divided

1 shallot, thinly sliced

12 ounces extra-large shrimp (21 to 25 per pound), peeled, deveined, and tails removed

¼ teaspoon pepper

1 tablespoon extra-virgin olive oil

6 slices bacon, cut into ½-inch pieces

½ cup pecans or walnuts, chopped coarse

1 Fuji or Honeycrisp apple, halved, cored, and sliced thin

why this recipe works   We use baby spinach, juicy shrimp, and a warm bacon vinaigrette in this salad of many colors and flavors. The shrimp and a particularly sweet, fragrant, and crisp apple variety contrast with the spinach, and emphasize and off-set the bacon-pecan dressing's smoky, salty, nutty richness. We wanted the spinach leaves to be just gently softened by the warm vinaigrette. Too much or too-hot dressing, and the spinach would end up overly wilted and lifeless. Too little or too-cool dressing, and the spinach would stay chewy, raw, and less pleasant to eat. The trick for ensuring a properly wilted salad is to have everything at the ready—tongs and all—before beginning and then to toss the spinach and crisp endive and serve the salad the moment the vinaigrette is at the right temperature.

1   Place endive in large bowl along with spinach. Whisk vinegar, mustard, sugar, and ¼ teaspoon salt together in separate bowl. Measure out 2 tablespoons vinegar mixture and set aside in medium bowl. Add shallot to remaining vinegar mixture; cover; and microwave until steaming, 30 to 60 seconds. Stir briefly to submerge shallot; uncover and set aside to cool.

2   Pat shrimp dry with paper towels and sprinkle with pepper and remaining ¼ teaspoon salt. Heat oil in 12-inch nonstick skillet over medium-high heat until just smoking. Add shrimp in single layer and cook, without stirring, until spotty brown and edges turn pink on bottom, about 1 minute. Flip shrimp and continue to cook until all but very center is opaque, about 30 seconds; transfer shrimp to bowl with reserved 2 tablespoons vinegar mixture and cover to keep warm.

3   Cook bacon and pecans in now-empty skillet over medium heat, stirring frequently, until bacon is crispy and fat is well rendered, 8 to 10 minutes.

4   Off heat, whisk shallot mixture into skillet until combined. Pour warm vinaigrette over spinach and endive and toss until spinach is wilted slightly. Add apple and toss gently to combine. Divide salad among individual serving plates. Season with salt and pepper to taste. Serve immediately, topping individual portions with shrimp.

BRUSSELS SPROUTS SALAD WITH MUSTARD VINAIGRETTE

serves: 6

total time: 25 minutes

why this recipe works   In France, a warm vinaigrette is used to dress hardy or bitter greens like escarole or frisée in salads like salade lyonnaise. We tweak the technique by warming and then slightly cooling a dressing before adding it to thinly sliced, slightly warmed brussels sprouts. Quick pickled shallot and dried apricots add contrast; ricotta salata, toasted pistachios, and watercress bring richness. We dress the salad in the skillet before transferring it to a serving bowl. A food processor's slicing blade can be used to slice the brussels sprouts, but the salad will be less tender.

5	tablespoons white wine vinegar
1	tablespoon whole-grain mustard
1	teaspoon sugar
¼	teaspoon table salt
1	shallot, halved through root end and sliced thin crosswise
¼	cup dried apricots, chopped
5	tablespoons vegetable oil
⅓	cup shelled pistachios, chopped
1½	pounds brussels sprouts, trimmed, halved, and sliced thin
1½	ounces (1½ cups) watercress, chopped
4	ounces ricotta salata, shaved into thin strips using vegetable peeler

1   Whisk vinegar, mustard, sugar, and salt together in bowl. Add shallot and apricots, cover tightly with plastic wrap, and microwave until steaming, 30 to 60 seconds. Stir briefly to submerge shallot. Let cool to room temperature, about 15 minutes.

2   Heat oil in 12-inch skillet over medium heat until shimmering. Add pistachios and cook, stirring frequently, until pistachios are golden brown, 1 to 2 minutes. Off heat, whisk in shallot mixture. Add brussels sprouts and toss with tongs until dressing is evenly distributed and sprouts darken slightly, 1 to 2 minutes. Transfer to serving bowl. Add watercress and ricotta salata and toss to combine. Season with salt and pepper to taste, and serve immediately.

ARTICHOKE SOUP À LA BARIGOULE

serves: 4 to 6

total time: 1 hour

3 tablespoons extra-virgin olive oil, divided

3 cups jarred whole baby artichokes packed in water, quartered, rinsed, and patted dry

12 ounces white mushrooms, trimmed and sliced thin

1 leek, white and light green parts only, halved lengthwise, sliced ¼ inch thick, and washed thoroughly

4 garlic cloves, minced

2 anchovy fillets, rinsed, patted dry, and minced

1 teaspoon minced fresh thyme or ¼ teaspoon dried

3 tablespoons all-purpose flour

¼ cup dry white wine

3 cups chicken broth

3 cups vegetable broth

6 ounces parsnips, peeled and cut into ½-inch pieces

2 bay leaves

¼ cup heavy cream

2 tablespoons minced fresh tarragon

1 teaspoon white wine vinegar, plus extra for seasoning

why this recipe works Artichokes barigoule is an iconic Provençal springtime dish of seasonal ingredients—artichokes, mushrooms (the variety that was traditionally used is called barigoule in French), leeks, and turnips—braised in white wine. We thought the delicate but soothing dish would make a superb soup. We first sear artichokes to intensify their flavor. Cooking white mushrooms covered and then sautéing them uncovered evaporates their excess moisture before browning, while simmering the parsnips brings out their sweetness. Anchovies and garlic add depth, and leek contributes further sweetness and body. White wine and white wine vinegar brighten the dish, a little cream ties it all together, and tarragon adds freshness. We prefer the flavor and texture of jarred whole baby artichokes but you can substitute 18 ounces frozen artichoke hearts, thawed and patted dry.

1 Heat 1 tablespoon oil in Dutch oven over medium heat until shimmering. Add artichokes and cook until browned, 8 to 10 minutes. Transfer to cutting board, let cool slightly, then chop coarse.

2 Heat 1 tablespoon oil in now-empty pot over medium heat until shimmering. Add mushrooms, cover, and cook until they have released their liquid, about 5 minutes. Uncover and continue to cook until mushrooms are dry, about 5 minutes.

3 Stir in leek and remaining 1 tablespoon oil and cook until leek is softened and mushrooms are browned, 8 to 10 minutes. Stir in garlic, anchovies, and thyme and cook until fragrant, about 30 seconds. Stir in flour and cook for 1 minute. Stir in wine, scraping up any browned bits, and cook until nearly evaporated, about 1 minute.

4 Slowly whisk in chicken broth and vegetable broth, smoothing out any lumps. Stir in artichokes, parsnips, and bay leaves and bring to simmer. Reduce heat to low, cover, and simmer gently until parsnips are tender, 15 to 20 minutes. Off heat, discard bay leaves. Stir in cream, tarragon, and vinegar. Season with salt, pepper, and extra vinegar to taste. Serve.

CREAMY CAULIFLOWER SOUP WITH HAWAIJ

serves: 4 to 6

total time: 1½ hours

1 head cauliflower (2 pounds)

¼ cup extra-virgin olive oil, divided, plus extra for serving

1 leek, white and light green parts only, halved lengthwise, sliced thin, and washed thoroughly

1 small onion, halved and sliced thin

1½ teaspoons table salt

1 tablespoon Hawaij (page 83)

4½ cups water

1 recipe Green Zhoug, divided (page 20)

1 teaspoon white wine vinegar

why this recipe works   We like using cauliflower in soup, as it offers a wonderful blank canvas for flavoring. In France, creamy cauliflower soups might get their creaminess from a combination of chicken stock, butter, cream, potatoes, and leeks. Our vegetarian version only uses the leek and gets its earthy, sweet-savory taste from a Yemeni spice blend called hawaij. Also used in Israeli cuisine, hawaij is among the flavors finding their way into neo-bistro cooking. Here it highlights the cauliflower, which we cook in simmering water in two stages, first to bring out the nutty flavor of a long-cooked crucifer and also to get the grassy taste that comes from brief cooking. The soup is topped with Green Zhoug, browned cauliflower florets, and Pink Pickled Turnips (page 43) can be used as a garnish too.

1   Pull off outer leaves of cauliflower and trim stem. Using paring knife, cut around core to remove; slice core thin and reserve. Cut heaping 1 cup of ½-inch florets from head of cauliflower; set aside. Cut remaining cauliflower crosswise into ½-inch-thick slices.

2   Heat 3 tablespoons oil in large saucepan over medium-low heat until shimmering. Add leek, onion, and salt and cook, stirring often, until leek and onion are softened but not browned, about 7 minutes. Stir in hawaij and cook until fragrant, about 30 seconds. Stir in water, reserved sliced core, and half of sliced cauliflower. Increase heat to medium-high and bring to simmer. Reduce heat to medium-low and simmer gently for 15 minutes. Add remaining sliced cauliflower and simmer until cauliflower is tender and crumbles easily, 15 to 20 minutes.

3   Meanwhile, heat remaining 1 tablespoon oil in 8-inch skillet over medium heat until shimmering. Add reserved florets and cook, stirring often, until golden brown, 6 to 8 minutes. Transfer to bowl, add ¼ cup zhoug, and toss until well coated. Working in batches, process soup in blender until smooth, about 45 seconds. Return pureed soup to clean pot and bring to brief simmer over medium heat. Off heat, stir in vinegar and season with salt to taste. Spoon browned florets and remaining zhoug over individual serving bowls. Serve.

HAWAIJ

makes: about ½ cup

total time: 15 minutes

This golden Yemeni spice blend found its way into Israeli cooking by way of migration with Yemenite Jews. The multipurpose blend has a rich history of use in soups, stews, and curries in Yemen. We like to add it to soups and stews, and also use it as a marinade for chicken and fish. The spices found in this recipe are common. Cloves are optional, found only in some versions, but we love the depth they add.

- 2½   tablespoons black peppercorns
- 2   tablespoons cumin seeds
- 1½   tablespoons coriander seeds
- 10   cardamom pods
- 6   whole cloves
- 1½   tablespoons ground turmeric

Process peppercorns, cumin seeds, coriander seeds, cardamom pods, and cloves in spice grinder until finely ground, about 30 seconds. Transfer to bowl and stir in turmeric. (Hawaij can be stored in airtight container at room temperature for up to 1 month.)

FRENCH ONION SOUP

serves: 6

total time: 1 hour, 55 minutes

4 tablespoons unsalted butter

4 pounds onions, halved and sliced thin

1¾ teaspoons table salt, divided

1 teaspoon sugar

1 cup dry red wine

8 cups beef broth

4 sprigs fresh thyme

2 bay leaves

¾ teaspoon pepper, divided

6 ounces baguette, cut into 1-inch cubes

3 tablespoons extra-virgin olive oil

8 ounces Gruyère cheese, shredded (2 cups), divided

1½ ounces Parmesan cheese, shredded (½ cup)

why this recipe works   What could spell "bistro" more than French onion soup? The key to this classic is a shortcut-free, hour-long caramelization of the onions. We start with a mountain of sliced onions in a Dutch oven with some melted butter, salt to draw out moisture, and sugar to jump-start caramelization. We cook the onions covered at first to trap steam and soften them, and then cook them uncovered till soft and caramel-colored. Deglazing with red wine ensures that all the flavorful browned bits end up in the soup. We add rich, meaty beef broth, thyme, and bay leaves, and simmer it all together until the flavors meld. To make the soup easier to eat, we forgo the traditional toasted slice of baguette in favor of easily spoonable croutons. We ladle the soup into individual crocks and top them with the croutons, shredded Gruyère, and shredded Parmesan (for extra nuttiness). A bit of Gruyère under the croutons protects the bread from getting too soggy. Be patient when caramelizing the onions; the process takes 55 to 70 minutes. If you don't have ovensafe soup crocks, form six individual piles of croutons on a baking sheet, cover them with the cheese, and broil them on the middle oven rack until the cheese is melted, 1 to 3 minutes. Then use a spatula to transfer the crouton portions to the individual filled soup bowls.

1   Melt butter in Dutch oven over medium-high heat. Stir in onions, 1 teaspoon salt, and sugar. Cover and cook, stirring occasionally, until onions release their liquid and are uniformly translucent, about 20 minutes.

2   Uncover and cook until liquid has evaporated and browned bits start to form on bottom of pot, 5 to 10 minutes. Reduce heat to medium and continue to cook, uncovered, until onions are caramel colored, 30 to 40 minutes longer, stirring and scraping with wooden spoon as browned bits form on bottom of pot and spreading onions into even layer after stirring. (If onions or browned bits begin to scorch, reduce heat to medium-low.)

3   Stir in wine, scraping up any browned bits, and cook until nearly evaporated, about 1 minute. Stir in broth, thyme sprigs, bay leaves, ½ teaspoon pepper, and ½ teaspoon salt. Increase heat to high and bring to boil. Reduce heat to medium-low and simmer, uncovered, for 30 minutes.

4   While onions simmer, adjust oven rack to middle position and heat oven to 350 degrees. Toss baguette, oil, remaining ¼ teaspoon salt, and remaining ¼ teaspoon pepper together in bowl. Transfer to rimmed baking sheet and bake until golden and crisp, 15 to 18 minutes. Remove sheet from oven and set aside. Increase oven temperature to 500 degrees.

5   Set six 12-ounce ovensafe crocks on second rimmed baking sheet. Discard thyme sprigs and bay leaves and season soup with salt and pepper to taste. Divide soup evenly among crocks (about 1½ cups each). Divide 1 cup Gruyère evenly among crocks, top with croutons, and sprinkle with remaining Gruyère, then Parmesan. Bake until cheeses are melted and soup is bubbly around edges, 5 to 7 minutes. Let cool for 5 minutes before serving.

Soup Story

It is impossible to know when French-style onion soup was first conceived and cooked; cheap brothy meals were common fare in Medieval Europe and likely predate the very concept of France as a political entity. But in the 18th and 19th centuries, the soup's signature gratiné topping of relatively expensive cheese transformed the humble dish into something that even wealthy eaters rhapsodized over. The soup achieved renown among the myriad vendors and patrons of the vast Les Halles market in Paris, where it became prized for its restorative (and hangover-soothing) properties.

SOUPE AU PISTOU

serves: 6

total time: 40 minutes

pistou

¾ cup fresh basil leaves

1 ounce Parmesan cheese, grated
(½ cup)

⅓ cup extra-virgin olive oil

1 garlic clove, minced

soup

1 tablespoon extra-virgin olive oil

1 leek, white and light green parts only,
halved lengthwise, sliced ½ inch
thick, and washed thoroughly

1 celery rib, cut into ½-inch pieces

1 carrot, peeled and sliced ¼ inch thick

½ teaspoon table salt

2 garlic cloves, minced

3 cups vegetable broth

3 cups water

½ cup orecchiette or other short pasta

8 ounces haricots verts or green beans,
trimmed and cut into ½-inch lengths

1 (15-ounce) can cannellini or navy beans

1 small zucchini, halved lengthwise,
seeded, and cut into ¼-inch pieces

1 large tomato, cored, seeded, and cut
into ¼-inch pieces

why this recipe works   The French equivalent of minestrone, soupe au pistou is native to Provence in the south of France. This broth, chock-full of vegetables, beans, and herbs, is a celebration of the fresh produce that comes to the markets in early summer. Virtually any vegetable can go into the pot, but aromatics like carrots, celery, and leeks are typical, along with zucchini and the thin French green beans called haricots verts. Pasta often makes an appearance too, along with a white bean known as coco de Mollans. The only component that's an absolute constant is the pesto-like condiment or pistou for which the soup is named; stirring a spoonful into each bowl lends the broth a jolt of fresh basil and garlic, along with salty Parmesan.

1   **for the pistou**   Process all ingredients in food processor until smooth, scraping down sides of bowl as needed, about 15 seconds. (Pistou can be refrigerated for up to 4 hours.)

2   **for the soup**   Heat oil in large Dutch oven over medium heat until shimmering. Add leek, celery, carrot, and salt and cook until vegetables are softened, 8 to 10 minutes. Stir in garlic and cook until fragrant, about 30 seconds. Stir in broth and water and bring to simmer.

3   Stir in pasta and simmer until slightly softened, about 5 minutes. Stir in haricots verts and simmer until bright green but still crunchy, 3 to 5 minutes. Stir in cannellini beans and their liquid, zucchini, and tomato and simmer until pasta and vegetables are tender, about 3 minutes. Season with salt and pepper to taste. Serve, topping individual portions with generous tablespoon pistou.

PROVENÇAL FISH SOUP

serves: 6 to 8

total time: 1 hour

1 tablespoon extra-virgin olive oil, plus extra for serving

6 ounces pancetta, chopped fine

1 fennel bulb, 2 tablespoons fronds minced, stalks discarded, bulb halved, cored, and cut into ½-inch pieces

1 onion, chopped

2 celery ribs, halved lengthwise and cut into ½-inch pieces

1½ teaspoons table salt

4 garlic cloves, minced

1 teaspoon paprika

⅛ teaspoon red pepper flakes

Pinch saffron threads, crumbled

1 cup dry white wine or dry vermouth

4 cups water

2 (8-ounce) bottles clam juice

2 bay leaves

2 pounds skinless hake fillets, 1 to 1½ inches thick, sliced crosswise into 6 equal pieces

2 tablespoons minced fresh parsley

1 tablespoon grated orange zest

why this recipe works Every country with a coastline has its own version of fish soup and our Provence-inspired version is not only easy to make, it also boasts a richly flavored broth fragrant with fennel, paprika, saffron, and orange zest. Fish soup can often have a bland and flavorless broth and overcooked fish. We chose thick cuts of hake, wanting a firm fish that would not break apart too easily, and orange and fennel to pair well with the seafood. Premade fish stock produced soups that overpowered the hake's own mild flavor. Water-based versions were more delicate but lacked depth or richness. Instead, we deglaze the vegetables and spices with wine and bottled clam juice to bring out a more balanced flavor. We also brown pancetta and cook the vegetables in the rendered fat. This gives the soup a perfect balance of smokiness, richness, and a citrus aroma. We leave the hake in big slices. If simmered over low heat, the fish would be overcooked by the time it was served, so we use a more unconventional approach: We place the fish in the pot, shut off the heat, and let it poach gently in the warm broth. This way, the fish is perfectly cooked and the soup is hearty and fragrant. Cod or halibut can be substituted for the hake.

1 Heat oil in Dutch oven over medium heat until shimmering. Add pancetta and cook, stirring occasionally, until beginning to brown, 3 to 5 minutes. Stir in fennel pieces, onion, celery, and salt and cook until vegetables are softened and lightly browned, 12 to 14 minutes. Stir in garlic, paprika, pepper flakes, and saffron and cook until fragrant, about 30 seconds.

2 Stir in wine, scraping up any browned bits. Stir in water, clam juice, and bay leaves. Bring to simmer and cook until flavors meld, 15 to 20 minutes.

3 Off heat, discard bay leaves. Nestle hake into cooking liquid, cover, and let sit until fish flakes apart when gently prodded with paring knife and registers 140 degrees, 8 to 10 minutes. Gently stir in parsley, orange zest, and fennel fronds and break fish into large pieces. Season with salt and pepper to taste. Serve, drizzling individual portions with extra oil.

LOBSTER BISQUE

serves: 6

total time: 1½ hours

1½ cups dry white wine

4 (8-ounce) bottles clam juice, divided

3 (1-pound) live lobsters

2 tablespoons extra-virgin olive oil, divided

¼ cup brandy or cognac, warmed

6 tablespoons unsalted butter, divided

1 small carrot, chopped fine

1 small celery rib, chopped fine

1 small onion, chopped fine

1 garlic clove, minced

½ cup all-purpose flour

1 (14.5-ounce) can diced tomatoes, drained

½ teaspoon minced fresh tarragon, plus 1 small sprig

1 cup heavy cream

1 tablespoon lemon juice

Pinch ground cayenne

1 tablespoon dry sherry

why this recipe works   In France, a bisque traditionally refers to a rich, creamy soup typically made with shellfish. Here in the United States, the word is used to describe any smooth creamy soup, shellfish-based or not, that is more refined and flavorful than plainer creamed soups. This luxurious bisque does indeed contain chunks of shellfish—lobster—in its silky-smooth, rich cream base. It is flavored with tarragon and tomatoes as well as white wine, brandy, and dry sherry. First, we steam lobsters and remove the meat. To extract the most flavor, we grind the lobster shells and sauté them. Next we flambé the shells with brandy and add them to the steaming liquid, which is thickened and flavored with browned vegetables. For a classic presentation, float the meat from one claw in the center of each bowl. Before flambéing, be sure to roll up long shirtsleeves, tie back long hair, and turn off the exhaust fan and any lit burners.

1   Bring wine and 3 bottles clam juice to boil over high heat in large stockpot. Rinse lobsters, then add to pot. Cover and steam lobsters for 3 minutes. Shake pot to redistribute lobsters and steam for 4 minutes longer. Transfer lobsters to bowl; let cool. Strain liquid through fine-mesh strainer into separate bowl.

2   Remove lobster meat from tail and claws and dice; place in bowl, cover, and refrigerate. Split lobster bodies in half lengthwise, then remove and discard innards.

3   Grind shells in food processor in 2 or 3 batches. (Some pinkish paste may coat some of shells.) Heat 1 tablespoon oil in 12-inch skillet over high heat until just smoking, about 3 minutes. Add half of lobster shells and cook until lightly browned, about 3 minutes; transfer to bowl. Repeat with remaining 1 tablespoon oil and remaining shells. Off heat, return all shells to skillet, add brandy, and let warm through, about 5 seconds. Wave lit match over pan until brandy ignites, then shake pan to distribute flames.

4   Meanwhile, melt 2 tablespoons butter in Dutch oven over medium heat. Add carrot, celery, onion, and garlic and cook until vegetables are softened and lightly browned, 6 to 7 minutes. Stir in remaining 4 tablespoons butter until melted. Stir in flour until thoroughly combined and cook for 1 minute. Slowly stir in strained steaming liquid, scraping up any browned bits and smoothing out any lumps. Add tomatoes, tarragon sprig, and lobster shells. Add remaining 1 bottle clam juice to now-empty skillet and bring to boil over high heat, scraping up browned bits; add to Dutch oven.

5 Bring soup to boil, then cover and reduce heat to low. Simmer gently, stirring often, until thickened, about 20 minutes. Stir in cream and simmer for 10 minutes longer.

6 Strain bisque through fine-mesh strainer into bowl, pressing on solids with back of ladle to extract all liquid. Wash and dry Dutch oven. Return strained bisque to Dutch oven and stir in lemon juice and cayenne. Bring soup to simmer over medium-high heat. When hot, add diced lobster meat and sherry and season with salt and pepper to taste. Serve immediately, garnishing each bowl with minced tarragon.

How—and Why—We Flambé

French cuisine is renowned for its use of the technique of flambéing, most famously used in crêpes Suzette. The word "flambé" literally means "flamed" and the technique is used in dishes from soups to sauces, when alcohol is added to a pan and set alight. This not only removes some of the alcohol but also makes a real difference in the dish's flavor, producing a more complex-tasting finish through cara-melization and the Maillard reaction, both of which lead to an altered flavor perception. Adding the alcohol in two stages keeps the size of the flames manageable and shortens the amount of time it burns. For this recipe though, we flambé just once, after pouring brandy over the lobster shells. Instead of using a blowtorch, which might seem challenging to home cooks, we wave a lit match over the pan until the brandy ignites, then shake the pan to distribute the flames.

chapter four
poultry

———

RECIPE EXTRAS

CHICKEN SALAD WITH QUICK PICKLED FENNEL AND WATERCRESS

serves: 4 to 6

total time: 1¾ hours

¼ teaspoon table salt, plus salt for cooking chicken

4 (6- to 8-ounce) boneless, skinless chicken breasts, trimmed

1 recipe Quick Pickled Fennel (page 95)

2 tablespoons extra-virgin olive oil

10 ounces (10 cups) watercress, torn into bite-size pieces

2 tablespoons minced fennel fronds

½ cup macadamia nuts or cashews, toasted and chopped

why this recipe works In France, salads are often served at the end of a meal. But this rustic chicken salad—crunchy, nutty, and tangy—is hearty enough to serve as a meal in itself. The recipe doesn't use the usual go-tos of American chicken salad—roasted chicken, mayonnaise, and pickles. Instead we gently poach chicken breasts and then toss the cooled, shredded meat with watercress; macadamia nuts; and savory, floral Quick Pickled Fennel. We use some of the brine from our pickled fennel to make a lively, tangy vinaigrette. Fennel fronds add a fresh element to this salad; be sure to save them when making the pickles. If your fennel comes without fronds, however, they can be omitted.

1 Dissolve 2 tablespoons salt in 6 cups cold water in Dutch oven. Cover chicken with plastic wrap and pound to even 1-inch thickness. Submerge chicken in water and heat over medium heat until water registers 170 degrees. Turn off heat, cover, and let sit until chicken registers 160 degrees, 13 to 16 minutes.

2 Transfer chicken to paper towel–lined baking sheet and refrigerate until chicken is cool, about 30 minutes. Transfer chicken to cutting board and shred into bite-size pieces using 2 forks.

3 Drain pickled fennel, reserving ⅓ cup brine; discard solids. Whisk reserved brine, oil, and salt in large bowl. Add chicken, pickled fennel, watercress, and fennel fronds and toss to combine. Season with salt and pepper to taste. Sprinkle with macadamia nuts and serve.

QUICK PICKLED FENNEL

makes: 2 cups

total time: 45 minutes

These pickles give any salad a burst of sweet anise and fresh citrus flavor and pair really well with meat salads.

- ¾ **cup seasoned rice vinegar**
- ¼ **cup water**
- 1 **(1-inch) strip orange zest**
- 1 **garlic clove, peeled and halved**
- ¼ **teaspoon fennel seeds**
- ⅛ **teaspoon black peppercorns**
- ⅛ **teaspoon yellow mustard seeds**
- 1 **fennel bulb, stalks discarded, bulb halved, cored, and sliced thin**

Combine vinegar, water, orange zest, garlic, fennel seeds, peppercorns, and mustard seeds in 4-cup liquid measuring cup. Microwave until boiling, about 3 minutes. Stir in sliced fennel until completely submerged and let cool completely, about 30 minutes. (Pickled fennel can be refrigerated for up to 6 weeks; fennel will soften significantly after 6 weeks.)

SEARED DUCK BREAST WITH ORANGE AND BLACKBERRY SALAD

serves: 4

total time: 40 minutes

2 (8- to 10-ounce) boneless split duck breasts, trimmed

¼ teaspoon table salt

¼ teaspoon pepper

2 oranges

6 ounces (1¼ cups) blackberries, halved

½ head frisée (3 ounces), torn into bite-size pieces

2 ounces (2 cups) baby watercress or baby arugula

1 cup Quick Pickled Fennel (page 95)

6 tablespoons Orange-Ginger Vinaigrette (page 97), divided

Quick Pickling

Traditional pickles preserve food through anaerobic fermentation in which lactobacillus bacteria turn sugars into lactic acids. Quick pickling simply injects foods with flavor and tenderizes raw textures. Heat the brine, pour it over the vegetables, and cool them in the jar. Quick pickling won't create shelf-stable pickles but it adds superb flavor and crunch to salads, vegetables, steak, burgers, and more.

why this recipe works Some pairings are so perfect that they become classics. Duck a l'orange is one such French pairing. We make it into a beautiful modern main course salad, cooking two duck breasts slowly in a skillet skin side down to render the fat and creating a perfectly crispy cap of skin covering succulent, rosy meat. Lacy, delicately bitter frisée and soft and peppery baby watercress stand up to the duck's substantial presence. To complement the duck's affinity for oranges and to cut through its richness, we slice oranges into sweet, juicy triangles and also juice them for a punchy orange-ginger vinaigrette. We add blackberries for visual interest and pops of sweetness. Lastly, the Quick Pickled Fennel we use for our chicken salad makes a complexly flavored addition here, adding crunch, anise notes, and vinegary tartness. If you use mature watercress, trim its thicker, woodier stems before using and tear leaves into bite-size pieces.

1 Using sharp knife, cut slits ½ inch apart in crosshatch pattern in duck skin and fat cap, being careful not to cut into meat. Pat breasts dry with paper towels and sprinkle with salt and pepper.

2 Heat 12-inch skillet over medium heat for 3 minutes. Reduce heat to low; carefully place breasts skin side down in skillet; and cook until skin begins to render fat, about 5 minutes. Continue to cook, adjusting heat as needed for fat to maintain constant but gentle sizzle, until most of fat has been rendered and skin is deep golden and crispy, 10 to 15 minutes.

3 Flip breasts skin side up and continue to cook until duck registers 120 to 125 degrees (for medium-rare), 2 to 5 minutes. Transfer breasts to cutting board and let rest while finishing salad.

4 Meanwhile, cut away peel and pith from oranges. Quarter oranges, then slice crosswise ¼ inch thick. Slice breasts ¼ inch thick. Gently toss blackberries, frisée, watercress, fennel, oranges, and ¼ cup vinaigrette in large bowl to combine. Top salad with duck and serve, drizzling with remaining 2 tablespoons vinaigrette.

ORANGE-GINGER VINAIGRETTE

makes: about 1 cup

total time: 30 minutes

Fruit juices with some tang make a sweet-tart vinaigrette base. Here we use orange juice; reducing 2 cups of juice to ⅔ cup creates a pleasant glaze-like consistency and means we need far less oil than usual to make a full-bodied vinaigrette. A little fresh lime juice add bright acidity, and honey enhances its sweetness. To avoid off-flavors, reduce the juice in a nonreactive stainless-steel saucepan.

- 2 cups orange juice (4 oranges)
- 1 tablespoon honey
- 3 tablespoons lime juice (2 limes)
- 1 tablespoon minced shallot
- 1 teaspoon grated fresh ginger
- ½ teaspoon table salt
- ½ teaspoon pepper
- 2 tablespoons extra-virgin olive oil

Bring orange juice and honey to boil in small saucepan over medium-high heat. Reduce heat to maintain simmer and cook until mixture is thickened and measures about ⅔ cup, 15 to 20 minutes. Transfer syrup to medium bowl and refrigerate until cool, about 15 minutes. Whisk in lime juice, shallot, ginger, salt, and pepper until combined. Whisking constantly, slowly drizzle in oil until emulsified. Season with salt and pepper to taste. (Vinaigrette can be refrigerated for up to 1 week; whisk to recombine before using.)

BRIE-STUFFED TURKEY BURGERS WITH RED PEPPER RELISH

serves: 4

total time: 1½ hours, plus 30 minutes chilling

why this recipe works For a burger with a French accent, we take inspiration from our Baked Brie with Honeyed Apricots (page 28) and stuff turkey burgers with cheese, then top them with sweet tanginess. Simply packing cheese into the patty doesn't work; it melts too quickly and oozes out of the uncooked meat. Brie melts at around 130 degrees Fahrenheit, but the patty must reach 160 degrees to be fully cooked. So we wrap the cheese in two portions of the patty mixture and refrigerate it until the cheese chills. This delays melting enough for the burgers to cook through. We top the burgers with a sweet-and-sour bell pepper–jalapeño relish. Be sure to use ground turkey or chicken, not ground turkey or chicken breast (also labeled 99 percent fat-free).

relish

- 1 red bell pepper, stemmed, seeded, and cut into 1-inch pieces
- 1 jalapeño chile, stemmed, seeded, and cut into 1-inch pieces
- ⅓ cup chopped onion
- 1 garlic clove, peeled
- ¼ cup distilled white vinegar
- ¼ cup sugar
- ½ teaspoon yellow mustard seeds
- ¼ teaspoon table salt

burgers

- 4 ounces Brie cheese, rind removed, cut into ½-inch pieces
- 1½ pounds ground turkey or chicken
- 2 tablespoons unsalted butter, melted and cooled
- 2 teaspoons Worcestershire sauce
- ¼ teaspoon pepper
- ½ teaspoon table salt
- 2 teaspoons vegetable oil
- 4 hamburger buns, toasted if desired
- ½ head frisée (3 ounces), leaves separated

1 **for the relish** Pulse bell pepper and jalapeño in food processor until coarsely chopped into ¼-inch pieces, about 8 pulses; transfer to bowl. Pulse onion and garlic in now-empty food processor until coarsely chopped into ¼-inch pieces, about 8 pulses; transfer to bowl with bell pepper mixture.

2 Bring vinegar, sugar, mustard seeds, and salt to boil in large saucepan over medium-high heat. Add vegetable mixture, reduce heat to medium, and simmer, stirring occasionally, until mixture has thickened, about 15 minutes. Let relish cool slightly, then transfer to bowl and let cool to room temperature, about 10 minutes. (Relish can be refrigerated for up to 3 months; flavor will deepen over time.)

3 **for the burgers** Divide Brie into 4 equal portions; using your hands, mash each portion together into rough 2-inch disk. Break ground turkey into small pieces in large bowl. Add melted butter, Worcestershire, and pepper and gently knead with your hands until well combined.

4 Divide turkey mixture into 8 equal portions. Encase each disk of cheese with 1 portion of turkey mixture to form mini burger patty. Mold second portion of turkey around each mini patty and seal edges to form ball. Flatten ball to form ¾-inch-thick patty. Cover and refrigerate patties for at least 30 minutes or up to 24 hours.

5 Sprinkle patties with salt. Heat oil in 12-inch nonstick skillet over medium heat until shimmering. Transfer patties to skillet and cook until well browned on first side, 5 to 7 minutes. Flip patties, reduce heat to medium-low, and continue to cook until browned on second side and meat registers 160 degrees, 5 to 7 minutes. Transfer burgers to platter and let rest for 5 minutes. Serve burgers on buns, topped with relish and lettuce.

leek and white
wine pan sauce
(page 103)

mustard-cider sauce
(page 102)

CHICKEN PAILLARD

serves: 4

total time: 40 minutes

chicken

- 4 (6- to 8-ounce) boneless, skinless chicken breasts, tenderloins removed and breasts trimmed
- 2 tablespoons vegetable oil, divided

mustard-cider sauce

- 1 shallot, minced
- 1¼ cups apple cider
- 2 tablespoons cider vinegar
- 2 teaspoons whole-grain mustard
- 2 teaspoons minced fresh parsley
- 2 tablespoons unsalted butter, cut into 2 pieces

why this recipe works   Paillard is a French term that refers to boneless meat that has been pounded thin to tenderize it and help it cook faster. We halve the chicken breasts horizontally and pound them to an even thickness under plastic wrap, so they cook at the same rate and turn out moist, tender, and juicy. To further ensure juiciness, we brown them on only one side. Getting a brown crust is key, but browning both sides dries the meat out. These sautéed superthin chicken cutlets are satisfying midweek fare; they are easy to make and look so good, they evoke the feeling of an evening out. The cutlets can be paired with a number of sauces. We use the sweet, tangy combination of apple cider and cider vinegar with the kick of whole grain mustard. You can also try our leek and white wine pan sauce or dill and orange pan sauce. To make slicing the chicken easier, freeze it for 15 minutes.

1   for the chicken   Adjust oven rack to middle position and heat oven to 200 degrees. Halve chicken horizontally, then cover chicken halves with plastic wrap and use meat pounder to pound cutlets to even ¼-inch thickness. Season both sides of each cutlet with salt and pepper.

2   Heat 1 tablespoon oil in a 12-inch skillet over medium-high heat until just smoking. Place 4 cutlets in skillet and cook, without moving, until browned, about 2 minutes. Using spatula, flip cutlets and continue to cook until second sides are opaque, 15 to 20 seconds. Transfer to large heatproof plate. Add remaining 1 tablespoon oil to now-empty skillet and repeat with remaining cutlets. Cover plate loosely with foil and transfer to oven to keep warm while making sauce.

3   for the sauce   Pour off all but 1 tablespoon fat from skillet. (If necessary, add oil to equal 1 tablespoon). Add shallot and cook over medium heat until softened, about 1 minute. Adjust heat to medium-high and add cider and vinegar. Bring to simmer, scraping pan bottom with wooden spoon to loosen any browned bits. Simmer until reduced to ½ cup, 6 to 7 minutes. Off heat, stir in mustard and parsley, then whisk in butter 1 tablespoon at a time. Season with salt and pepper to taste, and serve immediately with cutlets.

LEEK AND WHITE WINE PAN SAUCE

makes: about: ¾ cup (serves 4)

total time: 15 minutes

- 1 leek, white and light green parts only, halved lengthwise, sliced ¼ inch thick, and washed thoroughly
- 1 teaspoon all-purpose flour
- ¾ cup chicken broth
- ½ cup dry white wine or dry vermouth
- 1 tablespoon unsalted butter, chilled
- 2 teaspoons chopped fresh tarragon
- 1 teaspoon whole-grain mustard

1 Pour off all but 2 tablespoons fat from skillet. (If necessary, add oil to equal 2 tablespoons.) Add leek and cook over medium heat until softened and lightly browned, about 5 minutes. Stir in flour and cook for 1 minute. Slowly whisk in broth and wine, scraping up any browned bits and smoothing out any lumps. Bring to simmer and cook until thickened and reduced to ¾ cup, 3 to 5 minutes.

2 Off heat, whisk in butter until melted and sauce is thickened and glossy, then whisk in tarragon, mustard, and any accumulated meat juices. Season with salt and pepper to taste. Serve.

DILL AND ORANGE PAN SAUCE

makes: about ½ cup (serves 4)

total time: 10 minutes

- 1 large shallot, minced
- 1 cup chicken broth
- ¼ teaspoon orange zest plus ¼ cup orange juice
- 3 tablespoons unsalted butter, cut into 3 pieces and chilled
- 1 tablespoon chopped fresh dill
- 1 teaspoon white wine vinegar

1 Pour off all but 1 tablespoon fat from skillet. (If necessary, add oil to equal 1 tablespoon.) Add shallot and cook over medium heat until softened, about 1 minute. Stir in broth and orange juice, scraping up any browned bits. Bring to simmer and cook until reduced to ¾ cup, about 3 minutes.

2 Off heat, whisk in butter, 1 piece at a time, until melted and sauce is thickened and glossy. Whisk in orange zest, dill, vinegar, and any accumulated meat juices. Season with salt and pepper to taste. Serve.

COQ AU VIN

serves: 4

total time: 2 hours

6 ounces thick-cut bacon (about 5 slices), chopped

Vegetable oil, as needed

4 pounds bone-in, skin-on chicken pieces (split breasts cut in half, drumsticks, and/or thighs)

¾ teaspoon table salt

½ teaspoon pepper

8 ounces (about 2 cups) frozen pearl onions

10 ounces white mushrooms, trimmed and quartered

2 garlic cloves, minced

1 tablespoon tomato paste

3 tablespoons all-purpose flour

1 (750-ml) bottle medium-bodied red wine

2½ cups chicken broth

1 teaspoon minced fresh thyme or ¼ teaspoon dried

2 bay leaves

2 tablespoons unsalted butter, cut into 2 pieces, chilled

2 tablespoons minced fresh parsley

why this recipe works For most American cooks, coq au vin (rooster cooked in wine) means chicken stewed in red wine, a dish Julia Child first popularized on *The French Chef*. Coq au vin has humble origins in France, a way to use old roosters or stewing hens. Cooking older birds for a long time in acidic wine helped tenderize tough, sinewy meat and lend it flavor. In turn, the wine, enriched by gelatin from the chicken, transformed into a rich, velvety sauce. Though cooking a whole chicken is traditional, you can use any chicken parts you like. To thicken the stewing liquid, we sprinkle flour over the sautéed vegetables and whisk in butter toward the end of cooking to add richness to the sauce. We make life easy by using store-bought chicken broth. Note that you really do need an entire bottle of red wine for so much chicken. It provides a great base of flavor. Tomato paste adds extra depth, while a sprinkling of crisp, salty bacon rounds out the wine's acidity. Use a $10 fruity, medium-bodied red wine, such as Pinot Noir, Côtes du Rhône, or Zinfandel. If using both chicken breasts and thighs/drumsticks, we recommend cutting the breast pieces in half so that each person can have some white meat and dark meat. The breasts and thighs/drumsticks do not cook at the same rate; if using both, note that the breast pieces are added partway through cooking so that all the chicken is finished at the same time. Serve with egg noodles.

1 Cook bacon in Dutch oven over medium heat until crispy, 5 to 7 minutes. Using slotted spoon, transfer bacon to paper towel-lined plate; set aside. If necessary, add vegetable oil to fat in pot to equal 2 tablespoons.

2 Pat chicken dry with paper towels and sprinkle with salt and pepper. Heat pot with fat on medium-high heat until shimmering. Brown half of chicken, 5 to 8 minutes per side, reducing heat if pan begins to scorch. Transfer chicken to large plate, leaving fat in pot. Return pot to medium-high heat and repeat with remaining chicken; transfer chicken to plate.

3   Pour off all but 1 tablespoon of fat in the pot
(or add vegetable oil if needed to make this amount).
Add onions and mushrooms and cook over medium
heat, stirring occasionally, until lightly browned,
about 10 minutes. Stir in garlic and tomato paste and
cook until fragrant, about 30 seconds. Stir in flour
and cook for 1 minute. Stir in wine, broth, thyme, and
bay leaves, scraping up any browned bits.

4   Nestle chicken, along with any accumulated
juices, into pot and bring to simmer. Cover, turn heat
to medium-low, and simmer until chicken is tender
and breasts register 160 degrees, about 20 minutes,
and/or thighs and drumsticks register 175 degrees,
about 1 hour. (If using both types of chicken, simmer thighs and drumsticks for 40 minutes before
adding breasts.)

5   Transfer chicken to serving dish and tent with
aluminum foil. Using wide spoon, skim as much fat as
possible from surface of sauce and return to simmer
until sauce is thickened and measures about 2 cups,
about 20 minutes. Off heat, remove bay leaves, whisk
in butter, and season with salt and pepper to taste.
Pour sauce over chicken, sprinkle with parsley and
reserved bacon, and serve.

Picking the Right Red Wine

When a recipe such as Coq au Vin or Beef
Burgundy (page 152) calls for red wine, it might
feel convenient to grab something that is inexpensive or already open on the counter. But your
choice can make the difference between a stellar
dish and an average one. So though you don't have
to break the bank to cook with wine, you should
keep these tips in your memory bank:

Many grapes
While a Pinot Noir (made with a single variety
of grape) makes for a smooth sauce, using a
wine like Côtes du Rhône (a blend of several
varieties of grape) produces even more potent,
well-rounded flavor.

No oak, please
Remember to steer clear of red wines aged in
oak, like Cabernet Sauvignon, because the flavors
of oak do not soften with cooking, they just add
harsh bitterness.

Low and slow
Even the right wine can taste all wrong if cooked
badly. As wine is heated, its delicate flavor compounds, known as esters, break apart, turning
fruity flavors and aromas muddy and sour. The
higher the heat, the more rapidly these esters will
change from good to horrid. So sauce made from
rapidly simmered wine can taste tart and edgy,
while that made from slowly reduced wine is round
and smooth.

Price matters . . . a bit
As wine cooks and reduces, it becomes an intensely
flavored version of itself. A $5 bottle is not your
best bet, and although wines in a more expensive
price range ($20–$30) do have more balanced and
refined flavors, the variety of $10 bottles available
gives us many great options.

coq au vin (page 104)

coq au riesling (page 108)

COQ AU RIESLING

serves: 4 to 6

total time: 1¾ hours

1 (4- to 5-pound) whole chicken, cut into 8 pieces (2 breasts cut in half, 2 drumsticks, 2 thighs), wings and back reserved, giblets discarded

1½ teaspoons table salt, divided

½ teaspoon pepper

2 slices bacon, chopped

3 shallots, chopped

2 carrots, peeled and chopped coarse

2 celery ribs, chopped coarse

4 garlic cloves, lightly crushed and peeled

3 tablespoons all-purpose flour

2½ cups dry Riesling

1 cup water

2 bay leaves

6 sprigs fresh parsley, plus 2 teaspoons minced

6 sprigs fresh thyme

1 pound white mushrooms, trimmed and halved if small or quartered if large

¼ cup crème fraiche

why this recipe works In France, coq au vin (see page 104) is also made with white wine. A common rendition hails from Alsace and features the local white wine, Riesling. For this understated and refined dish, instead of searing skin-on chicken, we remove the skin before cooking the meat, as it gets flabby during braising. We do, however, use the skin to build flavor, browning it separately with the back and wings and using the fat collected from the process. The other difference between the red and white versions of the dish is that we don't use a whole bottle of wine here—it makes the meat too sour. We use 2½ cups of an inexpensive dry white that we would want to drink; our rule of thumb for all wines we cook with. Once the chicken is slow-cooked to tender perfection, we strain the sauce and stir in some crème fraîche for richness, as crème fraîche is tarter and thicker than cream, so it does not thin out our sauce. For the garnish, mushrooms are typically sautéed in butter in a separate skillet until brown, but we make things easy by cooking them in a few tablespoons of reserved chicken fat in the Dutch oven, and return the strained sauce to the pot. A dry Riesling is the best wine for this recipe, but Sauvignon Blanc or Chablis also work. Avoid a heavily oaked wine such as Chardonnay. Serve the stew with egg noodles or mashed potatoes. For more information on cutting up a whole chicken, see page 109.

1 Remove skin from chicken breast pieces, drumsticks, and thighs and set aside. Sprinkle both sides of chicken pieces with 1¼ teaspoons salt and pepper; set aside. Cook bacon in Dutch oven over medium-low heat, stirring occasionally, until beginning to render, 2 to 4 minutes. Add chicken skin, back, and wings to pot; increase heat to medium; and cook, stirring frequently, until bacon is browned, skin is rendered, and chicken back and wings are browned on all sides, 10 to 12 minutes. Remove pot from heat; carefully transfer 2 tablespoons fat to small bowl and set aside.

2 Return pot to medium heat. Add shallots, carrots, celery, and garlic and cook, stirring occasionally, until vegetables are softened, 4 to 6 minutes. Add flour and cook, stirring constantly, until no dry flour remains, about 30 seconds. Slowly add wine, scraping up any browned bits. Increase heat to high and simmer until mixture is slightly thickened, about 2 minutes. Stir in water, bay leaves, parsley sprigs, and thyme sprigs and bring to simmer. Place chicken pieces in even layer in pot, reduce heat to low, cover, and cook until breasts register 160 degrees and thighs and legs register 175 degrees, 25 to 30 minutes, stirring halfway through cooking. Transfer chicken pieces to plate as they come up to temperature.

cutting up a whole chicken

Buying chicken parts is convenient, but packages often contain pieces of varying sizes. Cutting up a whole chicken yourself isn't difficult and it will guarantee evenly sized pieces of meat.

1. Using chef's knife, cut off legs, one at a time, by severing joint between leg and body.

2. Cut each leg into 2 pieces—drumstick and thigh—by slicing through joint that connects them (marked by thick white line of fat).

3. Flip chicken over and remove wings by slicing through each wing joint. Turn chicken (now without its legs and wings) on its side and, using scissors, remove back from chicken breast.

4. Flip breast skin side down and, using chef's knife, cut it in half through breast plate (marked by thin white line of cartilage), then cut each piece in half again.

3 Discard back and wings. Strain cooking liquid through fine-mesh strainer set over large bowl, pressing on solids to extract as much liquid as possible; discard solids. Let cooking liquid settle for 10 minutes. Using wide shallow spoon, skim fat from surface and discard.

4 While liquid settles, return pot to medium heat and add reserved fat, mushrooms, and remaining ¼ teaspoon salt; cook, stirring occasionally, until lightly browned, 8 to 10 minutes.

5 Return liquid to pot and bring to boil. Simmer briskly, stirring occasionally, until sauce is thickened to consistency of heavy cream, 4 to 6 minutes. Reduce heat to medium-low and stir in crème fraîche and minced parsley. Return chicken to pot along with any accumulated juices, cover, and cook until just heated through, 5 to 8 minutes. Season with salt and pepper to taste, and serve.

Picking the Right White Wine

Shopping for Riesling can be tricky. For this recipe, don't worry about the wine's origin, but do make sure to get a drier style of Riesling rather than a sugary one. Since this information isn't always clearly indicated on labels, here are a few tips:

- Alsatian and Austrian Rieslings are usually a safe bet; most are dry

- On bottles of German Riesling, look for the word "trocken," which means dry

- On the back label of some Rieslings, you'll find a sliding scale indicating where the wine falls on the dry-sweet spectrum. Make sure it falls on the drier half

- Look for Riesling that is 11 percent alcohol by volume or above. The higher the alcohol level, the drier the wine.

POULET AU VINAIGRE

serves: 4 to 6

total time: 1½ hours

8 (5- to 7-ounce) bone-in chicken thighs, trimmed

1¼ teaspoons table salt

¾ teaspoon pepper

1 tablespoon vegetable oil

1 large shallot, minced

2 garlic cloves, sliced thin

1 cup chicken broth

1 cup dry white wine

⅓ cup red wine vinegar, plus extra for seasoning

1 tablespoon tomato paste

2 tablespoons unsalted butter, chilled

1 tablespoon minced fresh tarragon

why this recipe works Poulet au vinaigre or chicken in vinegar is a dish that exemplifies the simple and stellar qualities of everyday French cooking (la cuisine traditionnelle française). As you might guess, the sauce features vinegar—the bright, tangy red wine type—but it also includes white wine, chicken broth, fresh tomato, anise-y tarragon, and a bit of heavy cream. White wine is used so as not to impart too much color to the chicken; the red wine vinegar adds tannic intensity and sharpness to the creamy, satisfying sauce. The dish comes together easily. Our version calls for using just chicken thighs rather than the usual mix of light and dark meat to ensure that all the meat cooks at the same rate. We brown the chicken to develop flavor and then braise it in a flavorful mix of chicken broth, white wine, and red wine vinegar until it reaches 195 degrees and is meltingly tender and juicy. To finish the sauce, we fortify the braising liquid with tomato paste and reduce it to a luxurious, lightly thickened consistency before adding minced fresh tarragon. The sauce is typically finished with heavy cream, but we prefer to whisk in a couple tablespoons of butter instead, as we find that cream dulls the sauce's vibrancy here. Use an inexpensive dry white wine for this recipe.

1 Adjust oven rack to lower-middle position and heat oven to 325 degrees. Pat chicken dry with paper towels and sprinkle both sides with salt and pepper. Heat oil in 12-inch ovensafe skillet over medium heat until shimmering. Add chicken, skin side down, and cook, without moving it, until well browned, about 8 minutes. Using tongs, flip chicken and brown on second side, about 3 minutes. Transfer chicken to large plate.

2 Pour off all but 2 tablespoons fat from skillet. Add shallot and garlic and cook, stirring frequently, until garlic is golden brown, about 1½ minutes. Add broth, wine, and vinegar; bring to simmer, scraping up any browned bits. Return chicken to skillet, skin side up (skin will be above surface of liquid). Transfer skillet to oven and bake, uncovered, until chicken registers 195 degrees, 35 to 40 minutes.

3 Using tongs, transfer chicken to clean serving platter and tent with aluminum foil. Place skillet over high heat. Whisk tomato paste into liquid and bring to boil. Cook, occasionally scraping sides of skillet to incorporate fond, until sauce is thickened and reduced to 1¼ cups, 5 to 7 minutes. Off heat, whisk in butter and tarragon. Season with salt, pepper, and up to 1 teaspoon extra vinegar (added ¼ teaspoon at a time) to taste. Pour sauce around chicken and serve.

CHICKEN WITH 40 CLOVES OF GARLIC

serves: 4

total time: 1¼ hours

40 garlic cloves, peeled

2 teaspoons vegetable oil, divided

½ teaspoon sugar

8 (5- to 7-ounce) bone-in chicken thighs, trimmed

½ teaspoon table salt

¼ teaspoon pepper

½ cup dry sherry

¾ cup chicken broth

½ cup heavy cream

2 teaspoons cornstarch dissolved in 1 tablespoon water

2 sprigs fresh thyme

1 bay leaf

to remove garlic peels in bulk

Put garlic cloves in zipper-lock bag. Shut tight. Beat bag gently with rolling pin to release peels.

why this recipe works In his youth, James Beard spent time in Paris where he learned about French cooking and ate frequently at Parisian bistros. In the 1970s, when he first published his recipe for chicken with 40 cloves of garlic, derived from French fricassées or stews, he told home cooks about its "wonderful, buttery paste perfumed with garlic." Indeed, this easy-to-make dish yields huge flavor dividends. The garlic gets a head start in the microwave to soften and begin to mellow it. Sugar also helps it brown more quickly. Chicken broth, heavy cream, dry sherry, and thyme help make the luscious sauce, and mashing half the garlic into it ensures sweet flavor in every bite. You need three or four heads of garlic to yield 40 cloves. You can substitute four bone-in, skin-on chicken breasts (halved crosswise) for the thighs; reduce the cooking time in step 4 to 15 to 20 minutes. Serve with crusty bread to scoop up the rich sauce.

1 Adjust oven rack to upper-middle position and heat oven to 450 degrees. Toss garlic in bowl with 1 teaspoon oil and sugar. Microwave garlic until slightly softened, with light brown spotting, about 4 minutes, stirring halfway through microwaving.

2 Pat chicken dry with paper towels and sprinkle with salt and pepper. Heat remaining 1 teaspoon oil in 12-inch ovensafe skillet over medium-high heat until just smoking.

3 Cook chicken skin side down until browned, 7 to 10 minutes. Transfer to plate, skin side up. Pour off all but 1 tablespoon fat from skillet. Reduce heat to medium-low, add garlic, and cook until evenly browned, about 1 minute.

4 Off heat, add sherry to skillet. Return skillet to medium heat and bring sherry to simmer, scraping up any browned bits. Cook until sherry coats garlic and pan is nearly dry, about 4 minutes. Stir in broth, cream, cornstarch mixture, thyme sprigs, and bay leaf and simmer until slightly thickened, about 3 minutes. Return chicken skin side up to skillet along with any accumulated juices. Transfer skillet to oven and roast until chicken registers 175 degrees, 18 to 22 minutes.

5 Using pot holders (skillet handle will be hot), remove skillet from oven. Transfer chicken and half of garlic to serving platter. Discard thyme sprig and bay leaf.

6 Using potato masher, mash remaining garlic into sauce and season with salt and pepper to taste. Pour half of sauce around chicken. Serve, passing remaining sauce separately.

CHICKEN PROVENÇAL WITH SAFFRON, ORANGE, AND BASIL

serves: 4

total time: 2½ hours

why this recipe works In France and beyond, Provençal recipes carry an air of romance and deliciousness because of their use of ingredients that celebrate the south of France, from herbes de Provence and niçoise olives to orange zest and basil. That is certainly true of this dish of meltingly tender, flavorful chicken. Its aromatic tomato sauce, also flavored with saffron, anchovy paste, and garlic, just asks to be mopped up with a thick slice of crusty bread. We use chicken thighs for their tender texture and oven-poach them gently in a combination of white wine, canned diced tomatoes, tomato paste, and herbs. Apart from bread, rice and soft polenta make a good accompaniment to the dish. Be sure to use niçoise olives here; other olives are too potent.

8 (5- to 7-ounce) bone-in chicken thighs, trimmed

Table salt

1 tablespoon extra-virgin olive oil, divided

1 small onion, chopped fine

6 garlic cloves, minced

1 anchovy fillet, rinsed and minced

⅛ teaspoon cayenne pepper

1 cup dry white wine

⅛ teaspoon saffron threads

1 (14.5-ounce) can diced tomatoes, drained

1 cup chicken broth

2½ tablespoons tomato paste

1½ tablespoons chopped fresh thyme

1 teaspoon chopped fresh oregano

1 teaspoon herbes de Provence (page 21) (optional)

1 bay leaf

1½ teaspoons grated orange zest, divided

½ cup pitted niçoise olives

1 tablespoon chopped fresh basil

1   Adjust oven rack to lower-middle position and heat oven to 300 degrees. Pat chicken dry with paper towels and sprinkle both sides with salt. Heat 1 teaspoon oil in Dutch oven over medium-high heat until shimmering. Add 4 thighs, skin side down, and cook without moving them until skin is crispy and well browned, about 5 minutes. Using tongs, flip chicken and brown on second side, about 5 minutes longer; transfer to large plate. Repeat with remaining 4 thighs and transfer to plate; set aside. Pour off all but 1 tablespoon fat from pot.

2   Add onion to pot and cook over medium heat, stirring occasionally, until browned, about 4 minutes. Add garlic, anchovy, and cayenne and cook, stirring constantly, until fragrant, about 1 minute. Add wine and saffron, scraping up any browned bits. Stir in tomatoes; broth; tomato paste; thyme; oregano; herbes de Provence, if using; and bay leaf.

3   Remove and discard skin from chicken, then submerge chicken in liquid and add any accumulated chicken juices to pot. Increase heat to high, bring to simmer, cover, and transfer pot to oven; cook until chicken offers no resistance when poked with tip of paring knife but still clings to bones, about 1¼ hours.

4   Using slotted spoon, transfer chicken to platter and tent with aluminum foil. Discard bay leaf. Set pot over high heat, stir in 1 teaspoon orange zest, bring to boil, and cook, stirring occasionally, until slightly thickened and reduced to 2 cups, about 5 minutes.

5   Stir in olives and cook until heated through, about 1 minute. Meanwhile, mix basil and remaining ½ teaspoon orange zest together. Spoon sauce over chicken, drizzle chicken with remaining 2 teaspoons oil, sprinkle with basil mixture, and serve.

pitting niçoise olives

Removing pits from tiny niçoise olives by hand is not an easy job. We found the following method to be the fastest:

Cover cutting board with clean dish towel and spread olives on top, spacing them about 1 inch apart. Place second clean towel over olives. Using mallet, pound olives firmly for 10 to 15 seconds, being careful not to split pits. Remove top towel and, using your fingers, press pit out of each olive.

CHICKEN BOUILLABAISSE WITH SAFFRON ROUILLE

serves: 6

total time: 1¼ hours

3 pounds bone-in chicken pieces (split breasts cut in half, drumsticks, and/or thighs), trimmed

½ teaspoon table salt

¼ teaspoon pepper

2 tablespoons extra-virgin olive oil

1 large leek, white and light green parts only, halved lengthwise, sliced thin, and washed thoroughly

1 small fennel bulb, stalks discarded, bulb halved, cored, and sliced thin

4 garlic cloves, minced

1 tablespoon tomato paste

1 tablespoon all-purpose flour

¼ teaspoon saffron threads, crumbled

¼ teaspoon cayenne pepper

3 cups chicken broth

1 (14.5-ounce) can diced tomatoes, drained

12 ounces Yukon Gold potatoes, unpeeled, cut into ¾-inch pieces

½ cup dry white wine

¼ cup pastis or Pernod

1 (3-inch) strip orange zest

1 tablespoon chopped fresh tarragon or parsley

1 recipe Saffron Rouille (page 18)

Croutons (page 117)

why this recipe works We thought the potent taste of bouillabaisse, a traditional French fish and shellfish stew (page 196) bursting with the aromatic flavors of Provence, could work well with chicken too. Adapting the recipe involved substituting chicken broth for fish stock. White wine and orange zest bring complexity. Adding pastis, an anise-flavored liqueur (Pernod is a good substitute) that is local to Provence early on gives the alcohol time to cook off and leave behind a hint of sweetness that marries well with the fennel. We brown the chicken and to help the skin stay crisp after browning, we switch from stovetop to oven cooking and rest the chicken on the potatoes as the bouilla-baisse cooks so that the skin stays out of the liquid and remains crisp. A finishing blast from the broiler before serving further enhances the crispness. The stew is often served with a dollop of a creamy garlicky pepper sauce called rouille, which gives the dish a hit of richness. We add flour and tomato paste to the saffron and cayenne to give the rouille extra body.

1 **for the stew** Adjust oven racks to upper-middle and lowest positions and heat oven to 375 degrees. Pat chicken dry with paper towels and sprinkle with salt and pepper. Heat oil in Dutch oven over medium-high heat until just smoking. Brown chicken well, 5 to 8 minutes per side; transfer to plate.

2 Add leek and fennel to fat left in pot and cook, stirring often, until beginning to soften and turn translucent, about 4 minutes. Stir in garlic, tomato paste, flour, saffron, and cayenne and cook until fragrant, about 30 seconds. Slowly whisk in broth, scraping up any browned bits and smoothing out any lumps. Stir in toma-toes, potatoes, wine, pastis, and orange zest. Bring to simmer and cook for 10 minutes.

3 Nestle chicken drumsticks and thighs into pot, with skin above surface of liquid. Cook, uncovered, for 5 minutes. Nestle breast pieces along with any accumulated juices into pot, adjusting pieces as necessary to ensure that skin stays above surface of liquid. Transfer pot to upper rack and cook, uncovered, until breasts register 145 degrees and drumsticks/thighs register 160 degrees, 10 to 20 minutes.

4   Remove pot from oven and heat broiler. Return pot to upper rack in oven and broil until chicken skin is crisp and breasts register 160 degrees and drumsticks/thighs register 175 degrees, 5 to 10 minutes (smaller pieces may cook faster than larger pieces; remove individual pieces as they reach correct temperature and return to pot before serving).

5   Transfer chicken pieces to large plate. Using large spoon, skim excess fat from liquid. Stir in tarragon and season with salt and pepper to taste. Divide broth and potatoes among large, shallow individual serving bowls and top with chicken pieces. Drizzle 1 tablespoon rouille over each portion and spread 1 teaspoon rouille on each crouton. Serve, floating 2 croutons in each bowl and passing remaining croutons and rouille separately.

CROUTONS

makes: about 12 slices

total time: 15 minutes

- 1   **(12-inch) baguette, sliced ¾ inch thick on bias**
- 2   **tablespoons extra-virgin olive oil**

Arrange baguette slices in single layer on rimmed baking sheet. Drizzle with oil and season with salt and pepper. Bake on lower rack until light golden brown, 10 to 15 minutes.

HERBES DE PROVENCE ROAST CHICKEN WITH FENNEL

serves: 4

total time: 1½ hours

why this recipe works The herbes de Provence blend is traditionally made in the south of France with herbs grown that summer and then dried, such as sage, rosemary, thyme, and sometimes lavender. Julia Child is often credited with popularizing the herb blend in the United States, and it is frequently used to flavor roast chicken and lamb. We use the blend to flavor our roast chicken but up the ante by roasting fragrant fennel bulbs with the chicken, too. They cook beautifully under the bird, which we butterfly so it is of a uniform thickness and cooks evenly. You'll need a 12-inch ovensafe skillet for this recipe.

- 2 tablespoons vegetable oil, divided
- 4 teaspoons herbes de Provence (page 21)
- 1½ teaspoons table salt, divided
- ¼ teaspoon pepper
- 1 (3½- to 4-pound) whole chicken, giblets discarded
- 3 fennel bulbs, stalks discarded, bulbs halved, cored, and sliced ½ inch thick
- 1 tablespoon minced fresh parsley
- 1 teaspoon sherry vinegar

1 Adjust oven rack to lower-middle position and heat oven to 450 degrees. Combine 1 tablespoon oil, herbes de Provence, 1 teaspoon salt, and pepper in bowl. With chicken breast side down on cutting board, use kitchen shears to cut through bones on either side of backbone. Discard backbone and trim away excess fat and skin around neck. Flip chicken, press firmly on breastbone to flatten, then pound breast to same thickness as legs and thighs.

2 Pat chicken dry with paper towels. Gently loosen skin covering breast and thighs. Rub 2 teaspoons spice mixture underneath skin, then rub remaining spice mixture all over chicken. Tuck wingtips underneath.

3 Toss fennel with remaining 1 tablespoon oil and ½ teaspoon salt and arrange in 12-inch ovensafe skillet. Place chicken skin side up on top of fennel. Transfer skillet to oven and roast chicken until breast registers 160 degrees and drumsticks/thighs register 175 degrees, 45 minutes to 1 hour. (If chicken begins to get too dark, cover loosely with aluminum foil.)

4 Using potholders, carefully remove skillet from oven. Transfer chicken to carving board and let rest while finishing fennel. Being careful of hot skillet handle, return skillet to oven and roast fennel until softened, 12 to 16 minutes. Using slotted spoon, transfer fennel to serving bowl. Add 1 tablespoon fat from skillet, parsley, and vinegar and toss gently to coat. Season with salt and pepper to taste. Carve chicken and serve with fennel.

WHOLE ROAST DUCK WITH CHERRY SAUCE

serves: 4

total time: 3 hours, plus
6 hours salting

duck

- 1 (5½- to 6-pound) Pekin duck, neck and giblets reserved if making stock
- 2 tablespoons kosher salt, divided
- 1 tablespoon maple syrup
- 1½ teaspoons soy sauce

cherry sauce

- 3 tablespoons maple syrup
- 2 tablespoons red wine vinegar
- 2 teaspoons soy sauce
- 1 teaspoon cornstarch
- ¼ teaspoon pepper
- 1 sprig fresh thyme
- 9 ounces frozen sweet cherries, quartered

why this recipe works For an intimate dinner party show-piece, try roasting duck, a popular main course at French bistros. Unlike chicken and turkey, duck is all dark meat, since both the breast and leg are well-exercised muscles with ample fat. Duck is also imbued with a sultry, bass-note richness that chicken and turkey lack; plus, duck breast is relatively flat, which enables its skin to brown remarkably evenly. The qualities that make duck special to eat also make it a challenge to cook well. For tender, evenly cooked meat and well-rendered, deeply browned skin, we crosshatch through the skin and fat to create escape routes for the rendered fat. Salting the meat for at least 6 hours ensures it is well seasoned and helps it retain moisture during cooking. First braising the legs in water while keeping the breast above the liquid level allows the legs, which need more time than the breast, to get a head start on cooking. A soy sauce–maple syrup glaze encourages deep browning. A bright, fruity sauce of cherries simmered with more soy sauce and maple syrup plus red wine vinegar, cornstarch, and thyme makes a vibrant accompaniment that balances the rich meat. Pekin ducks may also be labeled as Long Island ducks and are typically sold frozen. Thaw the ducks in the refrigerator for 24 hours. Do not thaw the cherries before using. If desired, pulse the cherries in a food processor until coarsely chopped. In step 4, the crumpled aluminum foil prevents the rendered fat from smoking. Even when the duck is fully cooked, its juices will have a reddish hue.

1 **for the duck** Use your hands to remove large fat deposits from bottom of cavity. Using kitchen shears, trim excess neck skin from top of breast; remove tail and first 2 segments from each wing, leaving only drumette. Arrange duck breast side up. With tip of sharp knife, cut slits spaced ¾ inch apart in crosshatch pattern in skin and fat of breast, being careful not to cut into meat. Flip duck breast side down. Cut parallel slits spaced ¾ inch apart in skin and fat of each thigh (do not crosshatch).

2 Rub 2 teaspoons salt into cavity. Rub 1 teaspoon salt into breast, taking care to rub salt into slits. Rub remaining 1 table-spoon salt into skin of rest of duck. Align skin at bottom of cavity so 1 side overlaps other by at least ½ inch. Use sturdy toothpick to pin skin layers to each other to close cavity. Place duck on large plate and refrigerate uncovered for 6 to 12 hours.

3 Place duck breast side up in Dutch oven. Add water until at least half of thighs are submerged but most of breast remains above water, about 6 cups. Bring to boil over high heat. Reduce heat to maintain vigorous simmer. Cook, uncovered, until thermometer inserted into thickest part of drumstick, all the way to bone, registers 145 to 160 degrees, 45 minutes to 1 hour 5 minutes. After 20 minutes of cooking, adjust oven rack to lower-middle position and heat oven to 425 degrees. Stir maple syrup and soy sauce together in small bowl.

4 Remove pot from heat. Crumple 20-inch length of aluminum foil into loose ball. Uncrumple foil and place in roasting pan. Set V-rack on foil and spray with vegetable oil spray. Using tongs and spatula, lift duck from pot, allow liquid to drain, and transfer to V-rack, breast side up. Brush breast and top of drumsticks with approximately one-third of maple syrup mixture. Flip duck and brush remaining mixture over back and sides. Transfer braising liquid to large bowl to cool. (Once cool, defat liquid and reserve liquid and/or fat for another use, if desired.) Roast until back is golden brown and breast registers 140 to 150 degrees, about 20 minutes.

5 Remove roasting pan from oven. Using tongs and spatula, flip duck breast side up. Continue to roast until breast registers 160 to 165 degrees, 15 to 25 minutes longer. Transfer duck to carving board and let rest for 20 minutes.

6 for the sauce Whisk maple syrup, vinegar, soy sauce, cornstarch, and pepper together in small saucepan. Add thyme sprig and bring to simmer over medium-high heat, stirring constantly with heatproof rubber spatula. Continue to cook, stirring constantly, until mixture thickens, about 2 minutes longer. Stir in cherries and cook, stirring occasionally, until sauce has consistency of maple syrup, 3 to 5 minutes. Discard thyme sprig and season with salt and pepper to taste. Transfer to serving bowl. Carve duck and serve, passing sauce separately.

Why (and How to) Roast Duck

Duck is the "red meat" of poultry. Its dark crimson color and rich, assertive flavor—even in the breast meat—come from the myoglobin in its abundant red muscle fibers, needed for endurance activities such as flying. Turkeys and chickens have fewer red muscle fibers because they perform only quick bursts of flight. Duck is also much fattier than other poultry, building up most of that fat as a thick layer of subcutaneous padding that adds to the bird's insulation and buoyancy in the water.

How to Prep Duck for Cooking

Trim the Fat
Because duck is so fatty, it's important to trim it thoroughly of excess fat around the neck and cavity.

Score the Skin
Treat duck skin like the fat cap on a pork or beef roast and score it extensively. These channels, which cut into the breast and the thighs, allow the salt rubbed over the skin to penetrate more deeply over a 6-hour rest.

Salt the Duck
Salt helps season the rich meat, keep it juicy, and highlight its full flavor.

First Braise
Give the leg portions a head start by braising them in the roasting pan.

Then Roast
Move the birds to a V-rack, glaze them, put them back in the roasting pan (emptied of braising liquid) and move them to the oven to finish cooking.

whole roast duck with
cherry sauce (page 120)

duck confit (page 124)

DUCK CONFIT

serves: 6

total time: 4 hours, plus
8 hours chilling

6 (11-ounce) duck legs,
   trimmed of excess fat

1 tablespoon kosher salt

¼ teaspoon pepper

10 sprigs fresh thyme

4 bay leaves, crumbled

6–8 cups duck fat

why this recipe works Duck confit, which boasts a rich, concentrated flavor and tender, silky texture, is the decadent darling of bistro-style restaurants, but with our recipe you can bring the French classic home and make a batch to keep on hand in the fridge. The meat can be separated from the bone and used in casseroles or to top salads, or you can crisp up whole legs on the stovetop or in the oven to serve them intact in all their golden glory. The salting time for the duck legs acts like a brine without the water, seasoning the meat and helping it retain moisture while it cooks. Thyme and bay leaves bring a hint of aromatic herbal flavor to the duck. If possible, let the legs chill in the fat for a few days (or even a week) before serving; they will taste even better. When it's time to remove the legs from the fat, just be sure to allow the fat to soften; otherwise you may tear the meat from the legs. Duck fat is crucial here for texture and flavor. It can be found at high-end butcher shops, specialty shops, and online. However, if needed, you can supplement the duck fat with vegetable oil. Duck fat can also be reused to make more confit or in other recipes like our Duck Fat-Roasted Potatoes (page 253). To store for up to a year, simply remelt the fat, strain through a fine-mesh strainer, and refrigerate in an airtight container (discard the fat when it begins to smell off).

1 Sprinkle duck legs evenly with salt and pepper. Toss with thyme sprigs and bay leaves in large bowl, cover tightly with plastic wrap, and refrigerate for 8 to 24 hours.

2 Adjust oven rack to middle position and heat oven to 300 degrees. Lay legs, skin side up, in single layer in Dutch oven and arrange thyme sprigs and bay leaves over top. Melt duck fat in medium saucepan over medium heat until liquefied, 5 to 10 minutes. Pour melted duck fat over legs until they are just covered.

3   Transfer pot to oven and bake, without moving legs, until skin has rendered most of its fat, meat is completely tender, and leg bones twist easily away from meat, about 3 hours (fat will be bubbling gently). Being very careful of hot fat, transfer pot to wire rack and let cool completely, about 2 hours. (At this point, with legs covered completely in fat, pot can be wrapped in plastic wrap and refrigerated for up to 1 month; if desired, transfer cooled legs to smaller airtight container and pour cooled fat over top to cover completely.)

4   To serve duck legs on their own, remove them from fat and scrape off as much fat as possible. Lay legs, skin side down, in 12-inch nonstick skillet and cook gently over medium-low heat until skin is crispy, 8 to 10 minutes. Gently flip legs and continue to cook until heated through, 4 to 6 minutes. Serve immediately.

Confit Confiture

Before refrigeration, the process of confit (conserving) was used in France as a simple and effective way to prolong the shelf life of foods, including duck or goose parts. The poultry was cured in salt and then gently poached in its own fat before being buried beneath the fat and stored in an airtight crock. At serving time, all that was needed was a blast of heat to crisp the skin. Today, all types of dark-meat poultry, pork, and game are given this treatment. Tender white meat breaks down too much with this method. Regardless of the protein, duck fat is the traditional choice for the poaching step. And what makes confit taste so darn good? A few simple ingredients, low heat, and a bit of patience results in deep, complex flavor, and tender meat with a moist, firm, dense texture. Vegetables and fruit can be made into a confit too, cooked in a seasoned liquid over low heat to preserve it for an extended period of time. No wonder the French word for jam is "confiture."

making duck confit

1. Trim excess skin and fat from duck legs. Sprinkle with salt and pepper and toss with herbs. Cover tightly with plastic and refrigerate for 8 to 24 hours.

2. Arrange legs, skin side up, in single layer in Dutch oven and arrange herbs over top. Pour melted duck fat over legs until just covered.

3. Bake duck until skin has rendered most of its fat, meat is completely tender, and leg bones twist easily away from meat (fat will be bubbling gently). Let duck and fat cool completely in pot.

4. Once cooled, entire pot can be wrapped in plastic wrap and refrigerated for up to 1 month. Or transfer cooled legs to smaller airtight container and pour cooled fat over top to cover completely.

DUCK CONFIT
BANH MI

serves: 4

total time: 50 minutes, plus
30 minutes chilling

pickles

- ¼ cup water
- 1 tablespoon fish sauce
- 1 tablespoon packed dark brown sugar
- ½ teaspoon grated lime zest plus ¼ cup juice (2 limes)
- ½ teaspoon table salt
- 8 ounces daikon radish, peeled and cut into 2-inch-long matchsticks
- 1 small carrot, peeled and cut into 2-inch-long matchsticks

banh mi

- 1 tablespoon fish sauce
- 1 teaspoon grated lime zest plus 1 tablespoon juice
- 2 teaspoons packed dark brown sugar
- ⅛ teaspoon red pepper flakes
- 2 legs Duck Confit (page 124)
- ⅓ cup mayonnaise
- 4 teaspoons sriracha
- 1 (18-inch) baguette, ends trimmed, cut crosswise into 4 equal lengths, and halved lengthwise
- ½ English cucumber, halved lengthwise and sliced thin
- 1 jalapeño chile, stemmed and sliced thin
- 1 cup fresh cilantro leaves and stems, trimmed and cut into 2-inch lengths

why this recipe works   A duck confit banh mi speaks to a delicious blending of French and Vietnamese culinary traditions, and is a great way to use your duck confit. A banh mi is a Vietnamese sandwich made with a soft baguette split in half and loaded with meat. The unctuous duck works just as well as beef or pork do. But the real star is the daikon radish and carrots pickled in brown sugar, lime juice, and fish sauce for sweet-citrusy-savory flavor. Sriracha mayo plus plenty of cucumbers, jalapeño, and cilantro complete the rich, satisfying flavor profile. Avoid pickling the radishes and carrots for longer than 1 hour; the radishes will begin to turn limp, gray, and bitter.

1   for the pickles   Bring water, fish sauce, sugar, lime zest and juice, and salt to simmer in 12-inch nonstick skillet; transfer to medium bowl. Stir in daikon and carrot and refrigerate for at least 15 minutes or up to 1 hour. Drain vegetables and set aside for serving.

2   for the banh mi   Whisk fish sauce, lime juice, sugar, and pepper flakes in large bowl until sugar has dissolved; set aside. Remove duck legs from fat and scrape off as much fat as possible. Lay legs, skin side down, in 12-inch nonstick skillet and cook gently over medium-low heat until skin is crispy, 8 to 10 minutes. Gently flip legs and continue to cook until heated through, 4 to 6 minutes. Remove bones and chop meat and skin into bite-size pieces. Toss with reserved fish sauce dressing.

3   Whisk mayonnaise, sriracha, and lime zest together in small bowl. Spread mayonnaise mixture evenly over cut sides of baguette. Layer pickled vegetables, duck, cucumber, jalapeño, and cilantro evenly over bottom halves. Top with baguette tops and serve.

TURKEY THIGH CONFIT WITH CITRUS-MUSTARD SAUCE

serves: 6 to 8

total time: 5½ hours, plus
4 days salting

3   large onions, chopped coarse
    (4¾ cups)

12 sprigs fresh thyme

2½ tablespoons table salt for curing

1½ tablespoons sugar

1½ teaspoons pepper

4   pounds bone-in turkey thighs

6   cups duck fat, chicken fat, or
    vegetable oil for confit

1   garlic head, halved crosswise

2   bay leaves

½   cup orange marmalade

2   tablespoons whole-grain mustard

¾   teaspoon grated lime zest plus
    2 tablespoons juice

¼   teaspoon table salt

⅛   teaspoon cayenne pepper

why this recipe works   One of our test cooks, Lan Lam, has roasted turkey many times in the test kitchen. But she says, "If I really wanted to wow you with a single unadorned bite of turkey—no drizzle of gravy, no sprinkle of flaky salt, no dollop of cranberry sauce—I would make turkey confit." She says the most important thing about confit is that its benefits go far beyond preservation. "The method is a near-miracle for turkey, producing satisfyingly dense, silky meat and concentrated savory flavor with very little effort." We make an onion–herb paste to coat turkey thighs and cure them for at least four days. The salt, sugar, and water-soluble compounds in the aromatics give the turkey a deeply savory flavor. After rinsing away the cure, we oven-poach the thighs in duck fat until tender. Now they can be refrigerated for up to six days or immediately browned and served with our citrus-mustard sauce. Start this recipe at least five days or up to 12 days before serving. Use table salt, not kosher salt, and measure it carefully. To ensure proper seasoning, make sure that the turkey's total weight is within 2 ounces of the 4-pound target weight; do not use enhanced or kosher turkey thighs. Duck fat is traditional; chicken fat or vegetable oil work nicely, too. Reserve the duck fat or chicken fat and remaining stock in step 4 for later use; used vegetable oil should be discarded. It is convenient to split the cooking over several days. If you prefer to do all the cooking in one day, go straight from step 2 to step 4 without letting the turkey cool.

1   Process onions, thyme sprigs, salt, sugar, and pepper in food processor until finely chopped, about 20 seconds, scraping down sides of bowl as needed. Spread one-third of mixture evenly in bottom of 13 by 9-inch baking dish. Arrange turkey thighs, skin side up, in single layer in dish. Spread remaining onion mixture evenly over thighs. Wrap dish tightly with plastic wrap and refrigerate for 4 to 6 days (whatever is most convenient).

2   Adjust oven rack to lower-middle position and heat oven to 200 degrees. Remove thighs from onion mixture and rinse well. Pat thighs dry with paper towels. Heat fat in large Dutch oven over medium heat to 165 degrees. Off heat, add turkey thighs, skin side down and in single layer, making sure thighs are completely submerged. Add garlic and bay leaves. Transfer to oven, uncovered, and cook until metal skewer inserted straight down into thickest part of largest thigh can be easily removed without lifting thigh, 4 to 5 hours. (To ensure that oven temperature remains steady, wait at least 20 minutes before retesting if turkey is not done.) Remove from oven. Let turkey cool completely in pot, about 2 hours; cover pot; and refrigerate for up to 6 days.

3   Uncover pot. Heat pot over medium-low heat until fat is melted, about 25 minutes. Increase heat to medium, maintaining bare simmer, and continue to cook until thickest part of largest thigh registers 135 to 140 degrees, about 30 minutes longer. (If turkey has been cooked in vegetable oil, heat pot over medium heat, maintaining bare simmer, until thickest part of largest thigh registers 135 to 140 degrees, about 30 minutes.)

4   Adjust oven rack to lower-middle position and heat oven to 500 degrees. While oven heats, crumple 20-inch length of aluminum foil into loose ball. Uncrumple foil, place in rimmed baking sheet, and top with wire rack. Using tongs, gently transfer thighs, skin side up, to prepared wire rack, being careful not to tear delicate skin. Set aside. Strain liquid through fine-mesh strainer into large bowl. Working in batches, pour liquid into fat separator, letting liquid settle for 5 minutes before separating fat from turkey stock. (Alternatively, use bulb baster to extract turkey stock from beneath fat.) Transfer 4 teaspoons turkey stock to small bowl; add marmalade; and microwave until mixture is fluid, about 30 seconds. Stir in mustard, lime zest and juice, salt, and cayenne. Transfer to serving bowl.

5   Transfer thighs to oven and roast until well browned, 12 to 15 minutes. Transfer thighs to cutting board, skin side up, and let rest until just cool enough to handle, about 15 minutes.

6   Flip 1 thigh skin side down. Using tip of paring knife, cut along sides of thighbone, exposing bone. Carefully remove bone and any stray bits of cartilage. Flip thigh skin side up. Using sharp chef's knife, slice thigh crosswise ¾ inch thick. Transfer to serving platter, skin side up. Repeat with remaining thighs. Serve, passing sauce separately.

chapter five
beef, pork & lamb

RECIPE EXTRAS

FRENCH ONION BURGERS

serves: 4

total time: 35 minutes

1½ teaspoons minced fresh thyme

½ teaspoon table salt

¼ teaspoon pepper

1 recipe Grind-Your Own Sirloin Burger Blend (page 133)

1 teaspoon vegetable oil

4 hamburger buns

½ cup Caramelized Onion Jam (page 21)

12 ounces Gruyère cheese, shredded (3 cups)

½ head frisée (3 ounces), leaves separated

why this recipe works Burgers, a classically American dish, are on the menu at many bistros stateside. We took ours back to France by pairing it with the components of French onion soup—an abundance of sweet onions and tangy Gruyère cheese. It makes a lot of sense, given that the soup itself has a deep beefy flavor. But the task proved elusive at first: Sautéing a mound of onions just didn't give us that complex, caramelized onion flavor we were after. Instead, we found that Caramelized Onion Jam, packed with savory sweetness and rich color, captures the essence of classic french onion soup far better. A homemade burger blend gives our patties exceptionally big, beefy flavor. To replicate the cheese-smothered crostini that float atop french onion soup, we toast our burger buns after spreading caramelized onion jam over the bun tops and then piling on shredded cheese. We then place the bun tops under the broiler until the cheese is melted, bubbly, and caramelized. A little frisée lends freshness to this rich burger. We prefer to use our homemade beef burger blend here; however, you can substitute 1¾ pounds of 85 percent lean ground beef if desired.

1 Adjust oven rack to middle position and heat oven to 300 degrees. Combine thyme, salt, and pepper in bowl. Divide ground beef into 4 lightly packed balls, then gently flatten into ¾-inch-thick patties. Using your fingertips, press center of each patty down until about ½ inch thick, creating slight divot.

2 Season patties with thyme mixture. Heat oil in 12-inch skillet over high heat until just smoking. Using spatula, transfer patties to skillet, divot side up, and cook until well browned on first side, 2 to 4 minutes. Gently flip patties and continue to cook until well browned on second side, 2 to 4 minutes. Transfer patties to rimmed baking sheet, divot side down, and bake until burgers register 120 to 125 degrees (for medium-rare) or 130 to 135 degrees (for medium), 3 to 8 minutes. Transfer burgers to platter and let rest for 5 minutes.

3 Meanwhile, adjust oven rack 6 inches from broiler element and heat broiler. Arrange buns on clean rimmed baking sheet, cut sides up, and broil until lightly toasted, about 1 minute. Transfer bun bottoms to plate. Spread onion jam over bun tops, then top evenly with Gruyère. Broil until Gruyère is melted and bubbly, about 2 minutes. Serve burgers on buns, topped with frisée.

GRIND-YOUR-OWN SIRLOIN BURGER BLEND

makes: enough for 4 patties
total time: 50 minutes

For strong beefy flavor, home-ground beef makes for a truly superior experience to store-bought. Sirloin steak tips give us good flavor and minimal gristly fat; we use the food processor to grind them. Butter gives the meat much-needed moisture and fat for juicy, tender burgers. If grilling, freezing the patties first helps them hold together. Sirloin steak tips are often sold as flap meat. When trimming meat, remove pieces of fat thicker than ⅛ inch along with any silverskin. After trimming, you should have about 1¾ pounds of meat. To double this recipe, spread beef over two baking sheets in step 1 and pulse in food processor in eight batches.

- **2 pounds sirloin steak tips, trimmed and cut into ½-inch pieces**
- **4 tablespoons unsalted butter, melted and cooled**

1 Arrange beef in single layer on rimmed baking sheet and freeze until very firm and starting to harden around edges but still pliable, 35 to 45 minutes.

2 Working in 4 batches, pulse beef in food processor until finely ground into ¹⁄₁₆-inch pieces, about 20 pulses, stopping to redistribute meat as needed; return to sheet. Spread ground beef over sheet, discarding any long strands of gristle and large chunks of fat. Drizzle with melted butter and toss gently with fork to combine.

BISTRO BURGERS WITH PÂTÉ, FIGS, AND WATERCRESS

serves: 4

total time: 40 minutes

8   ounces figs, stemmed and sliced thin

1   small shallot, halved and sliced thin

2   teaspoons balsamic vinegar

1   teaspoon honey

1¾ pounds 85 percent lean ground beef or
    1 recipe Grind-Your-Own Sirloin
    Burger Blend (page 133)

½   teaspoon table salt

¼   teaspoon pepper

1   teaspoon vegetable oil

6   ounces chicken or duck liver pâté

4   hamburger buns, toasted if desired

2   ounces (2 cups) watercress

why this recipe works   Pairing a rich home-ground burger with pâté and a fig salad may sound like gilding the lily, but we dress this extraordinary burger to impress. The beauty of pâté is that it adds intensely rich flavor but requires no prep beyond spreading a thick layer on the bun. The combined richness of the pâté and burger is a bit much on its own, so we add some fresh, bright ingredients for balance, creating a quick salad by tossing figs with honey to bring out their natural sweetness, balsamic for sweet tang, and shallot for a sharp counterpoint. Watercress, which needs no embellishment, lends texture and a pleasant vegetal flavor. We prefer to use our Grind-Your-Own Sirloin Burger Blend here; however, you can substitute 85 percent lean ground beef if desired. You can find pâté in the gourmet cheese section of most well-stocked supermarkets. Be sure to use a smooth-textured duck or chicken liver pâté, not a coarse country pâté.

1   Adjust oven rack to middle position and heat oven to 300 degrees. Combine figs, shallot, vinegar, and honey in bowl; set aside for serving.

2   Divide ground beef into 4 lightly packed balls, then gently flatten into ¾-inch-thick patties. Using your fingertips, press center of each patty down until about ½ inch thick, creating slight divot.

3   Sprinkle patties with salt and pepper. Heat oil in 12-inch skillet over high heat until just smoking. Using spatula, transfer patties to skillet, divot side up, and cook until well browned on first side, 2 to 4 minutes. Gently flip patties and continue to cook until well browned on second side, 2 to 4 minutes. Transfer patties to rimmed baking sheet, divot side down, and bake until burgers register 120 to 125 degrees (for medium-rare) or 130 to 135 degrees (for medium), 3 to 8 minutes. Transfer burgers to platter and let rest for 5 minutes.

4   Spread pâté evenly over bun tops. Serve burgers on buns, topped with fig mixture and watercress.

creamy black
pepper–tarragon
pan sauce (page 139)

sautéed radishes
with vadouvan and
almonds (page 244)

miso–butter pan sauce
(page 139)

PAN-SEARED STEAKS WITH BRANDY–PINK PEPPERCORN SAUCE

serves: 4

total time: 30 minutes

why this recipe works   A well-cooked steak with an appealing browned crust and rosy interior is immensely satisfying. Pair it with a flavorful sauce and it's the perfect special-occasion dinner: elegant and impressive but quick and simple to execute. We cook flavorful boneless strip steaks or rib eyes to medium-rare. While the steaks rest, we brown a shallot in the beef drippings and deglaze the pan with brandy. Then we throw in cracked pink peppercorns and chicken broth and reduce the sauce. Simmered with the broth, the fruity peppercorns add complexity while softening to a pleasantly chewy texture. If you prefer, you can use our Miso–Butter Pan Sauce or Creamy Black Pepper–Tarragon Pan Sauce instead.

2 (1-pound) boneless strip or rib-eye steaks, 1 to 1½ inches thick, trimmed and halved crosswise

½ teaspoon table salt

1 large shallot, minced

¼ cup brandy

¾ cup chicken broth

2 tablespoons pink peppercorns, cracked

1 tablespoon unsalted butter, plus 3 tablespoons cut into 3 pieces and chilled

¼ teaspoon red wine vinegar

1   Pat steaks dry with paper towels and sprinkle with salt. Heat oil in 12-inch skillet over medium-high heat until just smoking. Add steaks and cook, without moving them, until well browned on first side, about 4 minutes. Flip steaks and continue to cook, without moving, until well browned on second side and meat registers 120 to 125 degrees (for medium-rare), 3 to 7 minutes. Transfer steaks to plate, tent with aluminum foil, and let rest while preparing sauce.

2   Pour off all fat from skillet, melt 1 tablespoon butter in now-empty skillet, add shallot and cook over medium heat until softened, 1 to 2 minutes. Off heat, carefully add brandy, scraping up any browned bits.

3   Stir in broth and peppercorns and return skillet to medium heat. Bring to simmer and cook until reduced to ⅓ cup, 4 to 6 minutes. Off heat, whisk in remaining 3 tablespoons butter, 1 piece at a time, until melted and sauce is thickened and glossy. Whisk in vinegar and any accumulated steak juices. Season with salt to taste. Serve steaks with sauce.

MISO-BUTTER PAN SAUCE

makes: ¾ cup (serves 4)

total time: 40 minutes

Be sure to use unseasoned rice vinegar here because seasoned rice vinegar has added salt and sugar.

- 4 tablespoons unsalted butter, cut into 1-tablespoon pieces and chilled, divided
- 2 scallions, white and green parts separated and sliced thin
- 1 tablespoon red or white miso
- 1 garlic clove, minced
- ½ cup chicken broth
- 2 tablespoons soy sauce
- 1 tablespoon dry mustard
- 2 teaspoons packed light brown sugar
- 2 teaspoons unseasoned rice vinegar

1 Pour off all fat from skillet and melt 1 tablespoon butter in now-empty skillet over medium heat. Add scallion whites, miso, and garlic and cook until scallions are softened, about 2 minutes.

2 Stir in broth, soy sauce, mustard, and sugar and bring to simmer. Cook until slightly thickened, about 2 minutes. Reduce heat to low and whisk in remaining 3 tablespoons butter, 1 piece at a time, until melted and sauce is thickened and glossy. Off heat, stir in vinegar, scallion greens, and any accumulated meat juices. Season with salt and pepper to taste. Serve.

CREAMY BLACK PEPPER–TARRAGON PAN SAUCE

makes: 1 cup (serves 4)

total time: 40 minutes

You can substitute fresh thyme for the tarragon, if desired.

- 1 tablespoon unsalted butter
- 1 shallot, minced
- 1 garlic clove, minced
- 1 teaspoon coarsely ground pepper
- ¼ teaspoon kosher salt
- ¼ cup brandy
- ¾ cup heavy cream
- 1 tablespoon chopped fresh tarragon
- 2 teaspoons Worcestershire sauce
- 1 teaspoon Dijon mustard

1 Pour off all fat from skillet and melt butter in now-empty skillet over medium heat. Add shallot, garlic, pepper, and salt and cook until shallot is softened, about 2 minutes.

2 Off heat, add brandy. Return skillet to medium heat and cook until nearly evaporated, about 1 minute. Add cream and bring to simmer. Cook until slightly thickened, about 3 minutes. Off heat, stir in tarragon, Worcestershire, mustard, and any accumulated meat juices. Season with salt and pepper to taste. Serve.

STEAK AU POIVRE WITH BRANDIED CREAM SAUCE

serves: 4

total time: 40 minutes

sauce

- 4 tablespoons unsalted butter, divided
- 1 shallot, minced
- 1 cup beef broth
- ¾ cup chicken broth
- 5 tablespoons brandy, divided
- ¼ cup heavy cream
- 1 teaspoon lemon juice or champagne vinegar

steaks

- 4 (8- to 10-ounce) boneless strip steaks, ¾ to 1 inch thick, trimmed
- ½ teaspoon table salt
- 1 tablespoon black peppercorns, crushed
- 1 tablespoon vegetable oil

why this recipe works   Steak au poivre has a slightly sweet, smooth sauce with hints of shallot and brandy, a perfect counterpoint to its fiery peppercorn crust. We start with beefy, well-marbled boneless strip steaks and make a crust of cracked black peppercorns for the right balance of sharp bite, intense flavor, and subtle smokiness. So the peppercorns' heat doesn't overwhelm the dish, we coat only one side of each steak. Pressing the steaks with a cake pan as they cook guarantees a good sear and produces plenty of fond, which creates a rich foundation for the sauce. Do not substitute finely ground pepper for cracked peppercorns here. To save time, crush the peppercorns and trim the steaks while the broth mixture simmers in step 1. Many commercially sold pepper mills do not have a sufficiently coarse setting; we recommend roughly crushing peppercorns with a skillet, rolling pin, or mortar and pestle.

1   **for the sauce**   Melt 1 tablespoon butter in 12-inch skillet over medium heat; add shallot and cook, stirring occasionally, until softened, about 2 minutes. Add beef and chicken broths, increase heat to high, and boil until reduced to about ½ cup, about 8 minutes. Set aside reduced broth mixture.

2   **for the steaks**   Meanwhile, pat steaks dry with paper towels and sprinkle both sides with salt; rub 1 side of each steak with crushed peppercorns and, using your fingers, press peppercorns into steaks to make them adhere.

3   Heat oil in clean, dry skillet over medium heat until hot, about 4 minutes. Add steaks, unpeppered side down, and increase heat to medium-high. Firmly press on steaks with bottom of cake pan or flat pot lid, remove pan, and cook steaks without moving them until well browned on first side, about 6 minutes. Flip steaks. Firmly press down on steaks with bottom of cake pan or flat pot lid, remove pan, and cook on peppered side until meat registers 115 to 120 degrees (for rare), 120 to 125 degrees (for medium-rare), or 130 to 135 degrees (for medium), about 3 to 5 minutes. Transfer steaks to plate and tent with aluminum foil.

4   Pour ¼ cup brandy, cream, and reduced broth mixture into now-empty skillet; increase heat to high and bring to boil, scraping up any browned bits. Simmer until deep golden brown and thick enough to heavily coat back of metal tablespoon or soupspoon, about 5 minutes. Off heat, whisk in lemon juice, remaining 3 tablespoons butter, remaining 1 tablespoon brandy, and any accumulated steak juices. Season with salt to taste. Set steaks on individual plates, spoon portion of sauce over steaks, and serve immediately.

STEAK FRITES

serves: 4

total time: 1¾ hours

2½ pounds russet potatoes, unpeeled,
     sides squared off, and cut lengthwise
     into ¼-inch-thick batons

2   tablespoons cornstarch

3   quarts peanut oil or vegetable oil,
     for frying

1   tablespoon vegetable oil

2   (1-pound) boneless rib-eye steaks,
     trimmed and cut in half

½   teaspoon table salt

½   teaspoon pepper

1   recipe Herb Butter (page 143)

Entrecôte: Between the Ribs

In France, steak frites is usually prepared with a cut called entrecôte,
which literally means "between the
ribs." You won't find it in American
supermarkets but it's similar to rib eye
(both are cut from the same area as
prime rib). Entrecôte steaks are quite
thin, usually just ½ to ¾ inch thick, and
cook quickly, which is perfect for pow-
erful restaurant stovetops. For home
cooking, however, with four steaks in
the pan, we prefer thicker rib eyes so
we get a nice sear on the meat without
overcooking the middle.

why this recipe works   "When people go to Paris, the first
thing they do is visit Notre Dame, the Eiffel Tower, or the Louvre,"
says test cook Keith Dresser. He heads to a bistro and orders steak
frites because, "In Paris, the steak is always perfectly cooked, the
fries are fluffy on the inside and crispy on the outside, even when
bathed in juices from the meat." Keith wanted to re-create the
French way of making steak frites in the test kitchen. He found
that peanut oil is better than vegetable oil for frying but the real
key to crispier fries is an extra layer of starch, like cornstarch, to
absorb some of the potatoes' surface moisture. To fit four steaks
in the skillet, buy two 1-pound steaks; for 1¼ to 1¾ inch thick
steaks, cut them in half crosswise into small, wide steaks. For
steaks thicker than 1¾ inches, cut them in half lengthwise into two
narrower steaks. You can substitute strip steaks for the rib eyes.
Make sure to dry the potatoes well before tossing them with the
cornstarch. Use a Dutch oven that holds 6 quarts or more and
use refined peanut oil to fry the potatoes, not toasted peanut oil.
A 12-inch skillet is essential for cooking four steaks at once.
Ingredients can be halved to serve two—keep the oil amount the
same and forgo blanching and frying the potatoes in batches.

1   Rinse potatoes in bowl under cold running water until water
turns clear. Cover with cold water and refrigerate for at least
30 minutes or up to 12 hours.

2   Pour off water, spread potatoes on dish towels, and dry
thoroughly. Transfer potatoes to dry bowl and toss with
cornstarch until evenly coated. Transfer potatoes to wire rack set
in rimmed baking sheet and let rest until fine white coating forms,
about 20 minutes.

3   Meanwhile, add peanut oil to large Dutch oven until it
measures about 2 inches deep and heat over medium heat to
325 degrees. Line second baking sheet with triple layer of
paper towels.

4   Transfer half of potatoes, 1 handful at a time, to hot oil and
increase heat to high. Fry, stirring with spider skimmer or slotted
spoon, until potatoes start to turn from white to blond, 4 to
5 minutes. (Oil temperature will drop about 75 degrees during this
frying.) Transfer fries to prepared sheet. Return oil to 325 degrees
and repeat with remaining potatoes. Reduce heat to medium and
let fries cool while cooking steaks, at least 10 minutes. (Recipe
can be prepared through step 4 up to 2 hours in advance; turn
off heat under peanut oil, turning heat back to medium when you
start step 5.)

5   Pat steaks dry with paper towels and sprinkle with salt and pepper. Heat vegetable oil in 12-inch skillet over medium-high heat until just smoking. Add steaks and cook, without moving them, until well browned on first side, about 4 minutes. Flip steaks and cook, without moving, until well browned on second side and meat registers 115 to 120 degrees (for rare) or 120 to 125 degrees (for medium-rare), 3 to 7 minutes. Transfer steaks to plate, top with herb butter, and tent with aluminum foil.

6   Increase heat under pot to high and heat oil to 375 degrees. Add half of fries, 1 handful at a time, and fry until golden brown and puffed, 2 to 3 minutes. Transfer to sheet lined with clean paper towels. Return oil to 375 degrees and repeat with remaining fries. Season fries with salt to taste and serve with steak.

HERB BUTTER

makes: ¼ cup

total time: 10 minutes

- 4 tablespoons unsalted butter, softened
- ½ shallot, minced
- 1 tablespoon minced fresh parsley
- 1 tablespoon minced fresh chives
- 1 garlic clove, minced
- ¼ teaspoon table salt
- ¼ teaspoon pepper

Combine all ingredients in bowl.

PAN-ROASTED FILETS MIGNONS WITH GARLIC-HERB BUTTER

serves: 2

total time: 45 minutes

why this recipe works   Filet mignon is the most tender steak there is—and it is also one of the most expensive. However, when you're buying only two, we think filet mignon is well worth the price. For a foolproof way to cook filets well and ensure a deeply browned, rich crust and perfectly rosy interior every time, we like a dual method. We start by searing on the stovetop and then transfer the skillet to the oven to finish cooking the steaks through. A quick compound butter flavored with garlic, fresh tarragon, and parsley is a rich finishing touch to this date-night-worthy meal. Pan-Roasted Asparagus (page 229) makes the perfect side.

2   tablespoons unsalted butter, softened

2   teaspoons minced fresh tarragon

2   teaspoons minced fresh parsley

1   garlic clove, minced

⅛   plus ¼ teaspoon table salt, divided

⅛   plus ¼ teaspoon pepper, divided

2   (6- to 8-ounce) center-cut filets mignons, 1½ inches thick, trimmed

2   teaspoons vegetable oil

1   Adjust oven rack to lower-middle position, place rimmed baking sheet on rack, and heat oven to 425 degrees. Combine butter, tarragon, parsley, garlic, ⅛ teaspoon salt, and ⅛ teaspoon pepper in bowl; set aside.

2   Pat steaks dry with paper towels and sprinkle with remaining ¼ teaspoon salt and remaining ¼ teaspoon pepper. Tie kitchen twine around middles of steaks. Heat oil in 10-inch skillet over medium-high heat until just smoking. Add steaks and cook, without moving them, until well browned on first side, about 3 minutes. Flip steaks and continue to cook, without moving, until well browned on second side, about 3 minutes.

3   Transfer steaks to baking sheet and bake until steaks register 120 to 125 degrees (for medium-rare), 10 to 15 minutes. Transfer steaks to plate, tent with aluminum foil, and let rest for 5 minutes. Discard twine.

4   Evenly spoon garlic-herb butter over each steak and serve.

DAUBE PROVENÇALE

serves: 6 to 8

total time: 4 hours

¾ ounce dried porcini mushrooms, rinsed

4 pounds boneless beef chuck-eye roast, pulled apart at seams, trimmed, and cut into 1½-inch pieces

1 teaspoon table salt

1 teaspoon pepper

3 tablespoons extra-virgin olive oil, divided

5 ounces salt pork, rind removed

1 pound carrots, peeled and sliced 1 inch thick

2 onions, halved and sliced thin

2 tablespoons tomato paste

4 garlic cloves, sliced thin

⅓ cup all-purpose flour

1 (750-ml) bottle dry red wine

1 cup chicken broth, plus extra as needed

4 (3-inch) strips orange zest, sliced thin lengthwise

3 anchovy fillets, rinsed and minced

5 sprigs fresh thyme, tied together with kitchen twine

2 bay leaves

1 (14.5-ounce) can whole peeled tomatoes, drained and chopped

1 cup pitted niçoise or kalamata olives

2 tablespoons minced fresh parsley

why this recipe works Daube Provençale (also called daube Niçoise), is a rustic beef stew from the south of France. Country cooking at its best, this stew is bold, brash, and full-flavored with the flavors of local ingredients, including niçoise olives, bright tomatoes, mushrooms, garlic, floral orange zest, fresh thyme, and bay. A daube makes a rich and comforting dinner on a cold night; anchovies add complexity without a fishy taste, salt pork contributes body, and a whole bottle of wine lends rich, round flavor. With so much liquid in the pot, we find that only partially covering the Dutch oven before transferring it to the oven allows for enough evaporation to thicken the stew as the meat cooks. Cabernet Sauvignon is our favorite wine for this recipe, but Côtes du Rhône and Zinfandel also work. Because they are added just before serving, use canned whole tomatoes and dice them. Uncooked, they are more tender than canned diced tomatoes.

1 Microwave 1 cup water and mushrooms in covered bowl until steaming, about 1 minute. Drain mushrooms in fine-mesh strainer lined with coffee filter, reserving ¼ cup liquid, and chop mushrooms. Set mushrooms and reserved liquid aside.

2 Adjust oven rack to lower-middle position and heat oven to 325 degrees. Pat beef dry with paper towels and sprinkle with salt and pepper. Heat 2 tablespoons oil in Dutch oven over medium-high heat until shimmering. Brown half of beef on all sides, 8 to 10 minutes; transfer to large bowl. Repeat with remaining 1 tablespoon oil and remaining beef; transfer to bowl.

3 Reduce heat to medium and add salt pork, carrots, onions, tomato paste, and garlic to fat left in pot. Cook, stirring occasionally, until light brown, about 2 minutes. Stir in flour and cook for 1 minute. Slowly whisk in wine, scraping up any browned bits and smoothing out any lumps. Stir in broth, 1 cup water, and beef with any accumulated juices and bring to simmer.

4 Stir in mushrooms and their liquid, orange zest, anchovies, thyme bundle, and bay leaves, arranging beef so it is completely covered by liquid; partially cover pot and place in oven. Cook until beef is tender, 2½ to 3 hours.

5 Discard salt pork, thyme bundle, and bay leaves. Using wide, shallow spoon, skim excess fat from surface of stew. Stir in tomatoes and olives and let sit until heated through, about 2 minutes. Adjust consistency with extra hot broth as needed. Stir in parsley and season with salt and pepper to taste. Serve.

POT AU FEU

serves: 6 to 8

total time: 4 hours

meat

1   (3½- to 4-pound) boneless beef chuck-eye roast, pulled apart at seams and trimmed

1   tablespoon kosher salt

1½ pounds marrow bones

1   onion, quartered

1   celery rib, sliced thin

3   bay leaves

1   teaspoon black peppercorns

4   cups water

parsley sauce

⅔   cup minced fresh parsley

¼   cup Dijon mustard

¼   cup minced fresh chives

3   tablespoons white wine vinegar

10 cornichons, minced

1½ teaspoons pepper

vegetables

1   pound small red potatoes, halved

1   pound carrots, halved crosswise, thick halves quartered lengthwise, thin halves halved lengthwise

1   pound asparagus, trimmed

    Flake sea salt

why this recipe works   The French classic pot-au-feu ("pot on the fire") is typically made with several cuts of meat (beef is most common) simmered in a pot of water with potatoes and other root vegetables until tender. Then the meat is carved and portioned into bowls with the vegetables and the clear, complex-tasting broth ladled over the top. Pungent condiments such as mustard and cornichons on the side add some kick. French chef Raymond Blanc called pot-au-feu the "quintessence of French family cuisine ... It honors the tables of the rich and the poor alike." A winter dish that has been enjoyed in France for centuries, pot-au-feu might seem humble but its flavors are big. We use just one meat, chuck, so we add marrow bones to the boneless roast; bones give our broth a beguiling mix of butteriness and body since their collagen breaks down into gelatin during cooking and the marrow gives that meaty umami. Marrow bones (also called soup bones) can be found in the freezer section or the meat counter at most supermarkets. Use small red potatoes measuring 1 to 2 inches in diameter.

1   **for the meat**   Adjust oven rack to lower-middle position and heat oven to 300 degrees. Sprinkle beef with kosher salt. Using 3 pieces of kitchen twine per piece, tie each into loaf shape. Place roasts, bones, onion, celery, bay leaves, and peppercorns in Dutch oven. Add enough water to come halfway up roasts. Bring to simmer over high heat. Partially cover pot and transfer to oven. Cook until beef is tender and fork slips easily in and out of meat (beef should not be shreddable), 3¼ to 3¾ hours, flipping roasts halfway through cooking.

2   **for the parsley sauce**   While roasts cook, combine all ingredients in bowl. Cover and set aside.

3   Remove pot from oven and turn off oven. Transfer roasts to large platter, cover tightly with aluminum foil, and return to oven to keep warm. Transfer bones to cutting board; use handle of spoon to extract marrow. Mince marrow to paste and add 2 tablespoons marrow to parsley sauce (reserve any remaining marrow for other applications). Using ladle or large spoon, skim fat from surface of broth and discard fat. Strain broth through fine-mesh strainer into large liquid measuring cup; add water to equal 6 cups. Return broth to pot. (Meat can be returned to broth, cooled, and refrigerated for up to 2 days. Skim fat from cold broth, then gently reheat and proceed with recipe.)

4 for the vegetables Add potatoes to broth and bring to simmer over high heat. Reduce heat to medium and simmer for 6 minutes. Add carrots and cook 10 minutes longer. Add asparagus and continue to cook until all vegetables are tender, 3 to 5 minutes longer.

5 Using slotted spoon, transfer vegetables to large bowl. Toss with 3 tablespoons parsley sauce and season with salt and pepper to taste. Season broth with salt to taste.

6 Transfer roasts to carving board. Remove twine. Slice meat against grain ½ inch thick. Divide beef and vegetables among shallow bowls. Dollop beef with parsley sauce, drizzle with ⅓ cup broth, and sprinkle with sea salt. Serve, passing remaining parsley sauce and extra sea salt separately.

CARBONNADE À LA FLAMANDE

serves: 6

total time: 3 hours

3½ pounds blade steaks, 1 inch thick, trimmed and cut into 1-inch pieces

1 teaspoon table salt

1 teaspoon pepper

3 tablespoons vegetable oil, divided

2 pounds onions, halved and sliced ¼ inch thick

1 tablespoon tomato paste

½ teaspoon table salt

2 garlic cloves, minced

3 tablespoons all-purpose flour

¾ cup chicken broth

¾ cup beef broth

1½ cups beer

4 sprigs fresh thyme, tied with kitchen twine

2 bay leaves

1 tablespoon cider vinegar

why this recipe works One look at this fragrant stew with its deeply hued meat and rich broth, and you will want to eat. The Flemish dish that became popular in Belgium and came to be called Belgian beef, beer, and onion stew, carbonnade is also traditionally made in France and the Netherlands. Blade steaks (also called flat-iron steaks) are our first choice but any boneless roast from the chuck will work. If you use a chuck roast, look for chuck eye, a flavorful cut that can easily be trimmed and cut into 1-inch pieces. A copper-colored Belgian ale works best but you can substitute another dark or amber-colored ale of your liking. Buttered egg noodles, mashed potatoes, or fresh baguette make excellent accompaniments to this carbonnade.

1 Adjust oven rack to lower-middle position; heat oven to 300 degrees. Pat beef dry with paper towels and sprinkle with salt and pepper.

2 Heat 2 teaspoons oil in Dutch oven over medium-high heat until just smoking; add about one-third of beef to pot. Cook, without moving beef, until beef is well browned, 2 to 3 minutes; using tongs, flip each piece and continue to cook until second side is well browned, about 5 minutes longer. Transfer browned beef to medium bowl.

3 Repeat with 2 teaspoons oil and half of remaining beef. (If drippings in bottom of pot are very dark, add about ½ cup chicken broth or beef broth, scraping up any browned bits; pour liquid into bowl with browned beef, then proceed.) Repeat once more with 2 teaspoons oil and remaining beef.

4 Add remaining 1 tablespoon oil to now-empty pot; reduce heat to medium-low. Add onions, tomato paste, and salt and cook, scraping up any browned bits, until onions have released some moisture, about 5 minutes. Increase heat to medium and continue to cook, stirring occasionally, until onions are lightly browned, 12 to 14 minutes longer.

5   Stir in garlic and cook until fragrant, about 30 seconds. Add flour and stir until onions are evenly coated and flour is lightly browned, about 2 minutes.

6   Stir in chicken broth and beef broth, scraping up any browned bits, then stir in beer, thyme bundle, bay leaves, vinegar, and beef with any accumulated juices; season with salt and pepper to taste.

7   Increase heat to medium-high and bring to simmer, stirring occasionally; partially cover, then transfer pot to oven. Cook until fork slips easily in and out of beef, about 2 hours.

8   Discard thyme bundle and bay leaves. Season with salt and pepper to taste, and serve. (Stew can be refrigerated for up to 2 days.)

BEEF BURGUNDY

serves: 6 to 8

total time: 4½ hours

- 1 (4-pound) boneless beef chuck-eye roast, trimmed and cut into 1½- to 2-inch pieces, scraps reserved
- 1½ teaspoons table salt
- 6 ounces salt pork, cut into ¼-inch pieces
- 3 tablespoons unsalted butter, divided
- 1 pound cremini mushrooms, trimmed and halved if medium or quartered if large
- 1½ cups frozen pearl onions, thawed
- 1 tablespoon sugar
- ⅓ cup all-purpose flour
- 4 cups beef broth
- 1 (750-ml) bottle red Burgundy or Pinot Noir, divided
- 5 teaspoons unflavored gelatin
- 1 tablespoon tomato paste
- 1 teaspoon anchovy paste
- 2 onions, chopped coarse
- 2 carrots, peeled and cut into 2-inch lengths
- 1 garlic head, cloves separated, unpeeled, and smashed
- ½ ounce dried porcini mushrooms, rinsed
- 10 sprigs fresh parsley, plus 3 tablespoons minced
- 6 sprigs fresh thyme
- 2 bay leaves
- ½ teaspoon black peppercorns

why this recipe works Julia Child once wrote that boeuf bourguignon "is the best beef stew known to man." Indeed this hearty braise, one of the most iconic dishes in French cuisine, is the ultimate example of how rich, savory, and satisfying a beef stew can be: By gently simmering large chunks of well-marbled meat in beef stock and red wine, you get fork-tender beef in a silky, full-bodied sauce. But most boeuf bourguignon recipes need 40 minutes just to brown bacon lardons and batch-sear the beef. Then there's the braising time. To speed things up, we use a braised meat discovery we made a few years back: Given enough time, and provided the pieces are not fully submerged in liquid, meat braised in the oven can develop color because its exposed surface will eventually reach 300 degrees—the temperature at which meat begins to brown. We place raw meat chunks on the aromatics so that they break the liquid line. After 3 hours in a roasting pan (for greater surface area) in the oven, the bare surfaces look almost seared. This technique takes 45 minutes off Child's recipe and produces a stew similar to hers, but rich and luxurious in its own right. If the pearl onions have a papery outer coating, remove it by rinsing the onions in warm water and gently squeezing individual onions between your fingertips. Two minced anchovy fillets can replace anchovy paste. Salt the meat and let it stand while you prep the remaining ingredients. Serve with mashed potatoes or buttered noodles.

1 Toss beef and salt together in bowl; let stand at room temperature for 30 minutes.

2 Adjust oven racks to lower-middle and lowest positions and heat oven to 500 degrees. Place salt pork, 2 tablespoons butter, and beef scraps in large roasting pan. Roast on upper rack until well browned and fat has been rendered, 15 to 20 minutes.

3 While salt pork and beef scraps roast, toss cremini mushrooms, pearl onions, sugar, and remaining 1 tablespoon butter together on rimmed baking sheet. Roast on lower rack, stirring occasionally, until moisture released by mushrooms evaporates and vegetables are lightly glazed, 15 to 20 minutes. Transfer vegetables to large bowl, cover, and refrigerate.

4   Remove roasting pan from oven and reduce temperature to 325 degrees. Sprinkle flour over rendered fat and whisk until no dry flour remains. Whisk in broth, 2 cups wine, gelatin, tomato paste, and anchovy paste until combined. Add onions, carrots, garlic, porcini mushrooms, parsley sprigs, thyme sprigs, bay leaves, and peppercorns to pan. Arrange beef in single layer on top of vegetables. Add water as needed to come three-quarters up sides of beef pieces (beef should not be submerged). Return roasting pan to oven and cook until meat is tender, 3 to 3½ hours, stirring after 1½ hours and adding water to keep meat at least half-submerged.

5   Using slotted spoon, transfer beef to bowl with cremini mushrooms and pearl onions; cover and set aside. Strain braising liquid through fine-mesh strainer set over large bowl, pressing on solids to extract as much liquid as possible; discard solids. Stir in remaining wine and let cooking liquid settle, about 10 minutes. Using wide, shallow spoon, skim fat from surface and discard.

6   Transfer liquid to Dutch oven and bring mixture to boil over medium-high heat. Simmer briskly, stirring occasionally, until sauce has thickened to consistency of heavy cream, 15 to 20 minutes. Reduce heat to medium-low, stir in beef and mushroom-onion mixture, cover, and cook until just heated through, 5 to 8 minutes. Season with salt and pepper to taste. Stir in minced parsley and serve.

wine in the kitchen

WHAT WINE BRINGS TO FOOD

Red Wine

Red wine adds a brawny, tannic, complex, fruit-forward flavor and a twist of acidity to many recipes, most commonly sauces and braising liquids for flavorful red meats.

With a few exceptions (such as short ribs braised in ruby port), we do not cook with sweet red wines.

White Wine

White wine brings brightness and acidity to recipes. It is typically used in recipes for poultry, seafood, or vegetables, all lighter foods more suited to white wine's lighter flavor.

Sherry

We often call for dry (not sweet) sherry in recipes. This Spanish wine is fortified with brandy, giving it a rich flavor and big kick.

RED, WHITE, AND YOU

This precious fermented juice adds brightness and complexity to countless dishes. Since flavor nuances are diminished with cooking, it makes sense to save super-expensive wines for sipping. That said, the rule of "cook only with wines you'd be happy drinking" has merit; as such, avoid the salty "cooking wine" sold next to the vinegar in the supermarket.

For red wines, we generally recommend medium-bodied wines for cooking and found that blends, such as Côtes du Rhône or "table" wines, produced more complex results.

If you prefer single varietals, Pinot Noir and Merlot are good choices. Steer clear of heavily oaked reds (those that have been aged in oak barrels that confer a strong, aromatic flavor) such as Cabernet Sauvignon, as the oak flavor can intensify through cooking and dominate the dish.

When cooking with white wine, we prefer dry, clean-tasting wines such as Sauvignon Blanc or a dry Riesling; as with red wines, we advise steering clear of oaky whites (like many Chardonnays).

Finally, boxed wines—both reds and whites—can be a great option in the kitchen, as many are high quality, affordable, and, once opened, keep for much longer than bottled wines.

WHAT ARE TANNINS?

Tannins are polyphenols, a group of chemical compounds that occur in naturally high concentrations in foods like pomegranates, cranberries, and—you guessed it—grape skins. Since white wines have less contact with grape skins than red wines, they are usually less tannic. Tannins taste bitter and have an astringent quality that makes your tongue feel dry. When used in pan sauces, the tannins in red wine become more concentrated as a sauce reduces. Luckily, the proteins and fats in meat neutralize their acidity and astringency, important in a dish like Beef Burgundy (page 152) that uses an entire bottle of wine. For vegetarian sauces, remember to use a less tannic wine.

THE COLOR OF WINE

White grapes produce white juice and so do red grapes! Almost all grapes have light-colored flesh. Thus, red wine gets its color from the contact the pale juice has with the crushed red grape skins, which contain high levels of pigment; redness is only skin deep. So you can make white wines from red grapes—as long as you don't let the pressed juice stay in contact with the crushed skins. Rosé wines get their pink hue from the juice having only a short stay with the red skins; orange wines are made from crushed white grapes that ferment with their skins (and seeds), which impart a light orange hue. Note that all wine is vegetarian; some winemakers use animal-derived products to help clarify and process their wines.

CHOUCROUTE GARNIE

serves: 8

total time: 3¼ hours

2   tablespoons lard, bacon fat, or extra-virgin olive oil

1   onion, sliced thin

1   teaspoon kosher salt, divided

1   (12-ounce) smoked ham hock

1   cup dry white wine

5   garlic cloves, smashed and peeled

6   sprigs fresh thyme

1   pound skinless pork belly, cut into 2 equal pieces, fat cap trimmed to ¼ inch

½   teaspoon pepper

2   pounds sauerkraut, rinsed and squeezed dry

1   teaspoon caraway seeds

14 ounces kielbasa sausage, cut into 6 equal pieces (about 3-inch segments)

12 ounces cooked bratwurst, each sausage halved crosswise

    Whole-grain mustard

why this recipe works   At its simplest, choucroute garnie is a rustic, rib-sticking, country-style dish that puts the focus on the meat. The dish has roots in the Alsace region of France: "Choucroute" means "sauerkraut" in French. And while there's plenty of sauerkraut in this dish, the trick with choucroute garnie is to create a dish that's rich and meaty but also tempered with enough acidity (from wine and sauerkraut) and contrasting texture (also from sauerkraut) to keep things in balance. While the specific meats and sausages used can change from kitchen to kitchen and are often very local (in Alsace, you may find Strasbourg sausages or blood sausages), a combination of garlicky kielbasa, sweet and herbal bratwurst, smoky ham hock, and rich pork belly provide balanced flavors. If you have lard on hand, this is a great place to use it to give the dish a little extra richness. But extra-virgin olive oil works well, too. Do seek out pork belly for this recipe; ask for it at the butcher counter if you don't see it in the case. If you just can't find it, substitute pork blade chops, pork butt, or slab bacon. Serve this dish with boiled potatoes or Pommes Purée (page 254). This recipe makes excellent leftovers, to be enjoyed cold or gently warmed up. Note that we call for fully cooked bratwurst here. We developed this recipe with 12 ounces of bratwurst and 14 ounces of kielbasa, but if you can find only slightly larger packages of these sausages, it's OK to use the whole package. You can substitute two 8- to 10-ounce bone-in blade-cut pork chops; 1 pound of boneless pork butt, cut in half; or 1 pound of slab bacon for the pork belly.

1   Adjust oven rack to middle position and heat oven to 325 degrees. Heat lard in Dutch oven over medium heat until shimmering. Add onion and ¼ teaspoon salt and cook until just softened, about 6 minutes. Remove pot from heat.

2   Add ham hock, wine, garlic, and thyme sprigs to pot. Sprinkle pork belly with pepper and remaining ¾ teaspoon salt, then add to pot. Cover contents of pot with sauerkraut, then sprinkle with caraway seeds. Cover pot, transfer to oven, and cook for 1½ hours.

3   Remove pot from oven and nestle kielbasa and bratwurst into sauerkraut. Cover; return to oven; and continue to cook until sausages are hot throughout and pork belly is tender when pierced with paring knife, about 45 minutes longer. Remove pot from oven and let rest, covered, for 20 minutes.

4   Transfer sauerkraut to shallow platter; place sausages on top. Discard thyme sprigs. Slice pork belly thin crosswise and add to platter. Remove meat from ham hock, slice thin, and add to platter; discard bone. Serve with mustard.

BRAISED LAMB SHANKS WITH BELL PEPPERS AND HARISSA

serves: 4

total time: 3 hours

4 (10- to 12-ounce) lamb shanks, trimmed

1 teaspoon table salt, divided

½ teaspoon pepper

1 tablespoon extra-virgin olive oil

1 onion, chopped fine

4 bell peppers (red, orange, and/or yellow), stemmed, seeded, and cut into 1-inch pieces

¼ cup Harissa (page 159), divided

2 tablespoons tomato paste

4 garlic cloves, minced

2½ cups chicken broth

2 bay leaves

1 tablespoon red wine vinegar

2 tablespoons minced fresh mint

why this recipe works The Tunisian condiment harissa is a favored ingredient in neo-bistros (newer establishments with more global menus), so you might well find braised lamb shanks with harissa on offer. The long, slow, moist cooking breaks down the collagen-rich connective tissue and fats, adds flavor and body to the braising liquid, and produces fall-apart-tender meat. Braising our shanks in the oven, turning them once halfway through cooking, provides more even heat than braising on the stovetop, and browning them over high heat before braising creates complex flavor. But the dish's unique character is in the sauce made with bell peppers and harissa. To keep the sauce clean and light, we trim our shanks of all visible fat before cooking, and we strain and defat the cooking liquid after braising. You can substitute store-bought harissa; note that spiciness can vary greatly by brand. Serve with couscous, rice, or baguette to sop up the sauce.

1   Adjust oven rack to lower-middle position and heat oven to 350 degrees. Pat shanks dry with paper towels and sprinkle with ½ teaspoon salt and pepper. Heat oil in Dutch oven over medium-high heat until just smoking. Brown shanks on all sides, 8 to 10 minutes; transfer to bowl.

2   Add onion, peppers, and remaining ½ teaspoon salt to fat left in pot and cook over medium heat until softened, about 5 minutes. Stir in 3 tablespoons harissa, tomato paste, and garlic and cook until fragrant, about 30 seconds. Stir in broth and bay leaves, scraping up any browned bits, and bring to simmer.

3   Nestle shanks into pot and return to simmer. Cover, transfer pot to oven, and cook until lamb is tender and fork slips easily in and out of meat and peppers begin to break down, 2 to 2½ hours, turning shanks halfway through cooking. Transfer shanks to bowl, tent with aluminum foil, and let rest while finishing sauce.

4   Strain braising liquid through fine-mesh strainer into fat separator; discard bay leaves and transfer solids to blender. Let braising liquid settle for 5 minutes, then pour defatted liquid into blender with solids and process until smooth, about 1 minute.

5   Transfer sauce to now-empty pot and stir in vinegar and remaining 1 tablespoon harissa. Return shanks and any accumulated juices to pot, bring to gentle simmer over medium heat, and cook, spooning sauce over shanks occasionally, until heated through, about 5 minutes. Season with salt and pepper to taste. Transfer shanks to serving platter, spoon 1 cup sauce over top, and sprinkle with mint. Serve, passing remaining sauce separately.

HARISSA

makes: ½ cup

total time: 10 minutes

Harissa is a Tunisian chile paste that is popular all over North Africa and parts of the Middle East. Harissa is great for flavoring soups, sauces, and dressings and even for spreading on a turkey sandwich if you want a spicy condiment instead of mayo. If you can't find Aleppo pepper, you can substitute ¾ teaspoon of paprika and ¾ teaspoon of finely chopped red pepper flakes.

- 6 tablespoons extra-virgin olive oil
- 6 garlic cloves, minced
- 2 tablespoons paprika
- 1 tablespoon ground coriander
- 1 tablespoon ground dried Aleppo pepper
- 1 teaspoon ground cumin
- ¾ teaspoon caraway seeds
- ½ teaspoon table salt

Combine all ingredients in bowl and microwave until bubbling and very fragrant, about 1 minute, stirring halfway through microwaving. Let cool completely.

CASSOULET

serves: 8 to 10

total time: 3 hours, plus
12 hours soaking

pork and beans

2 pounds (5 cups) dried flageolet,
  cannellini, or navy beans, picked
  over and rinsed

1 tablespoon vegetable oil

1 pound boneless pork butt roast
  (Boston butt), trimmed and cut
  into 1-inch pieces

1 onion, chopped fine

9 garlic cloves, minced

2 tablespoons minced fresh thyme or
  2 teaspoons dried

½ teaspoon table salt

1 cup dry white wine

1 tablespoon tomato paste

10 cups chicken broth, plus extra
  as needed

1 (28-ounce) can diced
  tomatoes, drained

cassoulet

5 slices hearty white sandwich bread,
  cut into ½-inch cubes

3 tablespoons unsalted butter, melted

¼ teaspoon table salt

⅛ teaspoon pepper

1 pound (4- to 6-inch-long) garlic
  pork sausages

6 confit duck legs, scraped clean of
  confit fat

why this recipe works Cassoulet is an indulgent feast-in-a-pan that contrasts crunch with rich, aromatic, satisfying bites of meat and beans. The dish comes from France's Languedoc region and is typically composed of garlicky white beans, pork sausage, crispy-skinned duck confit, and other meats such as lamb and pork loin, capped with a buttery bread crumb topping. If you've made Duck Confit (page 124), definitely use it here. Do seek out garlic pork sausage or Irish bangers. You can substitute other sausages but the flavor and texture of the cassoulet will not be the same. Season this dish sparingly with salt; many of its components are already well seasoned.

1 **for the pork and beans** Combine beans and 2½ quarts cold water in large bowl and soak at room temperature for at least 12 hours or up to 24 hours. Drain beans and set aside.

2 Heat oil in large Dutch oven over medium-high heat until just smoking. Add pork and cook, stirring occasionally, until well browned, about 10 minutes, reducing heat if pan begins to scorch. Stir in onion, garlic, thyme, and salt and cook until onion begins to soften, about 3 minutes. Stir in wine and tomato paste, scraping up any browned bits. Stir in drained beans, broth, and tomatoes and bring to boil over high heat. Reduce heat to medium-low and simmer gently, uncovered, stirring occasionally, until beans and pork are just tender, about 1 hour (adjusting burner as needed to maintain gentle simmer).

3 **for the cassoulet** Meanwhile, adjust oven rack to middle position and heat oven to 400 degrees. Toss bread cubes with melted butter, salt, and pepper and spread over rimmed baking sheet. Bake until light golden and crispy, about 15 minutes, stirring bread cubes halfway through baking; set aside. Do not turn off oven.

4 Brown sausages in 12-inch nonstick skillet over medium heat until golden on all sides, 5 to 8 minutes; transfer to paper towel-lined plate and set aside.

5 When beans are just tender, level of broth and beans should be equal; if necessary, add extra broth. Nestle sausages into bean mixture and lay duck legs, skin side up, on top of beans (the duck skin should be exposed; do not nestle into beans). Bake, uncovered, until duck skin is golden and crispy and casserole is bubbling around edges, about 50 minutes.

6 Sprinkle croutons over top and continue to bake until they form crust, about 10 minutes longer. Let cassoulet cool and absorb some liquid, 15 to 20 minutes, before serving.

PORK AND WHITE BEAN CASSEROLE

serves: 8 to 10

total time: 2¾ hours, plus
8 hours soaking

- 2 tablespoons table salt for brining
- 1 pound (2½ cups) dried cannellini beans, picked over and rinsed
- 2 celery ribs
- 4 sprigs fresh thyme
- 1 bay leaf
- 1½ pounds fresh garlic pork sausage
- 4 ounces salt pork, rinsed
- ¼ cup vegetable oil, divided
- 1½ pounds boneless pork butt roast, cut into 1-inch chunks
- 1 large onion, chopped fine
- 2 carrots, peeled and cut into ¼-inch pieces
- 4 garlic cloves, minced
- 1 tablespoon tomato paste
- ½ cup dry white wine
- 1 (14.5-ounce) can diced tomatoes
- 4 cups chicken broth
- 4 large slices hearty white sandwich bread, torn into rough pieces
- ½ cup chopped fresh parsley

why this recipe works   Though it may look humble, traditional Cassoulet (page 161) is a masterpiece that takes time to make. For a simpler version, we omit the confit and replace it with salt pork for the necessary richness. We use the even, constant heat of the oven for most of the cooking so that the cook is largely off-duty. Pork shoulder fits the bill as the requisite stewing pork. We retain fresh garlic pork sausage and a crispy bread-crumb crust to cover the braise. To achieve crispness even with covered cooking, our trick is to use half of our crumbs to absorb the excess liquid in the casserole and then uncover the pot, add the remaining crumbs, and let the dish cook until they are crisp. If you can't find fresh garlic pork sausage, Irish bangers or bratwurst may be substituted.

1   Dissolve salt in 3 quarts cold water in large bowl or container. Add beans and soak at room temperature for 8 to 24 hours. Drain and rinse well.

2   Adjust oven rack to lower-middle position and heat oven to 300 degrees. Using kitchen twine, tie together celery, thyme sprigs, and bay leaf. Place sausage and salt pork in medium saucepan and add cold water to cover by 1 inch; bring to boil over high heat. Reduce heat to simmer and cook for 5 minutes. Transfer sausage to cutting board; let cool slightly, then cut into 1-inch pieces. Remove salt pork from water; set aside.

3   Heat 2 tablespoons oil in Dutch oven over medium-high heat until just smoking. Add sausage and brown on all sides, 8 to 12 minutes; transfer to bowl. Add pork shoulder and brown on all sides, 8 to 12 minutes total. Add onion and carrots; cook, stirring constantly, until onion is translucent, about 2 minutes. Add garlic and tomato paste and cook, stirring constantly, until fragrant, about 30 seconds. Return sausage to pot; add wine, scraping up any browned bits. Cook until slightly reduced, about 30 seconds. Stir in tomatoes, celery bundle, and reserved salt pork.

4   Stir in broth and beans, pressing beans into even layer. If any beans are completely exposed, add up to 1 cup water to submerge (beans may still break surface of liquid). Increase heat to high, bring to simmer, and cover; transfer pot to oven. Cook until beans are tender, about 1½ hours. Discard celery bundle and salt pork. (Alternatively, dice salt pork and return it to casserole.) Using wide spoon, skim fat from surface and discard. Season with salt and pepper to taste. Increase oven temperature to 350 degrees and bake, uncovered, for 20 minutes.

5   Meanwhile, pulse bread and remaining 2 tablespoons oil in food processor until crumbs are no larger than ⅛ inch, 8 to 10 pulses. Transfer to bowl, add parsley, and toss to combine. Season with salt and pepper to taste.

6   Sprinkle ½ cup bread-crumb mixture evenly over casserole; bake, covered, for 15 minutes. Remove lid and bake 15 minutes longer. Sprinkle remaining bread-crumb mixture over casserole and bake until topping is golden brown, about 30 minutes. Let rest for 15 minutes before serving.

ENCHAUD PÉRIGOURDIN

serves: 4 to 6

total time: 2¼ hours

2 tablespoons unsalted butter, divided

6 garlic cloves, sliced thin, divided

1 (2½-pound) boneless center-cut pork loin roast, trimmed

1 tablespoon kosher salt

1 teaspoon sugar

2 teaspoons herbes de Provence

2 tablespoons vegetable oil, divided

1 Granny Smith apple, peeled, cored, and cut into ¼-inch pieces

1 onion, chopped fine

⅓ cup dry white wine

2 sprigs fresh thyme

1 bay leaf

1 tablespoon unflavored gelatin

¼ cup chicken broth, plus extra as needed

1 tablespoon chopped fresh parsley

why this recipe works   French cuisine traditionnelle is known for dishes in which a lackluster cut of meat is made sumptuous and flavorful by surprisingly simple methods. One of these dishes is enchaud Périgourdin, from France's southwestern region of Périgord. For this dish, the loin—one of the least promising cuts for slow-cooking—is baked in a covered casserole with garlic and a trotter (pig's foot) for several hours. Since French pigs are bred to have plenty of fat but American pork contains far less marbling, we ensure the meat's tenderness in several ways. Lowering the temperature of the oven to 225 degrees gives us succulent meat. We also create tenderness by 'double-butterfly-ing'. With two sweeping cuts, we open up the loin like a trifold book and expose a vast amount of surface area, so we can add fat and flavor directly to the meat. Finally, we sear the roast to create a crusty layer of flavor. We sear the top and sides of the roast but not the bottom since the roast cooks with the bottom touching the Dutch oven and we don't want it to overcook. (Also any bottom browning would be washed off during the braise.) You'd expect a roast with so little fat or collagen to emerge dried-out and tasteless but it is astonishingly moist and flavorful, drizzled with lots of rich-tasting jus, which we make viscous by using gelatin in place of the pig's trotter. We prefer the flavor of natural pork in this recipe, but if you use enhanced pork (injected with a salt solution), reduce the salt to 2 teaspoons (1 teaspoon per side) in step 2.

1   Adjust oven rack to lower-middle position and heat oven to 225 degrees. Melt 1 tablespoon butter in 8-inch skillet over medium-low heat. Add half of garlic and cook, stirring frequently, until golden, 5 to 7 minutes. Transfer mixture to bowl and refrigerate.

2   Position roast fat side up. Insert knife one-third of way up from bottom of roast along 1 long side and cut horizontally, stopping ½ inch before edge. Open up flap. Keeping knife parallel to cutting board, cut through thicker portion of roast about ½ inch from bottom of roast, keeping knife level with first cut and stopping about ½ inch before edge. Open up this flap. If uneven, cover with plastic wrap and use meat pounder to even out. Sprinkle salt over both sides of loin (1½ teaspoons per side) and rub into pork until slightly tacky. Sprinkle sugar over inside of loin, then spread with cooled toasted garlic mixture. Starting from short side, fold roast back together like business letter (keeping fat on outside) and tie with twine at 1-inch intervals. Sprinkle tied roast evenly with herbes de Provence and season with pepper.

3   Heat 1 tablespoon oil in Dutch oven over medium heat until just smoking. Add roast, fat side down, and brown on fat side and sides (do not brown bottom of roast), 5 to 8 minutes. Transfer to large plate. Add remaining 1 tablespoon oil, apple, and onion; cook, stirring frequently, until onion is softened and browned, 5 to 7 minutes. Stir in remaining sliced garlic and cook until fragrant, about 30 seconds. Stir in wine, thyme, and bay leaf; cook for 30 seconds. Return roast, fat side up, to pot; place large sheet of aluminum foil over pot and cover tightly with lid. Transfer pot to oven and cook until pork registers 140 degrees, 50 minutes to 1½ hours (short, thick roasts will take longer than long, thin ones).

4   Transfer roast to carving board, tent with foil, and let rest for 20 minutes. While pork rests, sprinkle gelatin over chicken broth and let sit until gelatin softens, about 5 minutes. Remove and discard thyme sprigs and bay leaf from jus. Pour jus into 2-cup measuring cup and, if necessary, add extra chicken broth to measure 1¼ cups. Return jus to pot and bring to simmer over medium heat. Whisk softened gelatin mixture, parsley, and remaining 1 tablespoon butter into jus and season with salt and pepper to taste; remove from heat and cover to keep warm. Slice pork ½ inch thick, adding any accumulated juices to sauce. Serve pork, passing sauce separately.

variation

ENCHAUD PÉRIGOURDIN WITH PORT AND FIGS

Substitute ¾ cup chopped dried figs for apple and port for white wine. Add 1 tablespoon balsamic vinegar to sauce with butter in step 4.

FRENCH-STYLE PORK STEW

serves: 8 to 10

total time: 2½ hours

6 sprigs fresh parsley, plus
¼ cup chopped

3 large sprigs fresh thyme

5 garlic cloves, unpeeled

2 bay leaves

1 tablespoon black peppercorns

2 whole cloves

5 cups water

4 cups chicken broth

3 pounds boneless pork butt roast
(Boston butt), trimmed and cut into
1- to 1½-inch pieces

1 meaty smoked ham shank or 2 to
3 smoked ham hocks (1¼ pounds)

2 onions, halved through root end, root
end left intact

4 carrots, peeled, narrow end cut
crosswise into ½-inch pieces, wide
end halved lengthwise and cut into
½-inch pieces

1 pound Yukon Gold potatoes, unpeeled,
cut into ¾-inch pieces

12 ounces kielbasa sausage, halved
lengthwise and cut into
½-inch-thick slices

½ head savoy cabbage, shredded (8 cups)

why this recipe works   A French dish called potée, a stew that uses multiple parts of the pig, at least one of which is always smoked, was the inspiration for this recipe. To yield a deep, meaty flavor, we use a mix of pork butt for a base of tasty, succulent meat; collagen-rich smoked ham shanks for smokiness and a silky consistency; and kielbasa for a firm bite and additional smokiness. We build a flavorful backbone by cooking onion, garlic, and herbs together. Using mostly water and some chicken broth as our liquid keeps our stew flavorful but not heavy. We add potatoes, carrots, and cabbage halfway through cooking the pork and ham shanks to prevent the vegetables from becoming mushy, and we remove the shanks to shred the meat, which we add back to the stew. A final sprinkling of parsley rounds out the flavors and contributes freshness. Pork butt roast in the supermarket is a very fatty cut, so don't be surprised if you lose a pound or even a little more in the trimming process (the weight called for in the recipe takes this loss into account). Serve with crusty bread.

1   Adjust oven rack to middle position and heat oven to 325 degrees. Cut 10-inch square of triple-thickness cheesecloth. Place parsley sprigs (fold or break to fit), thyme sprigs, garlic, bay leaves, peppercorns, and cloves in center of cheesecloth and tie into bundle with kitchen twine.

2   Bring water, broth, pork, ham shank, onions, and herb bundle to simmer in large Dutch oven over medium-high heat, skimming off scum that rises to surface. Cover pot and transfer to oven. Cook until pork chunks are tender and skewer inserted in meat meets little resistance, 1¼ to 1½ hours.

3   Using slotted spoon, discard onions and herb bundle. Transfer ham shank to plate. Add carrots and potatoes to pot and stir to combine. Cover pot and return to oven. Cook until vegetables are almost tender, 20 to 25 minutes. When ham shank is cool enough to handle, using 2 forks, shred ham into bite-size pieces, discarding skin and bones.

4   Add kielbasa, cabbage, and shredded ham to pot. Stir to combine, cover, and return to oven. Cook until kielbasa is heated through and cabbage is wilted and tender, 15 to 20 minutes. Season with salt and pepper to taste, then stir in chopped parsley. Ladle into bowls and serve. (Stew can be made up to 3 days in advance.)

LEG OF LAMB
EN COCOTTE

serves: 6 to 8

total time: 1½ hours

1 (4- to 5-pound) boneless half leg of lamb, trimmed and tied

Table salt and pepper

2 tablespoons extra-virgin olive oil

8 garlic cloves, peeled and sliced thin

2 sprigs fresh rosemary

why this recipe works Cooking en cocotte (see page 186) is a technique that involves cooking proteins in a covered pot over low heat for an extended period of time, which results in incredibly moist, tender meat. The technique is often used in bistros because the meat doesn't need to be watched as it cooks. Lamb's gamy flavor comes mostly from the fat so we trim it before cooking to give the finished roast a milder flavor. We add rosemary and garlic cloves to the lamb before it goes into the oven; their aroma perfumes the meat. In an hour, we have a simple, beautifully flavored dish to add to our en cocotte repertoire and a lamb roast that slices like a dream into tender pieces and becomes more succulent with lamb jus from the pot.

1 Adjust oven rack to lowest position and heat oven to 250 degrees. Pat lamb dry with paper towels and sprinkle with salt and pepper.

2 Heat oil in Dutch oven over medium-high heat until just smoking. Brown lamb well on all sides, 7 to 10 minutes, reducing heat if pot begins to scorch. Transfer lamb to large plate.

3 Pour off fat from pot. Add garlic and rosemary and nestle lamb, with any accumulated juices, into pot. Place large piece of aluminum foil over pot and cover tightly with lid; transfer pot to oven. Cook until lamb registers 120 to 125 degrees (for medium-rare), 45 minutes to 1 hour.

4 Transfer lamb to carving board, tent with foil, and let rest for 20 minutes. Remove rosemary from pot, then cover to keep jus warm. Remove twine, slice lamb ¼ inch thick, and transfer to serving platter. Spoon jus over lamb and serve.

chapter six

seafood

———————

RECIPE EXTRAS

OVEN-STEAMED MUSSELS

serves: 2 to 4

total time: 45 minutes

1 tablespoon extra-virgin olive oil

3 garlic cloves, minced

Pinch red pepper flakes

1 cup dry white wine

3 sprigs fresh thyme

2 bay leaves

4 pounds mussels, scrubbed and debearded

¼ teaspoon table salt

2 tablespoons unsalted butter, cut into 4 pieces

2 tablespoons minced fresh parsley

Mussel Knowledge

1. Mussels are routinely tested by state and local agencies for algae-derived toxins.

2. Most mussels are cultivated on long ropes suspended from rafts so they have no sand and grit. Just rinsing them under the tap gets them clean.

3. A live mussel's shell should close when lightly tapped.

4. A dead mussel deteriorates rapidly and smells almost immediately. Discard it, along with mussels with cracked or broken shells or shells that won't close.

5. Store mussels for up to three days. Place mussels in a bowl, cover with a wet paper towel, and refrigerate.

why this recipe works It is said that the French eat more mussels per capita than any other nation, and arguably the most popular mussel dish in France is moules frites: mussels served with french fries and mayonnaise. But no matter how you wish to serve them, we wanted a method of steaming that allows mussels of different sizes to cook at the same rate, so they are all wide open and perfectly tender. We found that the oven gives us that because its all-round heat ensures gentler, more even cooking than the stovetop, where the heat can't help but be more aggressive at the bottom of the pan. The next question: What pan to use? A Dutch oven is great for the stovetop but full of mussels, it's hard to turn the shellfish over to ensure they all get some heat. We found that a large roasting pan works beautifully: The mussels aren't crowded, and covering the pan with aluminum foil traps the moisture in so they don't dry out. Unopened cooked mussels just need more cooking time. To open them, microwave briefly for 30 seconds or so.

1   Adjust oven rack to lowest position and heat oven to 500 degrees. Heat oil, garlic, and pepper flakes in large roasting pan over medium heat; cook, stirring constantly, until fragrant, about 30 seconds. Add wine, thyme sprigs, and bay leaves and bring to boil. Cook until wine is slightly reduced, about 1 minute. Add mussels and salt. Cover pan tightly with aluminum foil and transfer to oven. Cook until most mussels have opened (a few may remain closed), 15 to 18 minutes.

2   Remove pan from oven. Push mussels to sides of pan. Add butter to center and whisk until melted. Discard thyme sprigs and bay leaves, sprinkle parsley over mussels, and toss to combine. Serve immediately.

debearding mussels

When you buy mussels, you might notice that some of them have a weedy piece (known as a beard) protruding from their shells. Though the beard is harmless, it does look unattractive in dishes, so you should remove it.

Because it's fairly small, the beard can be difficult to tug out of place. To remove it easily, trap the beard in a towel and use your thumb and fingers to pull it out.

variations

OVEN-STEAMED MUSSELS WITH HARD CIDER AND BACON

Omit garlic and red pepper flakes. Heat oil and 4 slices thick-cut bacon, cut into ½-inch pieces, in roasting pan until bacon has rendered and is starting to crisp, about 5 minutes. Proceed with recipe as directed, substituting dry hard cider for wine and ¼ cup heavy cream for butter.

OVEN-STEAMED MUSSELS WITH LEEKS AND PERNOD

Omit red pepper flakes and increase oil to 3 tablespoons. Heat oil; 1 pound leeks, white and light green parts only, halved lengthwise, sliced thin, and washed thoroughly; and garlic in roasting pan until leeks are wilted, about 3 minutes. Proceed with recipe as directed, omitting thyme sprigs and substituting ½ cup Pernod and ¼ cup water for wine, ¼ cup crème fraîche for butter, and chives for parsley.

SCALLOPS WITH FENNEL AND BIBB SALAD

serves: 4

total time: 30 minutes

1½ pounds large sea scallops, tendons removed

¾ teaspoon table salt, divided

½ teaspoon pepper, divided

7 tablespoons extra-virgin olive oil, divided

1 small shallot, minced

½ teaspoon grated lemon zest plus 1½ tablespoons juice

1 teaspoon Dijon mustard

2 heads Bibb lettuce (1 pound), torn into bite-size pieces

1 fennel bulb, 1 tablespoon fronds minced, stalks discarded, bulb halved, cored, and sliced thin

4 radishes, trimmed and sliced thin

¼ cup hazelnuts, toasted, skinned, and chopped

2 tablespoons minced fresh tarragon

why this recipe works Scallops are known as coquilles in France; their pristinely smooth flesh and superlative sweetness doesn't have to be accompanied by a luxurious sauce. They make an ideal weeknight meal because they cook quickly and are healthful, giving heft to a salad when paired with flavorful greens. We quickly sear our scallops to browned perfection using a non-stick skillet, after blotting them dry first (see our other searing tips, below). Then we toss delicate Bibb lettuce, crisp sliced fennel, and radishes with a lemon vinaigrette. Finally, we top individual portions with warm scallops and chopped toasted hazelnuts, which bring out the natural sweet nuttiness of the scallops. Tarragon emphasizes the anise flavor of the fennel.

1 Pat scallops dry with paper towels and sprinkle with ½ teaspoon salt and ¼ teaspoon pepper. Heat 1 tablespoon oil in skillet over high heat until just smoking. Add half of scallops in single layer and cook, without moving, until well browned, 1½ to 2 minutes. Flip and cook until sides are firm and centers are opaque, 30 to 90 seconds (remove scallops as they finish cooking). Transfer scallops to plate and tent with aluminum foil. Wipe out skillet with paper towels and repeat with 1 tablespoon oil and remaining scallops.

2 Whisk shallot, lemon zest and juice, mustard, remaining ¼ teaspoon salt, and remaining ¼ teaspoon pepper together in large bowl. While whisking constantly, slowly drizzle in remaining 5 tablespoons oil until combined. Add lettuce, sliced fennel, and radishes and toss to combine. Season with salt and pepper to taste. Divide salad among individual serving dishes, then top with scallops and sprinkle with hazelnuts, tarragon, and fennel fronds. Serve.

Searing Tips for Beautifully Browned Scallops

1. Blot scallops dry and add them to the nonstick skillet when the oil begins to smoke, an indication of high heat

2. Cook scallops in batches, so as not to crowd the pan and lower its temperature

3. Resist the urge to move the scallops as they sear. Leave them alone until it's time to flip them!

SOLE MEUNIÈRE

serves: 4

total time: 40 minutes

4 (6- to 8-ounce) skinless sole fillets, split lengthwise down natural seam

½ teaspoon table salt

¼ teaspoon pepper

½ cup all-purpose flour

2 tablespoons vegetable oil, divided

6 tablespoons unsalted butter, divided

1½ tablespoons lemon juice

2 tablespoons chopped fresh parsley

Splitting Down the Natural Seam

We came up with the idea of splitting thin white fish down its natural seam before cooking. Why? The thick half of a thin, wide fillet rests flat in the pan and browns nicely during sautéing, but the thin half tilts up, hardly making contact at all. The only way around this is to split them at their seams and cook the thick halves in one batch and the thin halves in a second batch. The move actually enhances rather than detracts from their aesthetic: We like uniform, evenly browned fish fillets. High heat gets the fish, both thick and thin pieces, remarkably brown and evenly crisp on both sides. This step works well for sole and for other flat fish like flounder and tilapia, too.

why this recipe works Sole Meunière, the classic French dish that made Julia Child fall in love with French cuisine, consists of lightly browned flour-crusted fillets of sole served with a nutty, golden-brown butter sauce. We find that the perfect crust comes from simply drying the fillets, seasoning them with salt and pepper, and then dredging them in flour. We get the most even cooking and best browning by first splitting the fish down the natural seam. Try to purchase fillets that are of similar size. If using smaller fillets (3 ounces each), serve two fillets per person and reduce the cooking time on the second side to about 1 minute. You will need to cook smaller fillets in three or four batches and wipe out the skillet with paper towels after the second and third batches to prevent any browned bits from scorching. You can substitute catfish, flounder, or tilapia for the sole.

1 Adjust oven rack to middle position and heat oven to 200 degrees. Pat sole dry with paper towels and sprinkle with salt and pepper. Spread flour in shallow dish. Dredge fillets in flour, shaking off excess, and transfer to large plate.

2 Heat 1 tablespoon oil in 12-inch nonstick skillet over medium-high heat until shimmering. Add 1 tablespoon butter and swirl until melted. Add thick halves of fillets to skillet and cook until golden on first side, about 3 minutes. Using 2 spatulas, flip fillets and cook until second sides are golden and fish flakes apart when gently prodded with paring knife, about 2 minutes. Transfer to ovensafe platter and keep warm in oven. Wipe skillet clean with paper towels and repeat with remaining 1 tablespoon oil, 1 tablespoon butter, and thin halves of fillets. Transfer to platter.

3 Melt remaining 4 tablespoons unsalted butter in medium saucepan over medium-high heat. Continue to cook, swirling saucepan constantly, until butter is golden brown and has nutty aroma, 1 to 1½ minutes longer. Remove saucepan from heat, add lemon juice, and season with salt to taste. Spoon sauce over sole and sprinkle with parsley. Serve immediately.

PAN-SEARED TROUT WITH BRUSSELS SPROUTS AND BACON

serves: 4

total time: 40 minutes

why this recipe works Brussels sprouts rarely appear in seafood recipes but we love the heft they provide to an otherwise delicate fish, and trout, especially when given a crispy skin, has a presence that easily stands up to the vegetable. Smoky bacon, a classic with brussels sprouts, also pairs well with the trout and ties the dish together, making a hearty bistro-style main course. We use the rendered fat from the crispy bacon to sauté the Brussels sprouts, which we jump-start in the microwave to get them tender enough to cook through in the skillet. A little cornstarch on the trout helps it achieve extra-crispy skin.

1 pound brussels sprouts, trimmed and halved

1 teaspoon table salt, divided

½ teaspoon pepper, divided

3 slices bacon, cut into ½-inch pieces

1 shallot, minced

2 garlic cloves, minced

½ teaspoon minced fresh thyme

3 tablespoons cornstarch

3 (8- to 10-ounce) boneless, butterflied whole trout, halved between fillets

¼ cup vegetable oil, divided

1 Adjust oven rack to middle position and heat oven to 200 degrees. Combine brussels sprouts, 1 tablespoon water, ½ teaspoon salt, and ¼ teaspoon pepper in bowl. Microwave, covered, until brussels sprouts are just tender, about 5 minutes; drain.

2 Meanwhile, cook bacon in 12-inch nonstick skillet over medium-high heat until crispy, about 5 minutes. Using slotted spoon, transfer bacon to paper towel–lined plate. Add shallot to fat left in skillet and cook until softened, about 2 minutes. Stir in garlic and thyme and cook until fragrant, about 30 seconds. Add drained sprouts and cook until lightly browned, about 3 minutes; transfer to ovensafe platter and keep warm in oven.

3 Spread cornstarch in shallow dish. Pat trout dry with paper towels, sprinkle with remaining ½ teaspoon salt and remaining ¼ teaspoon pepper, then dredge in cornstarch, pressing gently to adhere. Wipe out now-empty skillet with paper towels, add 2 tablespoons oil, and heat over high heat until shimmering. Lay 3 pieces trout skin side down in skillet and reduce heat to medium-high. Cook until golden on both sides and fish flakes apart when gently prodded with paring knife, about 4 minutes per side; transfer to platter with sprouts and keep warm in oven.

4 Wipe out now-empty skillet with paper towels and repeat with remaining 2 tablespoons oil and remaining 3 trout pieces. Serve with brussels sprouts and sprinkle with bacon.

SEARED TUNA STEAKS WITH WILTED FRISÉE AND MUSHROOM SALAD

serves: 4

total time: 40 minutes

why this recipe works We give fish and salad a modern bistro touch with layers of flavor and texture by drizzling lightly seared tuna with harissa and pairing it with an elegant frisée and mushroom salad. First we cook cremini and shiitake mushrooms, add spicy harissa, and then wilt the frisée by adding the hot harissa-coated mushrooms to it. A mint garnish adds a fresh hint of coolness to the dish. Tuna steaks can be pricey. To get your money's worth, purchase only tuna steaks that are deep purplish red, firm to the touch, and devoid of any "fishy" odor. We prefer to use our Harissa for this dish but you can substitute store-bought. Remember that different brands vary in spiciness. You will need a 12-inch nonstick skillet with a tight-fitting lid for this recipe.

- 3 tablespoons Harissa (page 159), divided
- 1 tablespoon lemon juice plus lemon wedges for serving
- 6 tablespoons extra-virgin olive oil, divided
- 1–3 tablespoons hot water (110 degrees)
- 1 shallot, halved and sliced thin
- 1¼ pounds cremini mushrooms, trimmed and halved if small or quartered if large
- 12 ounces shiitake mushrooms, stemmed and sliced ½ inch thick
- 1 teaspoon table salt, divided
- 1 head frisée (6 ounces), cut into 1-inch pieces
- 4 (6- to 8-ounce) tuna steaks, 1 inch thick
- ¼ teaspoon pepper
- ½ teaspoon sugar
- 2 tablespoons chopped fresh mint

1 Whisk 2 tablespoons harissa, lemon juice, and 1 tablespoon oil together in bowl. Whisk in hot water, 1 tablespoon at a time, until sauce is pourable; set aside until ready to serve.

2 Heat 2 tablespoons oil in 12-inch nonstick skillet over medium heat until shimmering. Add shallot and cook until softened, about 2 minutes. Add cremini mushrooms, shiitake mushrooms, and ½ teaspoon salt, cover, and cook, stirring occasionally, until mushrooms have released their liquid, 8 to 10 minutes.

3 Uncover skillet, add 2 tablespoons oil, and cook, stirring occasionally, until mushrooms are deep golden brown and tender, 10 to 12 minutes. Add remaining 1 tablespoon harissa and cook until fragrant, about 30 seconds. Transfer mushrooms to large bowl, add frisée, and toss to combine; set aside. Wipe skillet clean with paper towels.

4 Pat tuna dry with paper towels and sprinkle with remaining ½ teaspoon salt and pepper. Sprinkle sugar evenly over 1 side of each steak. Heat remaining 1 tablespoon oil in now-empty skillet over medium-high heat until just smoking. Place steaks sugared sides down in skillet and cook, flipping every 1 to 2 minutes, until center is translucent red when checked with tip of paring knife and registers 110 degrees (for rare), 2 to 4 minutes.

5 Transfer steaks to cutting board and slice ½ inch thick. Sprinkle mint over mushroom mixture and season with salt and pepper to taste. Drizzle tuna with reserved harissa sauce and serve with salad and lemon wedges.

CRISPY PAN-SEARED SEA BASS WITH RAMP PISTOU

serves: 4

total time: 1¼ hours

2 teaspoons table salt, divided

1½ teaspoons sugar

4 (6- to 8-ounce) skin-on sea bass fish fillets, 1 to 1½ inches thick

6 ounces ramps, white parts sliced thin, green parts cut into 1-inch pieces, divided

½ cup extra-virgin olive oil, divided

3 tablespoons chopped toasted pistachios

2 tablespoons water, plus extra as needed

1 tablespoon lemon juice, plus lemon wedges for serving

¼ cup grated Parmesan cheese

why this recipe works April Fool's Day is Poisson d'Avril in France, when kids try to pin the picture of a fish on adults' backs. We'd rather eat fish! We pair crisp-skinned sea bass with seasonal ramps in a stunning main you might see at your favorite bistro. Scoring the skin and sprinkling the fish with salt and sugar ensures well-seasoned fillets. We sauté sliced ramp bulbs till softened, add most of the greens, and cook until just wilted. Then we process the cooked ramps and reserved ramp greens into a bright but mild pistou. This recipe makes about 1 cup of pistou. It can be refrigerated for up to three days. Skin-on arctic char, bluefish, farmed or wild salmon, or red snapper fillets make good substitutes for sea bass.

1 Combine 1½ teaspoons salt and sugar in small bowl. Using sharp knife, make 3 or 4 shallow slashes, about ½ inch apart, lengthwise in skin side of each fillet, being careful not to cut into flesh and stopping ½ inch from top and bottom edge of skin. Season flesh side of fillets evenly with salt mixture and place skin side up on wire rack set in rimmed baking sheet. Sprinkle skin side with ¼ teaspoon salt. Refrigerate for 45 minutes.

2 Meanwhile, measure out ¼ cup ramp greens and set aside. Heat 2 tablespoons oil in 12-inch nonstick skillet over medium heat until shimmering. Add ramp whites and cook until softened, about 2 minutes. Stir in remaining ramp greens and cook until just wilted, about 1 minute. Transfer to food processor and let cool slightly, about 10 minutes.

3 Add pistachios, water, lemon juice, remaining ¼ teaspoon salt, ¼ cup oil, and reserved ramp greens to food processor and process until smooth, about 30 seconds, scraping down sides of bowl as needed. Transfer to bowl and stir in Parmesan. Adjust consistency with additional water as needed; set aside until ready to serve.

4 Pat fillets dry with paper towels. Heat remaining 2 tablespoons oil in now-empty skillet over high heat until just smoking. Place fillets skin side down in skillet. Immediately reduce heat to medium-low and, using fish spatula, firmly press fillets for 20 to 30 seconds to ensure contact between skin and skillet. Continue to cook until skin is well browned and flesh is opaque except for top ¼ inch, 8 to 14 minutes. (If at any time during searing, oil starts to smoke or sides of fish start to brown, reduce heat so that oil is sizzling but not smoking.)

5 Off heat, flip fish and continue to cook using residual heat of skillet until fish registers 125 degrees, about 30 seconds longer. Transfer fish skin side up to large plate. Serve fish with pistou and lemon wedges.

BAKED SCALLOPS WITH COUSCOUS, LEEKS, AND ORANGE VINAIGRETTE

serves: 4

total time: 45 minutes

1 pound leeks, white and light green parts only, halved lengthwise, sliced thin, and washed thoroughly

1 cup pearl couscous

5 tablespoons extra-virgin olive oil, divided, plus extra for serving

4 garlic cloves, minced

1 teaspoon plus ⅛ teaspoon table salt, divided

½ teaspoon pepper, divided

Pinch saffron threads (optional)

¾ cup boiling water

¼ cup dry white wine

1½ pounds large sea scallops, tendons removed

2 tablespoons minced fresh tarragon

1 tablespoon white wine vinegar

½ teaspoon Dijon mustard

½ teaspoon grated orange zest plus 1 tablespoon juice

why this recipe works Scallops are often pan-fried but they benefit from gentle cooking, too. We cook them on a bed of pearl couscous, leeks, and white wine for a quick meal that allows the pearls of pasta to absorb the scallops' briny liquid while the flavors of orange, tarragon, and leeks add fresh earthiness to the dish. To ensure that the scallops finish cooking with the rest of the dish, we give the leeks and couscous some time in the microwave, adding garlic and a pinch of saffron. We stir in wine and boiling water, which starts the dish off hot and shortens the cooking time. Using a hot oven and sealing the baking dish with foil gives us perfectly cooked scallops that steam atop the couscous. A tarragon-orange vinaigrette complements the delicate scallops and leeks without overpowering them. For an accurate measurement of boiling water, bring a full kettle of water to a boil and then measure out the desired amount.

1   Adjust oven rack to middle position and heat oven to 450 degrees. Combine leeks; couscous; 2 tablespoons oil; garlic; ½ teaspoon salt; ¼ teaspoon pepper; and saffron, if using, in bowl. Microwave covered, stirring occasionally, until leeks are softened, about 6 minutes. Stir in boiling water and wine, then transfer mixture to 13 by 9-inch baking dish.

2   Pat scallops dry with paper towels and sprinkle with ½ teaspoon salt and remaining ¼ teaspoon pepper. Nestle scallops into couscous mixture and cover dish tightly with aluminum foil. Bake until couscous is tender, sides of scallops are firm, and centers are opaque, 20 to 25 minutes.

3   Meanwhile, whisk tarragon, vinegar, mustard, orange zest and juice, remaining 3 tablespoons oil, and remaining ⅛ teaspoon salt together in bowl.

4   Drizzle vinaigrette over scallops and serve, passing extra oil separately.

Are Your Scallops Wet or Dry?

"Dry" scallops are natural. They look translucent and fleshy and taste sweet and tender. "Wet" scallops are treated with chemicals and preservatives. They look pale and opaque, and have a soapy, watery, often bitter taste. Buy dry ones if you can. They sear well, caramelize nicely, and taste great.

COD EN PAPILLOTE WITH LEEKS AND CARROTS

serves: 4

total time: 50 minutes

4 tablespoons unsalted butter, softened

1 teaspoon minced fresh thyme

2 garlic cloves, minced, divided

1¼ teaspoons grated lemon zest, divided, plus lemon wedges for serving

1 teaspoon table salt, divided

½ teaspoon pepper, divided

2 tablespoons minced fresh parsley

2 carrots, peeled and cut into matchsticks

1 pound leeks, white and light green parts only, halved lengthwise, washed thoroughly, and cut into matchsticks

¼ cup dry white wine

4 (6- to 8-ounce) skinless cod fillets, 1 inch thick

En Papillote versus en Cocotte

En papillote and en cocotte are ways of cooking proteins and vegetables without added liquid. For en papillote, food is tightly sealed in a parchment package and baked. The food steams in its own juices quickly. To cook en cocotte means to bake food in a tightly covered pot at a very low temperature. Again, no liquid is added so natural juices flavor and cook the food until tender.

why this recipe works Cooking fish en papillote, or folded in a pouch, is a classic French technique that, in addition to being incredibly easy (and virtually cleanup-free), allows the fish to steam in its own juices and thus emerge flavorful but also moist. We find that aluminum foil is even easier to work with than parchment and creates a leakproof seal. Placing the packets on the lower-middle rack of the oven, close to the heat source, concentrates the exuded liquid in the packets and deepens its flavor. Vegetable selection is important: Hardier vegetables like potatoes and squash fail to cook evenly in the packets, and more water-absorbing vegetables like eggplant turn to mush when enclosed. But carrots and leeks, cut into elegant matchsticks, cook at the same rate as the fish and make a nice presentation as a bed for the fish when everything emerges from the packets. A zesty compound butter atop the fish adds richness and flavor as it melts. Open each packet promptly after baking to prevent overcooking. To test for doneness without opening the foil packets, use a permanent marker to mark an "X" on the outside of the foil where the fish fillet is the thickest, then insert an instant-read thermometer through the "X" into the fish to measure its internal temperature. You can substitute black sea bass, haddock, hake, or pollock for the cod.

1   Adjust oven rack to lower-middle position and heat oven to 450 degrees. Mash butter, thyme, half of garlic, ¼ teaspoon lemon zest, ¼ teaspoon salt, and ⅛ teaspoon pepper in bowl. Combine parsley, remaining garlic, and remaining 1 teaspoon lemon zest in second bowl. Combine carrots, leeks, ¼ teaspoon salt, and ⅛ teaspoon pepper in third bowl.

2   Lay four 16 by 12-inch rectangles of aluminum foil on counter with short sides parallel to counter edge. Divide vegetable mixture evenly among foil rectangles, arranging in center of lower half of each sheet of foil. Mound vegetables slightly and sprinkle with wine. Pat cod dry with paper towels, sprinkle with remaining ½ teaspoon salt and remaining ¼ teaspoon pepper, and place on top of vegetables. Spread butter mixture over fillets. Fold top half of foil over fish, then tightly crimp edges into rough 9 by 6-inch packets.

3   Place packets on rimmed baking sheet (they may overlap slightly) and bake until cod registers 135 degrees, about 15 minutes. Carefully open packets, allowing steam to escape away from you. Using thin metal spatula, gently slide cod and vegetables, and any accumulated juices, onto individual plates. Sprinkle with parsley mixture and serve with lemon wedges.

HALIBUT EN COCOTTE WITH ROASTED GARLIC AND CHERRY TOMATOES

serves: 4

total time: 1¼ hours

¼ cup extra-virgin olive oil, divided

2 garlic cloves, sliced thin

⅛ teaspoon red pepper flakes

Pinch plus ½ teaspoon table salt, divided

12 ounces cherry tomatoes, quartered

1 tablespoon capers, rinsed

1 teaspoon minced fresh thyme

4 (6- to 8-ounce) skinless halibut fillets, 1 inch thick

¼ teaspoon pepper

why this recipe works Cooking en cocotte is a variation on braising: It uses a covered pot, a low oven temperature, no added liquid, and an extended cooking time to yield tender results. The cover seals in moisture so the protein cooks in its own juices. We create a bold sauce with olive oil, garlic, thyme, capers, red pepper flakes, and cherry tomatoes that serves as a bright, briny counterpoint to the succulent halibut. Cooking sliced garlic in olive oil draws out its flavor, and once the garlic is golden brown, we stir in the cherry tomatoes and place the halibut on top. As the fish cooks, the tomatoes begin to break down, releasing their juices and helping to build the sauce, which we then spoon over the fish. Finishing with a splash of extra-virgin olive oil rounds out the flavors and gives the dish a lush feel. You can substitute mahi-mahi, red snapper, striped bass, or swordfish for the halibut.

1 Adjust oven rack to lowest position and heat oven to 250 degrees. Cook 2 tablespoons oil, garlic, pepper flakes, and pinch salt in Dutch oven over medium-low heat until garlic is light golden, 2 to 4 minutes. Off heat, stir in tomatoes, capers, and thyme.

2 Pat halibut dry with paper towels, sprinkle with remaining ½ teaspoon salt and pepper, and lay on top of tomatoes in pot. Place large piece of aluminum foil over pot and cover tightly with lid; transfer pot to oven. Cook until fish flakes apart when gently prodded with paring knife and registers 130 degrees, 35 to 40 minutes.

3 Transfer halibut to platter and let rest for 10 minutes. Meanwhile, bring tomato mixture to simmer over medium-high heat until slightly thickened, about 2 minutes. Off heat, stir in remaining 2 tablespoons oil and season with salt and pepper to taste. Spoon sauce over halibut and serve.

POMEGRANATE-ROASTED SALMON WITH LENTILS AND SWISS CHARD

serves: 4

total time: 1½ hours

2 tablespoons plus 1 teaspoon extra-virgin olive oil, divided

12 ounces Swiss chard, stemmed, ½ cup stems chopped fine, leaves cut into 2-inch pieces

1 small onion, chopped fine

2 garlic cloves, minced

4 sprigs fresh thyme

¾ teaspoon table salt, divided

2 cups chicken or vegetable broth

1 cup lentilles du Puy, picked over and rinsed

4 (6- to 8-ounce) skin-on salmon fillets, 1 inch thick

2 tablespoons pomegranate molasses, divided

¼ teaspoon pepper

½ cup pomegranate seeds

why this recipe works Salmon with lentils is popular on bistro menus. Here, we use pomegranate molasses to brighten the flavors of both the rich salmon and the earthy lentils. Swiss chard adds a green bite, and fresh pomegranate seeds lend tartness and color. Lentilles du Puy, also called French green lentils, are our first choice here but brown, black, or regular green lentils will work, too (cooking times will vary). if you can't find pomegranate molasses, substitute 1 tablespoon lemon juice plus 1 tablespoon mild molasses. If your knife is not sharp enough to easily cut through the salmon skin, try a serrated knife. It's important to keep the skin on during cooking; remove it afterward if desired. You can substitute arctic char or wild salmon for the farmed salmon; cook those fillets to 120 degrees (for medium-rare).

1   Adjust oven rack to lowest position, place aluminum foil–lined rimmed baking sheet on rack, and heat oven to 500 degrees. Heat 1 tablespoon oil in large saucepan over medium-high heat until shimmering. Add chard stems, onion, garlic, thyme sprigs, and ¼ teaspoon salt and cook, stirring frequently, until softened, about 5 minutes. Stir in broth and lentils and bring to boil. Reduce heat to low, cover, and simmer, stirring occasionally, until lentils are mostly tender, 45 to 50 minutes.

2   Stir chard leaves into lentils. Increase heat to medium-low and continue to cook, uncovered, until chard leaves are tender, about 4 minutes. Off heat, discard thyme sprigs, stir in 1 tablespoon oil, and season with salt and pepper to taste; cover to keep warm.

3   Meanwhile, make 4 or 5 shallow slashes, about 1 inch apart, on skin side of each fillet, being careful not to cut into flesh. Pat salmon dry with paper towels. Brush with remaining 1 teaspoon oil, then brush with 1 tablespoon pomegranate molasses and sprinkle with remaining ½ teaspoon salt and pepper. Reduce oven temperature to 275 degrees and use oven mitts to remove sheet from oven. Carefully place salmon skin-side down on hot sheet. Roast until center is still translucent when checked with tip of paring knife and registers 125 degrees (for medium-rare), 8 to 12 minutes.

4   Brush salmon with remaining 1 tablespoon pomegranate molasses. Transfer salmon to individual plates or serving platter. Stir pomegranate seeds into lentil mixture and serve with salmon.

ROASTED SALMON WITH ORANGE BEURRE BLANC

serves: 4 to 6

total time: 50 minutes

salmon

- 15 juniper berries, toasted
- ¾ teaspoon fennel seeds, toasted
- 1 teaspoon grated orange zest
- ½ teaspoon sugar
- ½ teaspoon table salt
- ½ teaspoon pepper
- 1 (1¾- to 2-pound) center-cut skin-on salmon fillet, pin bones removed
- 1 tablespoon vegetable oil

beurre blanc

- 3 tablespoons dry white wine
- 2 tablespoons white wine vinegar
- 1 small shallot, minced

   Pinch table salt

- 1 tablespoon heavy cream
- 8 tablespoons unsalted butter, cut into 8 pieces and chilled
- ⅛ teaspoon sugar
- ⅛ teaspoon grated orange zest

why this recipe works Roasting a center-cut fillet of salmon rather than individual fillets is easy but looks impressive to those at your dinner table. We elevate the dish by serving the fish with an orange-scented beurre blanc, a classic French warm butter sauce. First we rub our salmon with juniper berries and fennel seeds; a little sugar balances their bitterness and promotes browning, orange zest adds brightness and echoes the sauce. We preheat our oven at a very high temperature so the salmon can start cooking as soon as it goes in, and then lower the heat so the fish doesn't cook too quickly and stays moist and tender. While the salmon roasts, we prepare the beurre blanc by reducing wine and vinegar, enriching them with cream and butter, and finishing with orange zest. Use heavy-duty aluminum foil measuring 18 inches wide. You can substitute arctic char or wild salmon. If doing so, make sure to cook the fillet until it reaches 120 degrees (for medium-rare) and start checking for doneness early.

1 **for the salmon** Adjust oven rack to lowest position, place rimmed baking sheet on rack, and heat oven to 500 degrees. Grind juniper berries and fennel seeds in spice grinder until coarsely ground, about 30 seconds. Transfer spices to bowl and stir in orange zest, sugar, salt, and pepper.

2 Cut piece of heavy-duty aluminum foil 12 inches longer than salmon fillet and fold lengthwise into thirds. Make 8 shallow slashes, about 3 inches long and 1 inch apart, on skin side of salmon, being careful not to cut into flesh. Pat salmon dry with paper towels and lay skin side down on foil. Rub flesh side of salmon with oil, then rub with spice mixture.

3 Reduce oven temperature to 275 degrees. Using foil sling, lay salmon on preheated sheet and roast until center is still translucent when checked with tip of paring knife and registers 125 degrees (for medium-rare), 14 to 18 minutes.

4 **for the beurre blanc** Meanwhile, bring wine, vinegar, shallot, and salt to simmer in small saucepan over medium heat and cook until about 2 scant tablespoons of liquid remain, 3 to 5 minutes. Reduce heat to medium-low and whisk in cream. Add butter, 1 piece at a time, whisking vigorously after each addition, until butter is incorporated and forms thick, pale yellow sauce, 30 to 60 seconds. Off heat, whisk in sugar. Strain sauce through fine-mesh strainer into bowl. Stir in orange zest and season with salt to taste.

5   Using foil sling, transfer salmon to cutting board or serving platter. Run thin metal spatula between salmon skin and salmon to loosen. Using spatula to hold salmon in place, gently pull foil (and skin) out from underneath salmon. Serve with beurre blanc.

Why Beurre Blanc?

The French sauce called beurre blanc is an emulsion of a flavorful liquid and butter that coats proteins and vegetables beautifully.

If you gradually whisk cold butter into hot liquid, you transform it into an oil-in-water emulsion. The water droplets in butter contain remnants of the cream from which it was made; that is, proteins. These proteins act as emulsifiers, coating and separating tiny fat droplets as they disperse into the liquid when the butter melts.

The resulting sauce is viscous and clings to moist foods because the fat droplets are surrounded by water. Remember, water is attracted to water but resists fat.

MONKFISH TAGINE

serves: 4 to 6

total time: 40 minutes

3 (2-inch) strips orange zest, divided

5 garlic cloves, minced, divided

2 tablespoons extra-virgin olive oil

1 large onion, halved and sliced
¼ inch thick

3 carrots, peeled, halved lengthwise,
and sliced ¼ inch thick

¾ teaspoon table salt, divided

1 tablespoon tomato paste

1¼ teaspoons paprika

1 teaspoon ground cumin

½ teaspoon dried mint

¼ teaspoon saffron threads, crumbled

1 (8-ounce) bottle clam juice

1½ pounds skinless monkfish fillets,
1 inch thick, trimmed and cut into
3-inch pieces

¼ teaspoon pepper

¼ cup pitted oil-cured black
olives, quartered

2 tablespoons minced fresh mint

1 teaspoon sherry vinegar

why this recipe works Moroccan food is hugely popular in Paris; and here, we use the signature sweet-and-sour flavors of a Moroccan-style tagine with fish instead of the more-often seen chicken or lamb. Meaty monkfish fillets have a pleasantly firm texture, so they keep their shape while simmering in the pot. For sweetness, we use orange zest, onion, carrots, and tomato paste, which, along with fragrant paprika, cumin, dried mint, and saffron, build the base for the tagine's alluring broth. Deglazing the sautéed aromatics with a bottle of clam juice adds a briny element, bolstering the seafood flavor. For a salty, sour punch, we finish the sauce by stirring in pungent Moroccan oil-cured olives and a little sherry vinegar. Fresh mint completes the dish with brightness and we achieve intense Moroccan flavors in just a half hour of cooking. Monkfish fillets are surrounded by a thin membrane that needs to be removed before cooking. Your fishmonger can do this for you, or you can remove it yourself.

1 Mince 1 strip orange zest and combine with 1 teaspoon garlic in bowl; set aside.

2 Heat oil in Dutch oven over medium heat until shimmering. Add onion, carrots, ¼ teaspoon salt, and remaining 2 strips orange zest and cook until vegetables are softened and lightly browned, 10 to 12 minutes. Stir in tomato paste, paprika, cumin, dried mint, saffron, and remaining garlic and cook until fragrant, about 30 seconds. Stir in clam juice, scraping up any browned bits.

3 Pat monkfish dry with paper towels and sprinkle with remaining ½ teaspoon salt and pepper. Nestle monkfish into pot, spoon some cooking liquid over top, and bring to simmer. Reduce heat to medium-low, cover, and simmer gently until monkfish is opaque in center and registers 160 degrees, 8 to 12 minutes.

4 Discard orange zest strips. Gently stir in olives, fresh mint, vinegar, and garlic–orange zest mixture. Season with salt and pepper to taste. Serve.

BOUILLABAISSE

serves: 8 to 10

total time: 2½ hours, plus 4 hours marinating

why this recipe works

This Provençal dish with humble origins, a fisherman's cost-effective meal likely made with seafood caught that day, has become an upscale seafood stew. Bouillabaisse gets its name from the way it was made; the stock was brought to a boil and possibly simmered for hours while the fisherman worked. When he arrived home, the fresh seafood was added to the pot and quickly cooked. Our fish stock (fumet) is flavored with sautéed aromatics and cooked with carrot, fennel, leeks, and white wine. We also marinate our seafood. Not all bouillabaisse recipes call for this but we find that marinating (we use Provençal ingredients: basil, Pernod, and saffron) intensifies the seafood's flavor because it gets only a short time in the stock. Once the seafood has simmered for a few minutes, we turn off the heat and let it gently poach in the hot liquid so its juices combine with the stock and produce deep flavor. Garlic–Rubbed Croutons topped with Red Pepper Rouille finish the dish. Chop the vegetables for the stock evenly, making them no larger than 1 inch in diameter. More surface area means more flavor. We use white Côtes de Provence in this recipe because it belongs to the region where bouillabaisse comes from, but any inexpensive light white wine will work.

fish and shellfish marinade

- 1½ pounds skinless fish fillets, cut into 1- to 1½-inch cubes
- 8 ounces medium shrimp (41 to 50 per pound), peeled and deveined, shells reserved
- 8 ounces large sea scallops, tendons removed and each scallop halved
- ⅓ cup shredded fresh basil
- ¼ cup extra-virgin olive oil
- 3 tablespoons Pernod
- 3 garlic cloves, minced
- 2 teaspoons table salt
- ¼ teaspoon red pepper flakes
- ½ teaspoon saffron threads

fish stock

- ¼ cup extra-virgin olive oil
- 2 onions, chopped
- 1 fennel bulb, stalks discarded, bulb chopped
- 1 large carrot, chopped
- 3 garlic heads, outer papery skin removed
- 1 (750-ml) bottle dry white wine
- 2 (28-ounce) cans diced tomatoes
- 3 pounds fish frames, gills removed and discarded, frames rinsed and cut into 6-inch pieces
- 1 pound leeks, white and light green parts only, halved lengthwise, chopped, and washed thoroughly
- 4 cups water
  Reserved shrimp shells
- 1 bunch fresh parsley, stems only
- 5 sprigs fresh thyme
- 2 bay leaves
- 2 teaspoons whole black peppercorns
- 2 teaspoons table salt
  Large strips of zest from 2 oranges
- ½ teaspoon saffron threads

stew

- 2 pounds mussels, scrubbed and debearded
- 1 recipe Garlic-Rubbed Croutons (page 197)
- 1 recipe Red Pepper Rouille (page 18)

1   for the fish and shellfish marinade
Combine all ingredients in large bowl and toss until fish is thoroughly coated with herbs and oil. Cover with plastic wrap and refrigerate for 4 hours.

2   for the fish stock   Meanwhile, heat oil in 8-quart stockpot or Dutch oven over medium-low heat until shimmering. Add onions, fennel, and carrot to pot, cover, and cook, stirring frequently, until vegetables are fragrant, about 15 minutes. Place garlic in large zipper-lock bag and seal. Smash garlic with rolling pin or meat pounder until flattened. Add smashed garlic to vegetables and continue to cook, stirring frequently, until vegetables are dry and just beginning to stick, about 15 minutes longer. (Take care not to let garlic burn.) Add wine and stir to scrape pot bottom, then add tomatoes and their juice, fish frames, leeks, water, shrimp shells, parsley stems, thyme sprig, bay leaves, peppercorns, and salt. Bring to simmer over medium-high heat, reduce heat to medium-low, and simmer, pressing down on fish bones occasionally with wooden spoon to submerge, until stock is rich and flavorful, about 1 hour.

3.   Strain stock through large fine-mesh strainer (you should have about 9 cups); rinse and wipe out pot and return strained stock to pot. Bring stock to boil over high heat and simmer briskly until reduced to 8 cups, about 10 minutes. Off heat, add orange zest and saffron. Let stand for 10 minutes to infuse flavors. Strain stock through fine-mesh strainer and set aside. (Stock can be refrigerated in airtight container for up to 2 days or frozen for up to 1 month and then defrosted.)

4   for the stew   Return fish stock to clean 8-quart pot and bring to rolling boil over high heat. Stir in mussels and marinated fish and shellfish, cover pot, and return to simmer; simmer for 7 minutes, stirring a few times to ensure even cooking. Remove pot from heat, cover, and let stand until fish is cooked through and mussels have opened, about 2 minutes. Season with salt and pepper to taste, ladle into bowls, and float 1 crouton topped with dollop of rouille in each bowl. Serve.

GARLIC-RUBBED CROUTONS

makes: 10 croutons

total time: 10 minutes

Buy a 1-pound loaf of French bread and reserve the remainder for another use.

- **10   (½-inch-thick) slices country-style French bread**
- **6   garlic cloves, peeled and halved**
- **3   tablespoons extra-virgin olive oil**

Adjust oven rack to highest position and heat broiler. Arrange bread slices in single layer on baking sheet; broil until bread is lightly toasted, about 1½ minutes. Flip bread slices, then rub second side of each bread slice with raw garlic and brush with oil. Broil bread slices until light golden brown, about 1½ minutes longer.

chapter seven

vegetable mains & cheese dishes

———————

SAVORY FENNEL-APPLE TARTE TATIN

serves: 4 to 6

total time: 40 minutes

1 (9½ by 9-inch) sheet puff pastry, thawed

3 tablespoons extra-virgin olive oil, divided

1 tablespoon sugar

½ teaspoon plus pinch table salt, divided

2 fennel bulbs, stalks discarded (1 bulb cut into 6 wedges, 1 bulb halved, cored, and cut lengthwise into ½-inch-thick slices)

2 Granny Smith apples, peeled, cored, halved, and sliced ½ inch thick

4 teaspoons chopped fresh sage

2 teaspoons sherry vinegar

¼ teaspoon Dijon mustard

6 ounces (6 cups) watercress, torn into bite-size pieces

2 tablespoons chopped toasted and skinned hazelnuts

2 ounces (½ cup) goat cheese, crumbled (optional)

why this recipe works How could we turn tarte Tatin, a classic French dessert that is flipped upside down after baking to reveal caramelized apples and a flaky crust (page 318), into a savory appetizer? By adding sweet licorice-y fennel and earthy sage to the sweet-tart Granny Smith apples, and topping them with layered puff pastry. The fennel picks up beautiful caramelization while its center turns meltingly dense and silky. We start with olive oil and a little sugar in a cold skillet, carefully arrange fennel wedges in an attractive pinwheel; then fill in the gaps with sliced fennel and set the pan over high heat to jump-start browning on the vegetable's underside. Then we place some sliced apple and sage on top, cover it with convenient store-bought puff pastry, and finish it in the oven. The apples gently steam over the fennel and turn into a sage-infused apple sauce. We cut through the richness of the dish with a peppery watercress–hazelnut salad. Look for fennel bulbs that are about 4 inches tall after trimming. Do not core the fennel bulb that is cut into wedges. To thaw frozen puff pastry, let it sit either in the refrigerator for 24 hours or on the counter for 30 minutes to 1 hour.

1   Adjust oven rack to middle position and heat oven to 375 degrees. Unfold pastry onto lightly floured counter and roll into 11-inch square. Using pizza cutter or sharp knife, cut pastry into 11-inch circle. Transfer to parchment paper–lined rimmed baking sheet, cover loosely with plastic wrap, and refrigerate while preparing filling.

2   Swirl 2 tablespoons oil over bottom of 10-inch ovensafe nonstick skillet, then sprinkle with sugar and ¼ teaspoon salt. Arrange fennel wedges in pinwheel shape, fanning out from center of circle. Fill in gaps with sliced fennel. Cook, without stirring, over high heat until fennel turns deep golden brown, 7 to 9 minutes (if pan is not sizzling after 2 minutes, adjust cook≈time accordingly).

3　Off heat, sprinkle with apples, sage, and ¼ teaspoon salt. Carefully transfer chilled dough to skillet, centering over filling. Being careful of hot skillet, gently fold excess dough up against skillet wall (dough should be flush with skillet edge). Using paring knife, pierce dough evenly over surface 10 times. Transfer skillet to oven and bake until crust is deep golden brown, about 45 minutes. Transfer skillet to wire rack and let cool for 10 minutes.

4　Meanwhile, whisk vinegar, mustard, remaining 1 tablespoon oil, and remaining pinch salt together in large bowl. Add watercress and hazelnuts and toss to coat. Season with salt and pepper to taste.

5　Run paring knife around edge of crust to loosen. Using dish towels or potholders, carefully place serving platter on top of skillet, and, holding platter and skillet firmly together, invert tart onto serving platter. Transfer any fennel slices that stick to skillet to tart. Sprinkle with goat cheese, if using, and serve with salad.

assembling savory fennel-apple tarte tatin

1. Arrange fennel wedges in pinwheel shape in skillet.

2. Fill in remaining gaps with sliced fennel.

3. Slide prepared puff pastry on top of filling in skillet and press any excess dough up sides of skillet.

savory fennel-apple tarte tatin
(page 200)

upside-down tomato tart
(page 204)

UPSIDE-DOWN TOMATO TART

serves: 4 to 6

total time: 2¼ hours

⅓ cup sherry vinegar

2½ tablespoons sugar

¾ teaspoon table salt, divided

½ teaspoon pepper, divided

1 shallot, chopped fine

1 tablespoon unsalted butter

2½ teaspoons minced fresh thyme, divided

2 pounds plum tomatoes (about 10), cored, halved lengthwise, seeds and gel removed

1 (9½ by 9-inch) sheet puff pastry, thawed but still cool

why this recipe works Savory-sweet plum tomatoes pair beautifully with buttery puff pastry and sherry vinegar syrup to make a juicy, flavorful upside down tart. Plum tomatoes have a low moisture content, but to ensure a crisp—not soggy—crust, we halve the tomatoes and remove their jelly and seeds before roasting them. We reduce sherry vinegar and sugar syrup to develop caramelized notes, finish it with butter, shallot, and thyme, and then roast the tomatoes in the syrup for a full hour. This not only evaporates excess moisture and concentrates their fruity taste, it also gives their edges some flavorful browning and enhances their meaty texture. We top the roasted tomatoes with store-bought puff pastry. After about 30 minutes of baking, the pastry is puffed, crisp, and golden brown. If you don't have sherry vinegar, use cider vinegar. To thaw frozen puff pastry, let it sit either in the refrigerator for 24 hours or on the counter for 30 minutes to 1 hour. The dimensions of puff pastry sheets vary by brand; if your pastry will accommodate a 10-inch circle, skip the rolling in step 3. This tart is best eaten within a couple hours of baking. Cut the tart into four wedges and serve with a salad as a main course, or cut it into six wedges and serve as an appetizer.

1   Adjust oven rack to middle position and heat oven to 400 degrees. Bring vinegar, sugar, ½ teaspoon salt, and ¼ teaspoon pepper to simmer in 10-inch ovensafe skillet over medium-high heat, swirling skillet to dissolve sugar. Simmer vigorously, swirling skillet occasionally, until consistency resembles that of maple syrup, about 2 minutes. Add shallot, butter, and 2 teaspoons thyme and whisk until butter is fully incorporated, about 1 minute.

2   Remove skillet from heat; add tomatoes and toss to coat lightly with syrup. Arrange tomatoes cut side up in as close to single layer as possible (some overlap is OK; tomatoes will shrink as they cook) and sprinkle with remaining ¼ teaspoon salt and remaining ¼ teaspoon pepper. Transfer skillet to oven and cook until liquid has evaporated and tomatoes are very lightly browned around edges and softened but not fully collapsed, about 1 hour. While tomatoes cook, prepare pastry.

3   Unfold pastry onto lightly floured counter and roll pastry into 10-inch square. Using plate, bowl, or pot lid as template, cut out 10-inch round. Discard trimming. Transfer pastry round to large plate and refrigerate until needed. Remove skillet from oven and place pastry round over tomatoes. Bake until pastry is puffed, crisp, and deep golden brown, about 30 minutes, rotating skillet halfway through baking.

4   Let tart cool for 8 minutes. Run paring knife around edge of crust to loosen, then invert plate over skillet. Using pot holders, swiftly and carefully invert tart onto plate (if tomatoes shift or stick to skillet, arrange with spoon). Let cool for 10 minutes, then sprinkle with remaining ½ teaspoon thyme. Serve warm or at room temperature.

Buying the Best

Good plum tomatoes are available year-round, but for seasonally ripe tomatoes, buy them at the height of summer. Also try these paths to ripe flavor.

Go for Local

Buy locally grown tomatoes. The shorter the distance the tomato has to travel, the riper it can be when picked. Commercial high-yield production strains the tomato plant, resulting in fruit without enough sugars and other flavor compounds that make them tasty. To with-stand the rigors of machine harvesting and long-distance transport, commercial varieties are bred to be sturdier, with thicker walls but less of the jelly and seeds that add flavor.

Looks Aren't Everything

Oddly shaped tomatoes are fine. Only com-mercial tomatoes are bred to be perfectly symmetrical. Even cracked skin is OK. Just avoid bruised, overly soft tomatoes, or ones leaking juice. Choose tomatoes that smell fruity and feel heavy.

how to core and seed plum tomatoes

1. Hold tomato in your hand with stem scar facing out. Insert tip of paring knife at an angle into tomato at edge of stem scar, about ½ to 1 inch deep. Using sawing motion, cut around stem scar while rotating tomato until core is cut free.

2. Thoroughly excavate seeds and gel: Use your fingers or spoon to get deep into crevices on either side of core to remove seeds and gel. (Save this flavorful jelly—which is packed with savory glutamates—to spoon over crusty bread; top it with a sprinkling of flake sea salt.)

NETTLE AND MUSHROOM GALETTE

serves: 4 to 6

total time: 1¾ hours, plus 1½ hours chilling

dough

- 1¼ cups (6¼ ounces) all-purpose flour
- ½ cup (2¾ ounces) whole-wheat flour
- 1 tablespoon sugar
- ¾ teaspoon table salt
- 10 tablespoons unsalted butter, cut into ½-inch pieces and chilled
- 7 tablespoons ice water
- 1 teaspoon distilled white vinegar

filling

- ¼ cup extra-virgin olive oil, divided
- 8 ounces cremini mushrooms, trimmed and sliced thin
- ¼ teaspoon table salt
- 1 garlic clove, minced
- 6 ounces (12 cups) stinging nettle leaves
- 2 ounces Parmesan cheese, grated (1 cup), divided
- 2 tablespoons crème fraîche
- 1 tablespoon Dijon mustard
- 1 large egg, lightly beaten
- 1 tablespoon minced fresh tarragon

why this recipe works Nettles are herbaceous perennial flowering plants. They are used in France in tarts, soups, and omelets, sometimes with another foraged plant, dandelion greens. In the Vosges mountains, nettles and garlic flavor a local cheese. Here we pair them with mushrooms for a savory galette. We sauté nettles and creminis with garlic, and then combine them with Parmesan, crème fraîche, and Dijon mustard. For a sturdy, tender crust, we swap some white flour for nutty whole wheat. To punch up the crust's flakiness and introduce more structure, we make a series of folds in the crust to create numerous interlocking layers. Poking a few small holes in the dough circle prevents it from lifting off the pan and "doming" as it bakes. Always wear food-handling gloves (we recommend a double layer) when handling nettles and wash your hands well with warm soapy water afterward. If any of the little hairs cling to your skin, remove them with duct tape.

1 **for the dough** Process all-purpose flour, whole-wheat flour, sugar, and salt in food processor until combined. Scatter chilled butter over top and pulse until butter is pea-sized, about 10 pulses; transfer to medium bowl.

2 Sprinkle ice water and vinegar over flour mixture. Using rubber spatula, fold mixture until loose, shaggy mass forms with some dry flour remaining (do not overwork). Transfer to center of large sheet of plastic wrap, press gently into rough 4-inch square, and wrap tightly. Refrigerate for 45 minutes.

3 Transfer dough to lightly floured counter and roll into 11 by 8-inch rectangle with short side parallel to edge of counter. Using bench scraper, fold bottom third of dough away from you, then fold upper third toward you (as for business letter) into 8 by 4-inch rectangle. Turn dough 90 degrees counterclockwise. Repeat rolling dough into 11 by 8-inch rectangle and folding into thirds. Turn dough 90 degrees counterclockwise and repeat rolling and folding into thirds. After third set of folds, fold dough in half to create 4-inch square. Press top of dough gently to seal. Wrap with plastic and refrigerate for at least 45 minutes or up to 2 days.

4 **for the filling** Heat 1 tablespoon oil in 12-inch skillet over medium heat until shimmering. Add mushrooms and salt, cover, and cook, stirring occasionally, until mushrooms have released their liquid, 3 to 5 minutes. Stir in 2 tablespoons oil and garlic and cook, uncovered, until fragrant, about 30 seconds. Add nettles, 1 handful at a time, and cook, stirring occasionally, until mushrooms begin to brown and nettles are tender, 5 to 7 minutes. Transfer to bowl and stir in ¾ cup Parmesan, crème fraîche, and mustard. Season with salt and pepper to taste; set aside.

5 Adjust oven rack to lower-middle position, set baking stone on rack, and heat oven to 400 degrees. Line rimmed baking sheet with parchment paper. Remove dough from refrigerator and let sit at room temperature for 15 to 20 minutes. Roll dough into 14-inch circle about ⅛ inch thick on well-floured counter. (Trim edges as needed to form rough circle.) Transfer dough to prepared sheet. Using straw or tip of paring knife, poke five ¼-inch circles in dough (one at center and four evenly spaced halfway from center to edge of dough). Brush top of dough with 1 teaspoon oil.

6 Spread filling evenly over dough, leaving 2-inch border around edge. Drizzle remaining 2 teaspoons oil over filling, then sprinkle with remaining ¼ cup Parmesan. Grasp 1 edge of dough and fold outer 2 inches over filling. Repeat around circumference of tart, overlapping dough every 2 to 3 inches; gently pinch pleated dough to secure, but do not press dough into filling. Brush dough with egg wash.

7 Reduce oven temperature to 375 degrees. Set sheet on stone and bake until crust is deep golden brown and filling is well browned, 35 to 45 minutes. Let tart cool on sheet on wire rack for 10 minutes. Using offset spatula or wide metal spatula, loosen tart from parchment and carefully slide tart onto cutting board. Sprinkle tarragon over filling and cut tart into wedges. Serve.

MUSHROOM BOURGUIGNON

serves: 8

total time: 1¾ hours

½ cup extra-virgin olive oil, divided

5 pounds portobello mushroom caps, quartered, divided

1½ cups frozen pearl onions, thawed, divided

½ teaspoon table salt, divided

¼ teaspoon pepper, divided

⅓ cup all-purpose flour

4 cups chicken or vegetable broth

1 (750-ml) bottle red wine, divided

2 tablespoons unflavored gelatin

2 tablespoons tomato paste

1 tablespoon anchovy paste

2 onions, chopped

2 carrots, peeled and chopped

1 garlic head, cloves separated (unpeeled) and smashed

1 ounce dried porcini mushrooms, rinsed

10 sprigs fresh parsley, plus 3 tablespoons minced

6 sprigs fresh thyme

2 bay leaves

½ teaspoon black peppercorns

why this recipe works In this excellent recipe, chunks of portobello mushrooms are napped with a silky, luscious sauce with pearl onions, carrots, garlic, and red wine that will make you forget traditional French bourguignon with beef (boeuf). The umami qualities of porcinis (called cèpes in France) and anchovy paste "beef up" flavor. To achieve the body that would normally come from the collagen in the meat breaking down into the sauce, we stir in a bit of powdered gelatin, which gives us a smooth, unctuous sauce and cuts the cooking time to boot. Use a good-quality medium-bodied red wine, such as a Burgundy or other Pinot Noir, for this stew. If the pearl onions have a papery outer coating, remove by rinsing the onions in warm water and gently squeezing individual onions between your fingertips. Serve this over pasta, grains, or polenta.

1 Heat 3 tablespoons oil in Dutch oven over medium-high heat until shimmering. Add half of portobello mushrooms, half of pearl onions, ¼ teaspoon salt, and ⅛ teaspoon pepper; cover; and cook, stirring occasionally, until mushrooms have released their liquid, 8 to 10 minutes.

2 Uncover and continue to cook, stirring occasionally and scraping bottom of pot, until mushrooms are tender and pan is dry, 12 to 15 minutes. Transfer vegetables to bowl, cover, and set aside. Repeat with 3 tablespoons oil, remaining portobello mushrooms and remaining pearl onions, remaining ¼ teaspoon salt, and remaining ⅛ teaspoon pepper.

3 Add remaining 2 tablespoons oil and flour to now-empty pot and whisk until no dry flour remains. Whisk in broth, 2 cups wine, gelatin, tomato paste, and anchovy paste until combined, scraping up any browned bits and smoothing out any lumps. Stir in chopped onions, carrots, garlic, porcini mushrooms, parsley sprigs, thyme sprigs, bay leaves, and peppercorns. Bring to boil and cook, stirring occasionally, until liquid is slightly thickened and onions are translucent and softened, about 15 minutes.

4 Strain liquid through fine-mesh strainer set over large bowl, pressing on solids to extract as much liquid as possible; discard solids. Return liquid to now-empty pot and stir in remaining wine.

5 Bring mixture to boil over medium-high heat. Cook, stirring occasionally, until sauce has thickened to consistency of heavy cream, 5 to 7 minutes. Reduce heat to medium-low, stir in reserved portobello-onion mixture, and cook until just heated through, 3 to 5 minutes. Stir in minced parsley and serve.

WALKAWAY RATATOUILLE

serves: 6 to 8

total time: 1¾ hours

⅓ cup plus 1 tablespoon extra-virgin olive oil, divided

2 large onions, cut into 1-inch pieces

8 large garlic cloves, peeled and smashed

1¾ teaspoons table salt, divided

¾ teaspoon pepper, divided

1½ teaspoons herbes de Provence

¼ teaspoon red pepper flakes

1 bay leaf

2 pounds plum tomatoes, peeled, cored, and chopped coarse

1½ pounds eggplant, peeled and cut into 1-inch pieces

2 small zucchini, halved lengthwise and cut into 1-inch pieces

1 red bell pepper, stemmed, seeded, and cut into 1-inch pieces

1 yellow bell pepper, stemmed, seeded, and cut into 1-inch pieces

2 tablespoons chopped fresh basil, divided

1 tablespoon minced fresh parsley

1 tablespoon sherry vinegar

why this recipe works Ratatouille, a dish made super famous by the animated film, has a slew of main ingredients that contain more than 90 percent water. If that liquid isn't dealt with, you can end up with a wet, pulpy mess of ingredients indistinguishable in taste, color, and texture. So cooks use techniques such as salting, microwaving, or pressing vegetables to extract excess moisture. After that, individual vegetables are sautéed to create flavorful browning before simmering them together. Our walkaway shortcut is to use the oven, so the ambient dry heat evaporates moisture with less risk of burning. Our eggplant becomes so soft that we mash it into a silky sauce. Zucchini and bell peppers go in last so they retain some texture. Finishing the dish with fresh herbs, sherry vinegar, and extra-virgin olive oil brings the flavors and aromas together. This dish is best prepared with ripe, in-season tomatoes but you can substitute one 28-ounce can of whole peeled tomatoes, drained and chopped. Ratatouille can be served warm, at room temperature, or chilled, as an accompaniment to meat or fish or on its own with crusty bread.

1 Adjust oven rack to middle position and heat oven to 400 degrees. Heat ⅓ cup oil in Dutch oven over medium-high heat until shimmering. Add onions, garlic, 1 teaspoon salt, and ¼ teaspoon pepper and cook, stirring occasionally, until onions are translucent and starting to soften, about 10 minutes. Stir in herbes de Provence, pepper flakes, and bay leaf and cook until fragrant, about 1 minute. Stir in tomatoes, eggplant, ½ teaspoon salt, and ¼ teaspoon pepper.

2 Transfer pot to oven and cook, uncovered, until vegetables are very tender and spotty brown, 40 to 45 minutes.

3 Remove pot from oven and, using potato masher, mash eggplant mixture to coarse puree. Stir in zucchini, bell peppers, remaining ¼ teaspoon salt, and remaining ¼ teaspoon pepper and return to oven. Cook, uncovered, until zucchini and bell peppers are just tender, 20 to 25 minutes.

4 Remove pot from oven, cover, and let stand until zucchini is translucent and easily pierced with tip of paring knife, 10 to 15 minutes. Using wooden spoon, scrape any browned bits from sides of pot and stir back into ratatouille. Discard bay leaf.

5 Stir in 1 tablespoon basil, parsley, and vinegar. Season with salt and pepper to taste. Transfer to large platter, drizzle with remaining 1 tablespoon oil, sprinkle with remaining 1 tablespoon basil, and serve.

CAMPANELLE WITH PORCINIS AND CREAM

serves: 4 to 6

total time: 45 minutes

2 ounces dried porcini mushrooms, rinsed

3 tablespoons unsalted butter

2 onions, chopped fine

¼ teaspoon table salt, plus salt for cooking pasta

½ cup heavy cream

1 pound campanelle

2 ounces Parmesan cheese, grated (1 cup), plus extra for serving

why this recipe works Pasta dishes have long been found on bistro menus, and when pasta is paired with earthy mushrooms and indulgent cream, there can be no more satisfying meal. This easy but luxuriant recipe is made with porcinis (cèpes), which are eaten raw as well as cooked in France. Along with cream, the porcinis create a simple but rich sauce. We use them dried for concentrated, robust flavor. To get the most out of them, first we soften them in the microwave and sauté them with chopped onions to form a rich foundation for our sauce. Next, we save the liquid left over from rehydrating the dried mushrooms and use it as the base of the sauce; this way, none of the hearty porcini flavor is lost. Heavy cream enriches the sauce, while grated Parmesan thickens it and adds a salty tang that enhances the mushrooms' savory meatiness.

1 Combine mushrooms with 2 cups water in bowl. Cover and microwave until steaming, about 1 minute. Let sit until softened, about 5 minutes. Drain mushrooms in fine-mesh strainer lined with coffee filter, reserve liquid, and chop mushrooms into ¾-inch pieces.

2 Melt butter in large saucepan over medium heat. Add onions and salt and cook until softened and lightly browned, 10 to 12 minutes.

3 Stir in mushrooms and cook until fragrant, about 2 minutes. Stir in strained mushroom liquid, scraping up any browned bits, and simmer until thickened, about 10 minutes. Stir in cream and simmer until thickened, about 2 minutes.

4. Meanwhile, bring 4 quarts water to boil in large pot. Add pasta and 1 tablespoon salt and cook, stirring often, until al dente. Reserve ½ cup cooking water, then drain pasta and return it to pot. Add sauce and Parmesan and toss to combine. Adjust consistency with reserved cooking water as needed and season with salt and pepper to taste. Serve with extra Parmesan.

GNOCCHI À LA PARISIENNE WITH PISTOU

serves: 4

total time: 1 hour, plus 30 minutes resting

gnocchi

- 3 large eggs
- 7 tablespoons unsalted butter, divided
- ¾ teaspoon table salt
- ¾ cup (3¾ ounces) all-purpose flour
- 2 ounces Gruyère cheese, shredded (½ cup)
- ⅛ teaspoon pepper

pistou

- 1¼ cups fresh basil leaves
- 1½ ounces Parmesan cheese, grated (¾ cup), plus extra for serving
- ½ cup extra-virgin olive oil
- 2 garlic cloves, minced
- 2 anchovy fillets, rinsed, patted dry, and minced
- 1 teaspoon grated lemon zest plus 2 teaspoons juice

why this recipe works   Pâte à choux has been a workhorse of the French culinary canon since the 1500s, serving as the foundation for airy pastries, including Gougères (page 31), éclairs, Profiteroles with Chocolate Sauce (page 306), and beignets. But our favorite use for the eggy dough is as the base of a somewhat lesser-known puffed delicacy: gnocchi à la Parisienne. It's a real game changer for gnocchi lovers. Mixing a light dough for Italian potato gnocchi and individually shaping each dumpling requires practice for airy results, but replacing the dough with pâte à choux promises tender, ethereal puffs, even if you're a newbie. We make our dough quickly on the stovetop and then transfer it to a food processor to incorporate the eggs. We pipe and cut the dough into simmering water to form gnocchi and then sear them in a hot skillet to lightly brown and puff them to tender, melt-in-your-mouth perfection. We finish our gnocchi with an emerald-hued pistou. Emmentaler can be used in place of the Gruyère. You'll need a pastry bag and a ½-inch round tip for this recipe. If these are unavailable, substitute a large zipper-lock bag with one corner snipped off to create a ½-inch opening. This recipe can be doubled, if desired. Serve the gnocchi in wide, shallow pasta bowls.

1   for the gnocchi   Fit pastry bag with ½-inch round tip. Beat eggs in 2-cup liquid measuring cup.

2   Bring ¾ cup water, 4 tablespoons butter, and salt to boil in small saucepan over medium heat, stirring occasionally. As soon as mixture boils, remove saucepan from heat and stir in flour until incorporated. Return saucepan to low heat and cook, stirring constantly, using smearing motion, until mixture looks like shiny, wet sand, about 2 minutes.

3   Immediately transfer mixture to food processor. Add Gruyère and pepper and process, with feed tube open, for 10 seconds. With processor running, gradually add eggs in steady stream. When all eggs have been added, scrape down sides of bowl with rubber spatula. Continue to process until smooth, thick, sticky paste forms, about 30 seconds longer. Fill prepared pastry bag with warm mixture. Twist top of bag to close and let rest at room temperature for 30 minutes.

4   **for the pistou**   While dough rests, add all ingredients to clean, dry processor and process until smooth, about 15 seconds, scraping down sides of bowl as needed.

5   Lightly grease rimmed baking sheet. Bring 4 quarts water to boil in large Dutch oven. Reduce heat to maintain gentle simmer. Using 1 hand, hold pastry bag at 45-degree angle so tip is about 3 inches away from surface of water and squeeze bag to force dough out of tip. Using paring knife, cut off ¾-inch lengths and let them fall into water. Continue to pipe until 20 to 30 gnocchi are in pot. Simmer until gnocchi float and are slightly firm, about 2 minutes. Using spider skimmer or slotted spoon, transfer gnocchi to prepared sheet. Repeat until all dough is cooked (4 to 6 batches). (If not serving immediately, allow gnocchi to cool completely. Transfer to airtight container and refrigerate for up to 3 days. Alternatively, freeze on sheet until solid, then transfer to zipper-lock bag and freeze for up to 2 months; sauté from frozen, adding 1 to 2 minutes to cooking time.)

6   **to serve**   Melt remaining 3 tablespoons butter in 12-inch nonstick skillet over medium heat. Add all gnocchi and shake skillet gently until gnocchi fall into single layer. Cook, tossing every 2 minutes, until gnocchi are golden brown and slightly puffed, about 6 minutes. Remove skillet from heat.

7   Divide pistou evenly among wide, shallow pasta bowls and spread to coat bottoms of bowls. Top pistou with gnocchi and serve with extra Parmesan.

FOOLPROOF CHEESE FONDUE

serves: 8

total time: 30 minutes

8 ounces Emmentaler cheese, shredded (2 cups), room temperature

8 ounces Gruyère cheese, shredded (2 cups), room temperature

2 tablespoons cornstarch

Pinch ground nutmeg

1½ cups dry white wine

1 garlic clove, peeled and halved

¼ teaspoon pepper

1 (12-inch) baguette, cut into 1-inch pieces

why this recipe works You don't need a fondue pot—or an invitation to a 1960s theme party—to make our foolproof fondue. All you need are the right ingredients and some know-how about grating and melting cheese. This flavorful fondue is easy to assemble and reheat. Apple slices, broccoli florets, and cauliflower are delicious dipping options, along with a baguette. You can also try dipping chunks of cured meats in the melted cheese. Don't substitute deli Swiss cheese for the Emmentaler—it will make the fondue stringy. Use a crisp, unoaked wine, such as Sauvignon Blanc.

1 Toss Emmentaler, Gruyère, cornstarch, and nutmeg in bowl until well combined. Bring wine and garlic to boil in medium saucepan over high heat; discard garlic.

2 Reduce heat to medium-low and slowly whisk in cheese mixture 1 handful at a time. Continue to cook, whisking constantly, until mixture is smooth and begins to bubble, 2 to 4 minutes. Stir in pepper. Serve with bread.

Reheating Fondue

Even our foolproof fondue eventually cools down and firms up. We tested dozens of ways to keep it warm and reheat it and found this method works best: Fill a microwaveable bowl one-third full of boiling water, then nest a slightly smaller microwaveable bowl inside it. Pour the fondue into the smaller bowl and serve. To reheat, microwave the double-bowl setup for 2 to 3 minutes, stirring halfway through microwaving.

Mon Dieu, Fondue!

Although fondue originated in Switzerland in the 18th century when both cheese and wine were staples of the Swiss kitchen, since country borders were so fluid at the time, thedish migrated to neighboring regions of France and Belgium, and is often associated with French cooking. The word "fondue" comes from the French verb "fonder," meaning "to melt." And this melty winter staple of shepherds transformed cheese, stale bread, and wine into dinner. Fondue, a rich, satiny mixture just begging to be scooped up with bread, was popular in the States in the 1960s. By the '80s, Americans had stowed their fondue pots in their attics, along with their leisure suits and eight-track players. Swiss-style fondue is made by melting at least two varieties of cheese (usually Gruyère, which comes from both France and Switzerland and Emmentaler, a Swiss Alpine cheese) in a dry white wine. Garlic and other flavorings are added to complement the cheese blend, and in many cases, kirsch (a clear cherry brandy) lends a tinge of tartness. Newer recipes use flour or cornstarch to keep the cheese from separating.

TARTIFLETTE

serves: 4

total time: 1¾ hours

8 ounces ripe Camembert or Taleggio cheese, rind left on

1¾ pounds Yukon Gold potatoes, unpeeled, halved lengthwise and sliced into ¼-inch half-moons

6 slices thick-cut bacon, cut into ½-inch pieces

1 large onion, chopped fine

1¼ teaspoons table salt, divided

2½ teaspoons minced fresh thyme

2 garlic cloves, minced

½ cup dry white wine

½ cup heavy cream

¼ teaspoon pepper

Crème Fraîche (optional, page 16)

why this recipe works   This fabulous Haute-Savoie dish was created in the 1980s by the Syndicat Interprofessionnel du Reblochon. The cheese consortium, hoping the dish would encourage sales of their washed-rind, cow's-milk specialty, came up with the idea of melting the cheese on péla, a hearty rustic dish of fried potatoes, onions, and bacon. They created a silky, satisfying gratin of tender potatoes, crisp-chewy poitrine fumée (smoked bacon), white wine, and cream, generously topped with nutty, milky Reblochon cheese, and renamed it tartiflette. It was a resounding success. We use Camembert instead of Reblochon, which is unavailable here. Taleggio, Pont l'Évêque, Delice du Jura, Vacherin Mont d'Or and domestic cheeses such as Jasper Hill's Harbison and Winnimere work, too. If your cheese is runny, chill it before cutting it and hold the pieces in the freezer until you're ready to use them. A 2-quart baking dish can be used in place of the 8-inch square baking dish. Serve with bread and a crisp salad.

1   Adjust oven rack to middle position and heat oven to 400 degrees. Line large plate with paper towels. Grease 8-inch square baking dish. Cut Camembert in half horizontally to create 2 pieces of equal thickness. Cut each half into ¾-inch pieces.

2   Place steamer basket in large saucepan. Add water to barely reach bottom of steamer and bring to boil over high heat. Add potatoes, cover, and reduce heat to medium (small wisps of steam should escape from beneath lid). Cook until potatoes are just cooked through and tip of paring knife inserted into potatoes meets little resistance, 15 to 17 minutes. Leaving potatoes in steamer, remove steamer from saucepan; set aside and let cool slightly, at least 10 minutes.

A Clandestine History

The raw cow's milk, full-cream cheese called Reblochon gets its name from the verb "reblocher" (to pinch a cow's udder again). Thirteenth century landowners taxed farmers on the amount of milk their herds produced. So some of them only partially milked their cows every morning. Once landowners had measured the yield, ranchers secretly milked their cows again. The fatty milk made creamy Reblochon.

3   While potatoes cool, cook bacon in 12-inch skillet over medium heat, stirring occasionally, until browned and chewy-crisp, 4 to 6 minutes. Using slotted spoon, transfer bacon to paper towel-lined plate; pour off all but 2 tablespoons fat. Add onion and ½ teaspoon salt to fat left in skillet and cook over medium heat, stirring occasionally, until onion is softened and beginning to brown, about 7 minutes. Add thyme and garlic and continue to cook, stirring occasionally, until fragrant, about 2 minutes longer. Add wine and cook until reduced by half, about 2 minutes. Off heat, stir in cream, pepper, and remaining ¾ teaspoon salt.

4   Add potatoes to skillet and stir gently to coat with onion mixture. Transfer half of potato mixture to prepared dish and spread into even layer. Top evenly with half of bacon. Add remaining potatoes and top evenly with remaining bacon. Arrange Camembert, rind side up, in even layer on top. Bake until bubbling and lightly browned, about 20 minutes. Let cool for 10 minutes before serving. Top each serving with spoonful of crème fraîche, if using.

GROWN-UP GRILLED CHEESE SANDWICHES WITH COMTÉ AND CORNICHON

serves: 4

total time: 30 minutes

- 7 ounces Comté cheese, cut into 24 equal pieces, room temperature
- 2 ounces Brie cheese, rind removed
- 2 tablespoons dry white wine or dry vermouth
- 4 teaspoons minced cornichon
- 3 tablespoons unsalted butter, softened
- 1 teaspoon Dijon mustard
- 8 slices hearty rye sandwich bread

variations

GROWN-UP GRILLED CHEESE SANDWICHES WITH GRUYÈRE AND CHIVES

Substitute Gruyère cheese for Comté and chives for cornichon.

GROWN-UP GRILLED CHEESE SANDWICHES WITH CHEDDAR AND SHALLOT

Substitute cheddar cheese for Comté, minced shallot for cornichon, and white sandwich bread for rye sandwich bread. For the best flavor, look for a cheddar aged for about one year (avoid cheddar aged for longer; it won't melt well in this recipe).

why this recipe works Melty American cheese on fluffy white bread is a childhood favorite, but sometimes we want a grilled cheese for adults that offers more robust flavor. French Comté gives us that complexity. Adding a splash of wine and some Brie helps the firm cheese melt evenly without separating or becoming greasy. Using a food processor to combine the ingredients ensures that our cheese-and-wine mixture is easy to spread. A smear of mustard butter livens up the bread. In one variation, shallot ramps up the flavor without detracting from the cheese. To quickly bring the cheese to room temperature, microwave the pieces until warm, about 30 seconds. The first two sandwiches can be held in a 200-degree oven on a wire rack set in a baking sheet while the second batch cooks.

1 Process Comté , Brie, and wine in food processor until smooth paste is formed, 20 to 30 seconds. Add cornichon and pulse to combine, 3 to 5 pulses. Combine butter and mustard in small bowl.

2 Working on parchment paper–lined counter, divide mustard butter evenly among slices of bread and then spread evenly over surface of bread. Flip 4 slices of bread over and spread cheese mixture evenly over slices. Top with remaining 4 slices of bread, buttered sides up.

3 Preheat 12-inch nonstick skillet over medium heat for 2 minutes. (Droplets of water should just sizzle when flicked onto pan.) Place 2 sandwiches in skillet, reduce heat to medium-low, and cook until both sides are crisp and golden brown, 6 to 9 minutes per side, moving sandwiches to ensure even browning. Remove sandwiches from skillet and let stand for 2 minutes before serving. Repeat with remaining 2 sandwiches.

Grown-Up Grilled Cheese Sandwiches
with Cheddar and Shallot

GROWN-UP STOVETOP MACARONI AND CHEESE

serves: 2 to 4

total time: 40 minutes

1¾ cups water

1 cup milk

8 ounces elbow macaroni

4 ounces American cheese, shredded (1 cup)

½ teaspoon Dijon mustard

Small pinch cayenne pepper

3½ ounces Gruyère cheese, shredded (¾ cup)

2 tablespoons crumbled blue cheese

⅓ cup panko bread crumbs

1 tablespoon extra-virgin olive oil

⅛ teaspoon table salt

⅛ teaspoon pepper

2 tablespoons grated Parmesan cheese

why this recipe works Macaroni and cheese is the kind of homey nostalgic treat you would find at a bistro stateside, and the French–American connection runs deep. Thomas Jefferson and his cook, James Hemings, are said to have tasted mac-and-cheese in Paris and brought a recipe back to the States. The rest is history. For our creamy, smooth dish, we were inspired by an innovative recipe calling for adding sodium citrate, an emulsifier, to cheese to keep it smooth when heated (instead of adding flour to make a béchamel). American cheese, which contains a similar stabilizing ingredient, is the solution. Because it tastes so plain, we combine it with Gruyère, blue cheese, mustard, and cayenne for more sophisticated flavor. We cook the macaroni in a smaller-than-usual amount of water, so that we don't have to drain it; the liquid left after the elbows are hydrated is enough to form the base of the sauce. Then, rather than baking the dish, we just sprinkle toasted panko bread crumbs on top. Because we cook the macaroni in a measured amount of liquid, we don't recommend using different shapes or sizes of pasta. Use a 4-ounce block of American cheese from the deli counter rather than presliced cheese.

1   Bring water and milk to boil in medium saucepan over high heat. Stir in macaroni and reduce heat to medium-low. Cook, stirring frequently, until macaroni is soft (slightly past al dente), 6 to 8 minutes. Add American cheese, mustard, and cayenne and cook, stirring constantly, until cheese is completely melted, about 1 minute. Off heat, stir in Gruyère and blue cheese until evenly distributed but not melted. Cover saucepan and let stand for 5 minutes.

2   Meanwhile, combine panko, oil, salt, and pepper in 8-inch nonstick skillet until panko is evenly moistened. Cook over medium heat, stirring frequently, until evenly browned, 3 to 4 minutes. Off heat, sprinkle Parmesan over panko mixture and stir to combine. Transfer panko mixture to small bowl.

3   Stir macaroni until sauce is smooth (sauce may look loose but will thicken as it cools). Season with salt and pepper to taste. Transfer to warm serving dish and sprinkle panko mixture over top. Serve immediately.

INDIVIDUAL CHEESE SOUFFLÉS WITH FRISÉE AND STRAWBERRY SALAD

serves: 6

total time: 1 hour

why this recipe works A soufflé is a classically French dish that people often wait to eat at a bistro because it feels intimidating to make at home. But our simple method mixes a cheese and béchamel sauce right into the beaten egg whites and needs no finicky folding. Making individual-size soufflés cuts down on cooking time and makes for an elegant presentation on the dinner table. If you don't have six 10-ounce ramekins, you can bake the soufflé in one 8-inch round 2-quart soufflé dish, extending the cooking time to 30 to 35 minutes. Comté, sharp cheddar, or Gouda cheese can be substituted for the Gruyère. A salad of sweet strawberries, slightly bitter frisée, and acidic balsamic vinegar is a perfect complement to the creamy soufflés. Use the large holes of a box grater to shred the Gruyère.

1 ounce Parmesan cheese, grated (½ cup), divided

¼ cup all-purpose flour

¼ teaspoon paprika

¾ teaspoon table salt, divided

⅛ teaspoon plus ¼ teaspoon pepper, divided

4 tablespoons unsalted butter

1⅓ cups whole milk

6 ounces Gruyère cheese, shredded (1½ cups)

6 large eggs, separated

¼ teaspoon cream of tartar

2 teaspoons fresh parsley, minced, divided

1 head frisée (6 ounces)

8 ounces strawberries

3 tablespoons extra-virgin olive oil

1 tablespoon balsamic vinegar

5 ounces (5 cups) baby spinach

1   Adjust oven rack to middle position and heat oven to 350 degrees. Spray six 10-ounce ramekins with vegetable oil spray, then sprinkle each with 1 teaspoon Parmesan. Place ramekins on rimmed baking sheet.

2   Combine flour, paprika, ¼ teaspoon salt, and ⅛ teaspoon pepper in bowl. Melt butter in small saucepan over medium heat. Stir in flour mixture and cook for 1 minute. Slowly whisk in milk and bring to simmer. Cook, whisking constantly, until mixture is thickened and smooth, about 1 minute. Off heat, whisk in Gruyère and 5 tablespoons Parmesan until melted and smooth. Let cool for 10 minutes.

3   After béchamel has cooled for 5 minutes, using stand mixer fitted with whisk attachment, whip egg whites and cream of tartar on medium-low speed until foamy, about 1 minute. Increase speed to medium-high and whip until stiff peaks form, 3 to 4 minutes. Whisk egg yolks and 1½ teaspoons parsley into béchamel in saucepan. Add béchamel to egg whites in stand mixer and whip until fully combined, about 15 seconds.

4   Give soufflé batter final stir by hand to fully incorporate cheese mixture. Pour batter into prepared ramekins, leaving ½ inch of space between top of batter and rims of dishes (discard any excess batter). Sprinkle ramekins evenly with remaining 1 tablespoon Parmesan. Bake until soufflés have risen above rims, tops are deep golden brown, and interiors register 170 degrees, 12 to 18 minutes.

5   While soufflés bake, chop frisée into 2-inch pieces. Hull and quarter strawberries. Whisk oil, vinegar, remaining ½ teaspoon salt, and remaining ¼ teaspoon pepper together in large bowl.

6   Add spinach, frisée, and strawberries to bowl with dressing, toss gently to coat, and season with salt and pepper to taste. Sprinkle soufflés with remaining ½ teaspoon parsley and serve immediately with salad.

chapter eight
vegetable sides
———————

RECIPE EXTRAS

PAN-ROASTED ASPARAGUS

serves: 3 to 4

total time: 20 minutes

1 tablespoon extra-virgin olive oil

1 tablespoon unsalted butter

2 pounds thick asparagus (about 2 bunches), tough ends trimmed

½ lemon (optional)

why this recipe works   We love to serve this asparagus with our Pan-Roasted Filets Mignons with Garlic-Herb Butter (page 144) but it makes a wonderful accompaniment to any bistro main, whether meat, poultry, or seafood. The simple stovetop method delivers crisp, nicely browned spears. We choose to use thick asparagus spears because thinner spears overcook too quickly. Taking a cue from restaurant chefs who blanch asparagus first, we developed a method to lightly steam and then brown the asparagus in the same skillet. To achieve both flavor and browning, we use olive oil and butter as many French recipes call for. Positioning half the spears in one direction and the other half in the opposite direction ensures a better fit in the pan. Browning just one side of the asparagus provides a contrast in texture and guarantees that the asparagus is firm and tender, never limp. This recipe works best with asparagus that is at least ½ inch thick near the base. If using thinner spears, reduce the covered cooking time to 3 minutes and the uncovered cooking time to 5 minutes. Do not use pencil-thin asparagus; it cannot withstand the heat and overcooks too easily.

1   Heat oil and butter in 12-inch skillet over medium-high heat. When butter has melted, add half of asparagus to skillet with tips pointed in 1 direction; add remaining asparagus with tips pointed in opposite direction. Using tongs, distribute spears in even layer (spears will not quite fit into single layer); cover and cook until asparagus is bright green and still crisp, about 5 minutes.

2   Uncover and increase heat to high; season asparagus with salt and pepper to taste. Cook until spears are tender and well browned along 1 side, 5 to 7 minutes, using tongs to occasionally move spears from center of pan to edge of pan to ensure all are browned. Transfer asparagus to dish, season with salt and pepper to taste, and squeeze lemon half, if using, over spears. Serve.

BLANCHED GREEN BEANS WITH MUSTARD VINAIGRETTE

serves: 4

total time: 30 minutes

1 pound green beans, trimmed

¼ teaspoon table salt, plus salt for cooking green beans

¼ cup extra-virgin olive oil

1 tablespoon whole-grain mustard

1½ teaspoons red wine vinegar

1 small shallot, minced

1 small garlic clove, minced

½ teaspoon minced fresh thyme

⅛ teaspoon pepper

Blanched and Shocked

Blanching, a word derived from the French "blanchir," meaning "to become pale," describes the process of briefly dunking fruits or vegetables in boiling water to set their color, flavor, and texture; relieve the bitterness of vegetables like broccoli rabe; or tenderize hard ones such as carrots. Shocking, which typically follows this brief process, means that blanched vegetables are plunged into ice water to immediately stop the cooking process and help them maintain vibrant color.

why this recipe works   Like asparagus, green beans make excellent sides. They're great candidates for the classic, simple cooking technique of blanching, but there's no need for them to be boring. We cook green beans quickly in rapidly boiling salted water and then shock them in ice water to stop their cooking instantly. The green beans hold their fresh flavor, bright color, and crisp-tender texture beautifully, and a rustic, slightly sharp mustard vinaigrette adds tang and saltiness to the beans without overshadowing their mild taste. Be sure to set up the ice water bath before cooking the green beans, as plunging them in the cold water immediately after blanching both retains their bright green color and ensures that they don't overcook. These beans are delicious at room temperature, slightly chilled, or briefly heated in the microwave. We like to use Dijon mustard here but any mustard will work well.

1   Bring 4 quarts water to boil in large pot. Fill large bowl halfway with ice and water. Add green beans and 1 tablespoon salt to boiling water and cook until crisp-tender, 2 to 4 minutes. Drain beans, then transfer immediately to ice water. Let beans cool completely, about 5 minutes, then drain again and pat dry with paper towels.

2   Whisk oil, mustard, vinegar, shallot, garlic, thyme, pepper, and salt together in bowl. Add green beans and toss to combine. Season with salt and pepper to taste. Serve.

MODERN CAULIFLOWER GRATIN

serves: 8 to 10

total time: 1½ hours

- 2   heads cauliflower (2 pounds each)
- 8   tablespoons unsalted butter, divided
- ½   cup panko bread crumbs
- 2   ounces Parmesan cheese, grated (1 cup), divided
- 2   teaspoons table salt
- ½   teaspoon pepper
- ½   teaspoon dry mustard
- ⅛   teaspoon ground nutmeg
-     Pinch cayenne pepper
- 1   teaspoon cornstarch dissolved in 1 teaspoon water
- 1   tablespoon minced fresh chives

why this recipe works   Cauliflower is not only a delicious vegetable to cook as a side for a meal, but also one that provides a blank canvas for flavorings. It also has a natural ability to become an ultracreamy purée so here we use it as a sauce for itself. To ensure that we have enough cauliflower to use in two ways, we use two heads, remove the cores and stems, and steam them with some florets until soft; we then blend them to make the sauce. We cut the remaining cauliflower into slabs, which make for a more compact casserole and help them cook more evenly. For a stream-lined, efficient cooking setup, we place the cauliflower cores and stems in water in the bottom of a Dutch oven and set our steamer basket filled with florets right on top. Butter and Parmesan (plus a little cornstarch) give the sauce a rich flavor and texture without making it heavy, and a few pantry spices add some complexity. Tossing the florets in the sauce before placing them in the dish ensure that they are completely coated. Topping the gratin with Parmesan and panko gives it savory crunch, and a final garnish of minced chives adds color. When buying cauliflower, look for heads without many leaves. Alternatively, if your cauliflower does have a lot of leaves, buy slightly larger heads—about 2¼ pounds each. This recipe can be halved to serve four to six; cook the cauliflower in a large saucepan and bake the gratin in an 8-inch square baking dish.

1   Adjust oven rack to middle position and heat oven to 400 degrees.

2   Pull off outer leaves of 1 head of cauliflower and trim stem. Using paring knife, cut around core to remove; halve core length-wise and slice thin crosswise. Slice head into ½-inch-thick slabs. Cut stems from slabs to create florets that are about 1½ inches tall; slice stems thin and reserve along with sliced core. Transfer florets to bowl, including any small pieces that may have been created during trimming, and set aside. Repeat with remaining head of cauliflower. (After trimming you should have about 3 cups of sliced stems and cores and 12 cups of florets.)

3   Combine sliced stems and cores, 2 cups florets, 3 cups water, and 6 tablespoons butter in Dutch oven and bring to boil over high heat. Place remaining florets in steamer basket (do not rinse bowl). Once mixture is boiling, place steamer basket in pot, cover, and reduce heat to medium. Steam florets in basket until translucent and stem ends can be easily pierced with paring knife, 10 to 12 minutes. Remove steamer basket and drain florets. Re-cover pot, reduce heat to low, and continue to cook stem mixture until very soft, about 10 minutes longer. Transfer drained florets to now-empty bowl.

4   While cauliflower is cooking, melt remaining 2 tablespoons butter in 10-inch skillet over medium heat. Add panko and cook, stirring frequently, until golden brown, 3 to 5 minutes. Transfer to bowl and let cool. Once cool, add ½ cup Parmesan and toss to combine.

5   Transfer stem mixture and cooking liquid to blender and add salt, pepper, mustard, nutmeg, cayenne, and remaining ½ cup Parmesan. Process until smooth and velvety, about 1 minute (purée should be pourable; adjust consistency with additional water as needed). With blender running, add cornstarch slurry. Season with salt and pepper to taste. Pour purée over cauliflower florets and toss gently to evenly coat. Transfer mixture to 13 by 9-inch baking dish (it will be quite loose) and smooth top with spatula. (To make ahead, gratin and bread-crumb mixture can be refrigerated separately for up to 24 hours. To serve, assemble and bake gratin as directed in step 6, increasing baking time by 13 to 15 minutes.)

6   Scatter bread-crumb mixture evenly over top. Transfer dish to oven and bake until sauce bubbles around edges, 13 to 15 minutes. Let stand for 20 to 25 minutes. Sprinkle with chives and serve.

CELERY ROOT PURÉE

serves: 4 to 6

total time: 1 hour

1¾–2	pounds celery root, peeled and cut into 2-inch chunks
1	(6-ounce) russet potato, peeled and cut into 2-inch chunks
2	tablespoons unsalted butter
1	cup water
½	teaspoon table salt
¼	teaspoon baking soda
⅓	cup heavy cream
1	recipe Bacon, Garlic, and Parsley Topping (optional, page 235)

why this recipe works   Celery root's earthiness and fresh celery flavor makes it a delicious and versatile vegetable to use as a side, whether you serve it raw in a rémoulade (page 61) or sautéed, roasted, even puréed, which makes it a buttery alternative to mashed potatoes. The problem is that celery root can take 45 minutes of cooking for the pieces to turn fully tender, but cooking times longer than 30 minutes produce less celery flavor and add a slightly cabbagey sourness. So we wanted to cook the root as quickly as possible. Small pieces soften faster, so we use the food processor to blitz the large, dense chunks into tiny bits, along with russet potato (which brings body and thickness to the purée). Then we cook the vegetables quickly in a small amount of water and butter, with a little baking soda to help them cook even more quickly. This alkaline cooking environment speeds up their breakdown. Once the vegetables and water have cooked into a thick mush, we process it with some heavy cream to make a smooth purée. When buying celery root, look for one with few roots for easy peeling and minimal waste. Use a che's knife to peel the celery root: Trim the top and bottom of the root first, and then cut the skin away from the sides. Once it's prepped, you should have about 1½ pounds of celery root. While the celery root purée can be made in advance, the Bacon, Garlic, and Parsley Topping should be made as close to serving as possible.

1   Working in 2 batches, pulse celery root and potato in food processor until finely chopped, about 20 pulses per batch; transfer to bowl. (You should have about 4½ cups chopped vegetables.)

2   Melt butter in large saucepan over medium heat. Stir in celery root–potato mixture, water, salt, and baking soda. Cover and cook, stirring often (mixture will stick but cleans up easily), until vegetables are very soft and translucent and mixture resembles applesauce, 15 to 18 minutes.

3   Uncover celery root mixture and cook, stirring vigorously to further break down vegetables and thicken remaining cooking liquid, about 1 minute. Transfer celery root mixture to clean, dry food processor. Add cream and process until smooth, about 40 seconds. Season with salt to taste. Transfer to serving bowl. Sprinkle topping over celery root puree and serve. (Ungarnished purée can be cooled and refrigerated for up to 2 days. Before serving, microwave purée on medium-high power in covered bowl, stirring often, until hot throughout, 7 to 10 minutes.)

BACON, GARLIC, AND PARSLEY TOPPING

makes: ½ cup

total time: 15 minutes

If you are looking for a flavorful topping that contrasts with the smoothness of celery root purée, try this. We fry bacon and garlic while the celery root cooks. When the bacon is browned and crispy, we finish the topping with fresh parsley. If desired, freeze the bacon for 15 minutes to make it easier to chop.

> 2 slices bacon, chopped fine
>
> ¼ cup water
>
> 4 garlic cloves, sliced thin
>
> 1 tablespoon minced fresh parsley

Combine bacon, water, and garlic in 8-inch nonstick skillet and cook over medium-high heat until water has evaporated and bacon and garlic are browned and crispy, 8 to 10 minutes. Off heat, stir in parsley.

FENNEL CONFIT

serves: 6 to 8

total time: 2¼ hours

3 fennel bulbs, 2 tablespoons fronds minced, stalks discarded, bulbs cut lengthwise into ½-inch-thick slabs, divided

¼ teaspoon table salt, divided

3 garlic cloves, lightly crushed and peeled

3 (2-inch) strips lemon zest, plus lemon wedges for serving

1 teaspoon caraway seeds

1 teaspoon fennel seeds

3 cups extra-virgin olive oil

why this recipe works The French confit technique is most often used with duck, but it's also a versatile way of transforming and preserving vegetables (for more on confit, turn to page 124). Fennel is a perfect candidate for confit since long cooking times coax out its hidden flavors and turn it luxuriously creamy. We wanted to confit enough fennel to serve as a side dish for a group, but most recipes called for up to 2 quarts of olive oil—an amount that would drain a home pantry. We found that arranging two layers of fennel slabs in the bottom of a large Dutch oven allows us to use just 3 cups of oil. The oil doesn't fully cover the fennel, but the fennel shrinks and releases liquid during cooking, causing it to sink. We flavor the oil with lemon zest, garlic, fennel seeds, and caraway seeds. The oven is perfect for our purpose: It provides even heat for the 2-hour cooking time and is completely hands-off. The fennel emerges buttery and aromatic, and the pieces that remain above the oil become golden and caramelized. We finish the dish prettily with a scattering of fennel fronds. Don't core the fennel before cutting it into slabs; the core will help hold the slabs together during cooking. This recipe will yield extra oil that can be strained, cooled, and stored for up to two weeks. The infused oil is great as a base for salad dressings or for dipping bread.

1 Adjust oven rack to middle position and heat oven to 300 degrees. Arrange half of fennel, cut side down, in single layer in Dutch oven. Sprinkle with ⅛ teaspoon salt. Repeat with remaining fennel and remaining ⅛ teaspoon salt. Scatter garlic, lemon zest, caraway seeds, and fennel seeds over top, then add oil (fennel may not be completely submerged).

2 Cover pot, transfer to oven, and cook until fennel is very tender and is easily pierced with tip of paring knife, about 2 hours.

3 Remove pot from oven. Using slotted spoon, transfer fennel to serving platter, brushing off any garlic, lemon zest, caraway seeds, or fennel seeds that stick to fennel. Drizzle ¼ cup cooking oil over fennel, sprinkle with fennel fronds, and sprinkle with flake sea salt to taste. Serve with lemon wedges.

LEEKS
VINAIGRETTE

serves: 4

total time: 1¼ hours

3 leeks (1 to 1½ inches in diameter, with 8 to 9 inches of white and light-green parts), white and light-green parts only

   Table salt for simmering leeks

2 teaspoons plus 3 tablespoons extra-virgin olive oil, divided

¾ cup fresh bread crumbs

2 tablespoons finely grated Parmesan cheese

2 tablespoons finely chopped fresh parsley, divided

¼ teaspoon pepper

1½ tablespoons red wine vinegar

1 tablespoon Dijon mustard

1 garlic clove, minced to paste

why this recipe works   This fresh-tasting dish is often a starter but can be served with a simple fish or chicken main course or as a bistro lunch for two. It makes the most of in-season leeks at their most tender. Leeks are part of the onion family, but when they're cooked, their flavor is sweeter and milder than that of their pungent relations. We start by trimming away the dark-green tops and halve each leek lengthwise, leaving the base intact, so we can rinse away any grit concealed between the layers. Though some recipes call for steaming leeks to prevent their becoming waterlogged, we prefer simmering them in heavily salted water because this enables us to get seasoning all the way to their bases. Tying up each leek with a piece of kitchen twine prevents the layers from splaying out and becoming detached as they cook, and a brief squeeze after cooling removes excess water. A punchy vinaigrette, served both under and atop the leeks, balances their sweet creaminess, and crispy bread crumbs spiked with a little bit of Parmesan for added savor and richness give a pleasing textural contrast to the tender leeks. You can use almost any unseeded bread for the bread crumbs; if you're using a rustic loaf, remove the crust before grinding in a food processor. For a bistro-style lunch, omit the bread crumbs and top the dressed leeks with two chopped hard-cooked eggs and two slices of crumbled crispy bacon; serve with crusty bread.

1   Trim roots from leeks, leaving base intact so layers stay together. Starting 1 inch above base, halve leeks lengthwise (they'll still be joined at base). Rinse thoroughly between layers to remove any dirt. Tie halves of each leek together with kitchen twine about 2 inches from top.

2   Bring 3 quarts water to boil in Dutch oven. Add leeks and 3 tablespoons salt and return to boil. Adjust heat to maintain simmer. Cover and cook until area just above base can be pierced easily with paring knife, 15 to 20 minutes. Using tongs, grasp 1 leek close to base and hold vertically over pot to drain briefly. Transfer to paper towel-lined plate and repeat with remaining leeks. Let sit until cool enough to handle, about 10 minutes.

3   While leeks cool, heat 2 teaspoons oil in 8-inch nonstick skillet over medium heat until shimmering. Add bread crumbs and cook over medium heat, stirring frequently, until deep golden brown, 4 to 5 minutes. Off heat, sprinkle with Parmesan and let sit until crumbs are just warm, about 5 minutes. Add 1 tablespoon parsley and pepper and stir, breaking up any clumps.

4   Whisk vinegar, mustard, 1 tablespoon water, and garlic in small bowl until combined. Whisking constantly, drizzle in remaining 3 tablespoons oil. Whisk in remaining 1 tablespoon parsley. Squeeze leeks over sink to remove excess water. Remove twine and finish cutting leeks in half lengthwise. Cut each half crosswise into thirds (do not remove bases of leeks; they're delicious). Spread half of vinaigrette over bottom of serving platter. Arrange leeks on platter, cut side up, opening layers slightly. Drizzle evenly with remaining vinaigrette. (Dressed leeks can be covered loosely and stored at room temperature for up to 3 hours.) Sprinkle with bread-crumb mixture and serve.

ROASTED KING TRUMPET MUSHROOMS

serves: 4

total time: 45 minutes

1¾ pounds king trumpet mushrooms

½ teaspoon table salt

4 tablespoons unsalted butter, melted

Lemon wedges

why this recipe works French mushroom foraging starts every autumn after the grape harvest is completed, so naturally mushrooms are an apropos side to pair with French meat mains in the colder months. The king trumpet or king oyster mushroom is a popular variety native to the Mediterranean regions of Europe, the Middle East, North Africa, and many parts of Asia. These large, stumpy mushrooms are transformed by cooking, becoming deeply savory, with the meaty texture of squid or tender octopus. To highlight this special quality, we prepare them almost like a piece of meat. We start by halving and cross-hatching each mushroom, creating attractive "fillets," and then salting them and letting them sit briefly. Roasting the mushrooms cut side down in a hot oven results in plump, juicy well-seasoned mushrooms with a nicely browned exterior crust. They are delicious on their own with just a squeeze of lemon, but you can also pair them with our Red Wine–Miso Sauce or Brown Butter–Lemon Vinaigrette (page 241). Serve the mushrooms as a side with Pan-Roasted Filets Mignons with Garlic-Herb Butter (page 144) or Poulet Au Vinaigre (page 111). Look for trumpet mushrooms that weigh 3 to 4 ounces each.

1 Adjust oven rack to lowest position and heat oven to 500 degrees. Trim bottom ½ inch of mushroom stems, then halve mushrooms lengthwise. Cut ¹⁄₁₆-inch-deep slits on cut side of mushrooms, spaced ½ inch apart, in crosshatch pattern. Sprinkle cut side of mushrooms with salt and let sit for 15 minutes.

2 Brush mushrooms evenly with melted butter, season with pepper to taste, and arrange cut side down on rimmed baking sheet. Roast until mushrooms are browned on cut side, 20 to 24 minutes. Transfer to serving platter. Serve with lemon wedges and sauce, if desired.

RED WINE–MISO SAUCE

makes: ⅓ cup

total time: 25 minutes

  1 cup dry red wine
  1 cup vegetable broth
  2 teaspoons sugar
  ½ teaspoon soy sauce
  5 teaspoons white miso
  1 tablespoon unsalted butter

Bring wine, broth, sugar, and soy sauce to simmer in 10-inch skillet over medium heat and cook until reduced to ⅓ cup, 20 to 25 minutes. Off heat, whisk in miso and butter until smooth.

BROWN BUTTER–LEMON VINAIGRETTE

makes: 6 tablespoons

total time: 10 minutes

  4 tablespoons unsalted butter
  2 tablespoons lemon juice
  1 teaspoon Dijon mustard
  1 teaspoon maple syrup
  ¼ teaspoon table salt
  ⅛ teaspoon pepper

Melt butter in 10-inch skillet over medium heat. Cook, swirling constantly, until butter is dark golden brown and has nutty aroma, 3 to 5 minutes. Off heat, whisk in lemon juice, mustard, maple syrup, salt, and pepper.

LEMONY ROASTED RADICCHIO, FENNEL, AND ROOT VEGETABLES

serves: 4 to 6

total time: 55 minutes

- 2 fennel bulbs, stalks discarded, bulbs halved, cored, and sliced into ½-inch-thick wedges
- 1 pound red potatoes, unpeeled, cut into 1-inch pieces
- 1 head Chioggia radicchio (10 ounces), halved, cored, and cut into 2-inch-thick wedges
- 8 ounces parsnips, peeled and cut into 2-inch pieces
- 8 shallots, halved
- 3 tablespoons extra-virgin olive oil, divided
- 6 garlic cloves, peeled
- 2 teaspoons minced fresh thyme
- 1 teaspoon minced fresh rosemary
- 1 teaspoon sugar
- ¾ teaspoon table salt
- ¼ teaspoon pepper
- 2 tablespoons chopped fresh basil
- 2 tablespoons minced fresh chives
- 1 tablespoon lemon juice, plus extra for seasoning

why this recipe works   In the spring and summertime, a bistro meal would not be complete without a fresh, light salad. But in the winter, a vegetable salad of radicchio, fennel, potatoes, parsnips, and shallots can create an intriguing and pleasing balance of flavors and textures, made fresh with a lemony vinaigrette. To ensure that the vegetables roast evenly, we cut them into comparably sized pieces. Arranging the radicchio in the center of the baking sheet, with the other vegetables around the perimeter, keeps the more delicate radicchio from charring in the hot oven. Before roasting, we toss the vegetables with olive oil, garlic, thyme, rosemary, and a little sugar (to promote browning). Once all the vegetables are perfectly tender and caramelized, we toss them with the bright-tasting dressing. When coring the radicchio, leave just enough core to hold each wedge together.

1   Adjust oven rack to middle position and heat oven to 450 degrees. Toss fennel, potatoes, radicchio, parsnips, shallots, 1 tablespoon oil, garlic, thyme, rosemary, sugar, salt, and pepper together in bowl.

2   Spread vegetables into single layer on rimmed baking sheet. Roast until tender and golden brown, 30 to 35 minutes, rotating sheet halfway through roasting.

3   Whisk basil, chives, lemon juice, and remaining 2 tablespoons oil together in large serving bowl. Add vegetables and toss to combine. Season with salt, pepper, and extra lemon juice to taste. Serve.

SAUTÉED RADISHES WITH VADOUVAN AND ALMONDS

serves: 4 to 6

total time: 30 minutes

3 tablespoons unsalted butter, divided

1½ pounds radishes with their greens, radishes trimmed and quartered, 8 cups greens reserved

¼ plus ⅛ teaspoon table salt, divided

1½ teaspoons Vadouvan Curry Powder (page 245)

2 tablespoons coarsely chopped toasted almonds

why this recipe works   While it is well known that the English colonized India, it is less commonly known that the French had colonized parts of the subcontinent long before the English arrived. One of the things the French took back to France from India was a blend of ground spices they called vadouvan. Here earthy-sweet vadouvan pairs nicely with spicy radishes, which themselves sweeten when cooked. We start by cooking quartered radishes in butter over moderate heat until they are browned and nutty, and then we stir in the vadouvan to release its flavor in the heat and thoroughly coat the radishes. To provide some textural variety and color, we cook the radish greens at the end in plenty of garlic. The greens retain a slight crispness that complements the heartier radish pieces. If you can't find radishes with their greens, skip step 2. We prefer to use our homemade Vadouvan Curry Powder but you can substitute any store-bought curry powder.

1   Melt 2 tablespoons butter in 12-inch skillet over medium-high heat. Add radishes and ¼ teaspoon salt and cook, stirring occasionally, until radishes are lightly browned and crisp-tender, 10 to 12 minutes. Stir in curry powder and cook until fragrant, about 30 seconds; transfer to bowl.

2   Melt remaining 1 tablespoon butter in now-empty skillet over medium heat. Add radish greens and ⅛ teaspoon salt and cook, stirring frequently, until wilted, about 1 minute. Off heat, stir in radishes and season with salt to taste. Sprinkle with almonds and serve.

VADOUVAN CURRY POWDER

makes: about 6 tablespoons

total time: 10 minutes

The French colonized Pondicherry in southeastern India in the 17th century. Inspired by a local spice mixture called vadakam or vadavam they tasted there, they created vadouvan, with aromatics such as onions or shallots and garlic, along with yellow mustard seed, cumin seeds, fenugreek seeds, and curry leaves.

- 4 **teaspoons cumin seeds**
- 1 **tablespoon yellow mustard seeds**
- 1 **cardamom pod**
- 5 **teaspoons dried minced onion**
- 4 **teaspoons ground turmeric**
- 1½ **teaspoons fennel seeds, cracked**
- ¼ **teaspoon ground cinnamon**

Process cumin seeds, mustard seeds, and cardamom pod in spice grinder until finely ground, about 30 seconds. Stir in dried onion, turmeric, fennel seeds, and cinnamon.

EASIER
FRENCH FRIES

serves: 4

total time: 45 minutes

2½ pounds Yukon Gold potatoes (about 6 medium), scrubbed, dried, sides squared off, and cut lengthwise into ¼-inch by ¼-inch batons

1½ quarts peanut or vegetable oil for frying

¼ cup bacon fat, strained, for frying (optional)

why this recipe works   When you don't have time to make classic french fries (page 142), this recipe gives you crisp, golden fries with less work. Oven-frying is the usual "quick" method, but we wanted real french fries. So we use an unorthodox procedure, starting the cut potatoes in cold oil. The usual choice for fries, russets, turn out a little dry with this method; instead we use Yukon Golds, which have more water and less starch than russets. They come out creamy and smooth inside and crisp outside. Leaving the fries undisturbed for 15 minutes, then stirring them, keeps them from sticking or breaking apart. Thinner batons are also less likely to stick. For those who like it, flavoring the oil with bacon fat gives the fries a mild meaty flavor. We prefer peanut oil for frying, but vegetable oil can be substituted. This recipe will not work with sweet potatoes or russets. Serve with our Chive and Black Pepper Dipping Sauce (page 247), if desired. Leftover frying oil may be saved for further use; strain the cooled oil into an air-tight container and store it in a cool, dark place for up to one month or in the freezer for up to two months.

1   Combine potatoes; oil; and bacon fat, if using, in large Dutch oven. Cook over high heat until oil reaches rolling boil, about 5 minutes. Continue to cook, without stirring, until potatoes are pale golden and exteriors are beginning to crisp, about 15 minutes.

2   Using tongs, stir potatoes, gently scraping up any that stick, and continue to cook, stirring occasionally, until golden and crisp, 5 to 10 minutes longer. Using skimmer or slotted spoon, transfer fries to thick paper bag or paper towels. Season with salt to taste, and serve immediately.

CHIVE AND BLACK PEPPER DIPPING SAUCE

makes: about ½ cup

total time: 10 minutes

- 5 tablespoons mayonnaise
- 3 tablespoons sour cream
- 2 tablespoons chopped fresh chives
- 1½ teaspoons lemon juice
- ¼ teaspoon table salt
- ¼ teaspoon pepper

Whisk all ingredients together in small bowl.

THICK-CUT SWEET POTATO FRIES

serves: 4 to 6

total time: 1 hour

spicy fry sauce

- 6 tablespoons mayonnaise
- 1 tablespoon chili-garlic sauce
- 2 teaspoons distilled white vinegar

fries

- ½ cup cornstarch
- Kosher salt for cooking sweet potatoes
- 1 teaspoon baking soda
- 3 pounds sweet potatoes, peeled and cut into ¾-inch-thick wedges, wedges cut in half crosswise
- 3 cups peanut oil for frying

why this recipe works   Sweet potato fries are often seen in American bistros so we wanted to include them here. Taking a cue from commercial frozen fries, we dunk the potato wedges in a slurry of water and cornstarch for thick-cut fries with crispy exteriors and creamy interiors. Blanching the potatoes with salt and baking soda before dipping them in the slurry helps the coating stick to the potatoes, giving the fries a super-crunchy crust that stays crispy. To keep the fries from sticking to the pan, we use a nonstick skillet, which has the added benefit of allowing us to use less oil. We like our fries plain, but for a finishing touch to complement their natural sweetness, we also make a spicy dipping sauce. If your sweet potatoes are shorter than 4 inches in length, do not cut the wedges crosswise. We prefer peanut oil for frying, but vegetable oil may be used instead. Leftover frying oil may be saved for further use; strain the cooled oil into an airtight container and store it in a cool, dark place for up to one month or in the freezer for up to two months.

1   **for the sauce**   Combine mayonnaise, chili-garlic sauce, and vinegar in small bowl and set aside.

2   **for the fries**   Adjust oven rack to middle position and heat oven to 200 degrees. Set wire rack in rimmed baking sheet. Whisk cornstarch and ½ cup cold water together in large bowl.

3   Bring 2 quarts water, ¼ cup salt, and baking soda to boil in Dutch oven. Add potatoes and return to boil. Reduce heat to simmer and cook until exteriors turn slightly mushy (centers will remain firm), 3 to 5 minutes. Whisk cornstarch slurry to recombine. Using wire skimmer or slotted spoon, transfer potatoes to bowl with slurry.

4   Using rubber spatula, fold potatoes with slurry until slurry turns light orange, thickens to paste, and clings to potatoes.

5   Heat oil in 12-inch nonstick skillet over high heat to 325 degrees. Using tongs, carefully add one-third of potatoes to oil, making sure that potatoes aren't touching one another. Fry until crispy and lightly browned, 7 to 10 minutes, using tongs to flip potatoes halfway through frying (adjust heat as necessary to maintain oil temperature between 280 and 300 degrees). Using wire skimmer or slotted spoon, transfer fries to prepared wire rack (fries that stick together can be separated with tongs or forks). Season with salt to taste, and transfer to oven to keep warm. Return oil to 325 degrees and repeat in 2 more batches with remaining potatoes. Serve immediately.

POTATO GALETTE

serves: 6 to 8

total time: 1¼ hours

2½ pounds Yukon Gold potatoes, unpeeled, sliced ⅛ inch thick

5 tablespoons unsalted butter, melted, divided

1 tablespoon cornstarch

1½ teaspoons chopped fresh rosemary

1 teaspoon table salt

½ teaspoon pepper

why this recipe works   Our savory galette has a crispy exterior, and its beautifully layered presentation makes it a simple but sophisticated side or brunch dish. For even cooking and great browning, we start it on the stovetop, then slide the pan onto the bottom rack of a hot oven. An ovensafe nonstick skillet prevents our galette from sticking to the pan's bottom. To keep the potatoes from sliding away from one another during slicing, we include cornstarch in the butter that coats the potatoes, and compress the galette with a cake pan filled with pie weights for the first half of cooking. Slicing the potatoes ⅛ inch thick is crucial for the success of this dish; use a mandoline, a V-slicer, or a food processor fitted with a ⅛-inch-thick slicing blade. You will need a 10-inch ovensafe nonstick skillet for this recipe. A pound of dried beans or rice can be substituted for the pie weights.

1   Adjust oven rack to lowest position and heat oven to 450 degrees. Place potatoes in large bowl and fill with cold water. Swirl to remove excess starch, then drain in colander. Spread potatoes on paper towels and dry thoroughly.

2   Whisk 4 tablespoons melted butter, cornstarch, rosemary, salt, and pepper together in large bowl. Add potatoes and toss until thoroughly coated. Add remaining 1 tablespoon melted butter to 10-inch ovensafe nonstick skillet and swirl to coat. Place 1 potato slice in center of skillet, then overlap slices in circle around center slice, followed by outer circle of overlapping slices. Gently place remaining sliced potatoes on top of first layer, arranging so they form even thickness.

3   Place skillet over medium-high heat and cook until potatoes are sizzling and slices around edge of pan start to turn translucent, about 5 minutes. Spray 12-inch square of aluminum foil with vegetable oil spray. Place foil, sprayed side down, on top of potatoes. Place 9-inch round cake pan on top of foil and fill with 2 cups pie weights. Firmly press down on cake pan to compress potatoes. Transfer skillet to oven and bake for 20 minutes.

4   Remove cake pan and foil from skillet. Continue to cook until paring knife can be inserted in center of with no resistance, 20 to 25 minutes. Being careful of hot skillet handle, return skillet to medium heat on stovetop and cook, gently shaking pan (skillet handle will be hot), until galette releases from sides of skillet, 2 to 3 minutes. Carefully slide galette onto large plate, place cutting board over galette, and gently invert plate and cutting board together, then remove plate. Using serrated knife, gently cut galette into wedges; serve immediately.

DUCK
FAT-ROASTED
POTATOES

serves: 6

total time: 1¼ hours

3½ pounds Yukon Gold potatoes, peeled and cut into 1½-inch pieces

1 teaspoon kosher salt, plus salt for boiling potatoes

½ teaspoon baking soda

6 tablespoons duck fat, melted, divided

1 tablespoon minced fresh rosemary

why this recipe works We often roast vegetables in olive oil but this bistro dish calls for a richer option, duck fat. The result is aromatic potatoes, crisp on the outside, moist inside, and exploding with meaty, savory flavor. Moist-yet-starchy Yukon Golds are the best potato choice; we peel and cut them into chunks to maximize their crispable surface area. We encourage thorough seasoning and deeper browning by boiling the chunks with a touch of baking soda and salt. We drain them and then vigorously stir them on the stovetop to rough up their exteriors before working in the duck fat. This step is enough to coat the potatoes with a film of starchy, fatty paste that creates a rich, crisp shell. Quickly turning the potatoes partway through roasting ensures even doneness. Just before the potatoes are done, we stir in an extra tablespoon of duck fat, seasoned with fresh rosemary, and roast the potatoes until well browned. Duck fat can be found at high-end butcher shops, specialty shops, and online. You can also use reserved rendered duck fat from Seared Duck Breast with Orange and Blackberry Salad (page 96). Alternatively, substitute chicken fat, lard, or a mixture of 3 tablespoons of bacon fat and 3 tablespoons of extra-virgin olive oil.

1 Adjust oven rack to top position. Place rimmed baking sheet on rack and heat oven to 475 degrees.

2 Bring 10 cups water to boil in Dutch oven over high heat. Add potatoes, ⅓ cup salt, and baking soda. Return to boil, cook for 1 minute, and drain. Return potatoes to pot and cook over low heat, shaking pot occasionally, until surface moisture has evaporated, about 2 minutes. Off heat, add 5 tablespoons melted fat and salt; mix with rubber spatula until potatoes are coated with thick paste, about 30 seconds.

3 Remove sheet from oven and add potatoes, spreading into even layer. Roast for 15 minutes.

4 Remove sheet from oven. Using thin metal spatula, turn potatoes. Roast until golden brown, 12 to 15 minutes. While potatoes roast, combine rosemary and remaining 1 tablespoon melted fat in bowl.

5 Remove sheet from oven. Spoon rosemary mixture over potatoes and turn again. Continue to roast until potatoes are well browned and rosemary is fragrant, 3 to 5 minutes longer. Season with salt and pepper to taste. Serve immediately.

POMMES PURÉE

serves: 8

total time: 1 hour

2 pounds Yukon Gold potatoes, peeled
and cut into 1-inch pieces

20 tablespoons (2½ sticks)
unsalted butter

1⅓ cups whole milk

1 teaspoon table salt

why this recipe works   Chef Joël Robuchon's recipe for ultrasilky, mashed potatoes is amazingly buttery and indulgent. This side is perfect to serve at dinner parties with dishes such as Chicken Provençal with Saffron, Orange, and Basil (page 114) or Roasted Salmon with Orange Beurre Blanc (page 192). However, it poses a number of challenges for the home cook, including peeling piping-hot whole boiled potatoes, beating a full pound of cold butter into the potatoes, and passing the purée multiple times through a special restaurant sieve called a tamis. Our version eliminates all those challenges. Instead of using water, we cook peeled, diced potatoes directly in the milk and 2½ sticks of butter that will be incorporated into the mash. This approach eliminates the need to laboriously beat in the butter after cooking and also captures the potato starch released during cooking, which is key to producing an emulsified texture in which the butter doesn't separate out. You will need a food mill or potato ricer for this recipe. When serving, keep the richness in mind: A small dollop on each plate should suffice.

1   Place potatoes in fine-mesh strainer and rinse under cold running water until water runs clear; set aside to drain.

2   Heat butter, milk, and salt in large saucepan over low heat until butter has melted. Add potatoes, increase heat to medium-low, and cook until liquid just starts to boil. Reduce heat to low, partially cover, and simmer gently until potatoes are tender and paring knife can be slipped in and out of potatoes with no resistance, 30 to 40 minutes, stirring every 10 minutes.

3   Drain potatoes in fine-mesh strainer set over large bowl, reserving cooking liquid. Wipe saucepan clean with paper towels. Return cooking liquid to now-empty saucepan and place over low heat.

4   Set food mill or ricer fitted with finest disk over saucepan. Working in batches, transfer potatoes to hopper and process. Using whisk, recombine potatoes and cooking liquid until smooth, 10 to 15 seconds (potatoes should almost be pourable). Season with salt and white pepper to taste. Serve immediately.

chapter nine

brunch & bread

———————

COCKTAILS & RECIPE EXTRAS

OMELET WITH CHEDDAR AND CHIVES

serves: 1 to 2 (makes 1 omelet)

total time: 10 minutes

3 large eggs

Pinch table salt

1 ounce extra-sharp cheddar cheese, shredded (¼ cup)

1½ teaspoons unsalted butter

1½ teaspoons chopped fresh chives

why this recipe works A traditional French omelet is all about using technique to create a tender interior and a smooth exterior. An American omelet is about hearty fillings. This version gives us the best of both worlds, the French tenderness and smoothness and the American filling that makes a satisfying brunch dish. The technique takes some practice to perfect but is well worth the effort and time. We start by cooking three beaten eggs in an 8-inch nonstick skillet; this yields an omelet that is delicate but thick enough to support our filling. Stirring constantly as the eggs cook breaks up the curds so that the texture of the finished omelet is even and fine. Once a small amount (about 10 percent) of liquid egg remains, it helps to cut the heat and smooth this "glue" over the curds so that the whole thing holds together in a cohesive round. We add the filling, prepared separately, to the omelet just before rolling and serving. Have your ingredients and equipment ready before you begin. To ensure success, work at a steady pace. Omelets can be held for 10 minutes in an oven set to the lowest temperature.

1 Beat eggs and salt in bowl until few streaks of white remain.

2 Sprinkle cheese in even layer on small plate. Microwave at 50 percent power until cheese is just melted, 30 to 60 seconds. Set aside.

3 Melt butter in 8-inch nonstick skillet over medium heat, swirling skillet to distribute butter across skillet bottom. When butter sizzles evenly across skillet bottom, add eggs. Cook, stirring constantly with rubber spatula and breaking up large curds, until eggs are mass of small to medium curds surrounded by small amount of liquid egg. Immediately remove skillet from heat.

4 Working quickly, scrape eggs from sides of skillet, then smooth into even layer. Using fork, fold cheese into 2-inch-wide strip and transfer to center of eggs perpendicular to handle. Cover for 1 minute. Remove lid and run spatula underneath perimeter of eggs to loosen omelet. Gently ease spatula under eggs and slide omelet toward edge of skillet opposite handle until edge of omelet is even with lip of skillet. Using spatula, fold egg on handle side of skillet over filling. With your nondominant hand, grasp handle with underhand grip and hold skillet at 45-degree angle over top half of plate. Slowly tilt skillet toward yourself while using spatula to gently roll omelet onto plate. Sprinkle chives over omelet and serve.

how to make an omelet

Cook Eggs
Cook, stirring constantly and scraping bits of egg from sides of skillet into middle. Remove from heat; scrape eggs from sides and smooth into even layer.

Add Cheese
Place cheese filling in center of eggs perpendicular to handle. Cover for 1 minute.

Loosen and Fold
Loosen omelet and slide to rim opposite handle. Fold eggs partway over filling.

Change Grip and Tilt
Grasp handle with your nondominant hand; hold skillet over plate at 45-degree angle. Slowly tilt skillet toward yourself while using spatula to roll omelet onto plate.

variations

HAM, PEAR, AND BRIE OMELET

serves: 1 to 2 (makes 1 omelet)

total time: 15 minutes

This unusual combination of filling ingredients makes for a hearty omelet, bringing savoriness from the ham and Brie and sweetness from the sautéed pear.

- 1 tablespoon unsalted butter, divided
- ¼ cup chopped ripe peeled pear
- 2 pinches table salt, divided
- ¼ cup chopped thinly sliced deli ham
- 1 (1-ounce) slice Brie cheese, rind removed
- 3 large eggs

1 Melt 1½ teaspoons butter in 10-inch nonstick skillet over medium heat. Add pear and 1 pinch salt and cook, stirring occasionally, until pear begins to brown, 1 to 2 minutes. Add ham and cook, stirring constantly, until ham is warmed through, about 1 minute. Remove skillet from heat. With rubber spatula, push pear-ham mixture to side of skillet opposite handle and top with Brie. Set aside.

2 Beat eggs and remaining pinch salt in bowl until few streaks of white remain. Melt remaining 1½ teaspoons butter in 8-inch nonstick skillet over medium heat, swirling skillet to distribute butter across skillet bottom. When butter sizzles evenly across skillet bottom, add eggs. Cook, stirring constantly with rubber spatula and breaking up large curds, until eggs are mass of small to medium curds surrounded by small amount of liquid egg. Immediately remove skillet from heat.

3 Working quickly, scrape eggs from sides of skillet, then smooth into even layer. Slide filling into center of eggs in 2-inch-wide strip perpendicular to handle. Cover for 1 minute. Remove lid and run spatula underneath perimeter of eggs to loosen omelet. Gently ease spatula under eggs and slide omelet toward edge of skillet opposite handle until edge of omelet is even with lip of skillet. Using spatula, fold egg on handle side of

skillet over filling. With your nondominant hand, grasp handle with underhand grip and hold skillet at 45-degree angle over top half of plate. Slowly tilt skillet toward yourself while using spatula to gently roll omelet onto plate. Serve.

KALE, FETA, AND SUN-DRIED TOMATO OMELET

serves: 1 to 2 (makes 1 omelet)

total time: 15 minutes

The sharpness of kale is offset here by tangy, creamy feta, with a bit of tart chew added by sun-dried tomatoes against the creamy eggs. Lacinato kale is also sold as cavolo nero, black, dinosaur, or Tuscan kale. Do not use other types of kale in this recipe because they take longer to cook.

1 tablespoon unsalted butter, divided

1 garlic clove, minced

¼ teaspoon ground cumin

1½ ounces lacinato kale, stemmed and sliced thin (1½ cups)

2 pinches table salt, divided

2 tablespoons oil-packed sun-dried tomatoes, rinsed, patted dry, and sliced thin

2 tablespoons crumbled feta cheese

3 large eggs

1 Melt 1½ teaspoons butter in 10-inch nonstick skillet over medium heat. Add garlic and cumin and cook, stirring constantly, until fragrant, about 30 seconds. Add kale and 1 pinch salt and cook, stirring occasionally, until wilted, about 2 minutes. Add tomatoes and cook, stirring frequently, until tomatoes are warmed through and no liquid remains in skillet, 1 to 2 minutes. Remove skillet from heat. Push kale mixture to side of skillet opposite handle and top with feta. Set aside.

2 Beat eggs and remaining pinch salt in bowl until few streaks of white remain. Melt remaining 1½ teaspoons butter in 8-inch nonstick skillet over medium heat, swirling skillet to distribute butter across skillet bottom. When butter sizzles evenly across skillet bottom, add eggs. Cook, stirring constantly with rubber spatula and breaking up large curds, until eggs are mass of small to medium curds surrounded by small amount of liquid egg. Immediately remove skillet from heat.

3 Working quickly, scrape eggs from sides of skillet, then smooth into even layer. Slide filling into center of eggs in 2-inch-wide strip perpendicular to handle. Cover for 1 minute. Remove lid and run spatula underneath perimeter of eggs to loosen omelet. Gently ease spatula under eggs and slide omelet toward edge of skillet opposite handle until edge of omelet is even with lip of skillet. Using spatula, fold egg on handle side of skillet over filling. With your nondominant hand, grasp handle with underhand grip and hold skillet at 45-degree angle over top half of plate. Slowly tilt skillet toward yourself while using spatula to gently roll omelet onto plate. Serve.

The Tools for Omelet Success

Set yourself up properly by having everything—the equipment, eggs, and filling—ready to go.

8-Inch Nonstick Skillet: A three-egg omelet made in this pan will be delicate but thick enough to support the filling. Make sure that the surface is slick; if the coating is scratched or worn, sliding the omelet out of the pan will be difficult.

Tight-Fitting Lid: Briefly covering the pan traps heat that helps the omelet set, making it easier to maneuver, and keeps the filling warm.

Heatproof Rubber or Silicone Spatula: Any size or shape will work.

Serving Plate: This is your landing pad for the omelet when you roll it out of the pan.

FLUFFY OMELET

serves: 2 (Makes 1 omelet)

total time: 25 minutes

4   large eggs, separated

1   tablespoon unsalted butter, melted,
    plus 1 tablespoon unsalted butter

¼   teaspoon table salt

¼   teaspoon cream of tartar

1   recipe filling (recipes follow)

1   ounce Parmesan cheese, grated
    (½ cup)

The Magic of Cream of Tartar

Cream of tartar (potassium bitartrate), a powdered byproduct of the wine-making process, is, along with baking soda, one of the two main ingredients in baking powder. When egg whites are whipped, their protein strands unwind and form a network that holds water and air bubbles in place, creating stiff peaks. But the sulfur atoms in egg whites can form strong bonds that over-strengthen this network. Then the protein structure becomes too rigid≈and the network that holds the whipped air and water in place starts to collapse. Acidic cream of tartar slows down the formation of sulfur bonds, preserving the network's stability and creating a strong, voluminous foam, the key to tall soufflés and this omelet.

why this recipe works   Two French classics—the lofty soufflé and the tender omelet—come together in this dish meant for two. The beauty of this tall omelet is in its ease—we use the oven—and forgiving nature, thanks to our secret ingredient, cream of tartar. This acid allows you to reach great heights by preventing whipped egg whites from collapsing during or after cooking. Once you've whisked egg yolks and separately whipped egg whites to stiff peaks with cream of tartar, you simply fold them together, spread them in a pan, and bake. A teaspoon of white vinegar or lemon juice can be used instead of cream of tartar, and a hand mixer or a whisk can be used in place of a stand mixer. The fillings that accompany this recipe are designed not to interfere with the cooking of the omelet.

1   Adjust oven rack to middle position and heat oven to 375 degrees. Whisk egg yolks, melted butter, and salt together in bowl. Place egg whites in bowl of stand mixer and sprinkle cream of tartar over surface. Fit stand mixer with whisk and whip egg whites on medium-low speed until foamy, 2 to 2½ minutes. Increase speed to medium-high and whip until stiff peaks just start to form, 2 to 3 minutes. Fold egg yolk mixture into egg whites until no white streaks remain.

2   Melt remaining 1 tablespoon butter in 12-inch ovensafe non-stick skillet over medium-high heat, swirling to coat bottom of pan. Quickly add egg mixture, spreading into even layer with spatula. Remove pan from heat and gently sprinkle filling and Parmesan evenly over top of omelet. Transfer to oven and cook until center of omelet springs back when lightly pressed, 4½ minutes for slightly wet omelet and 5 minutes for dry omelet.

3   Run spatula around edges of omelet to loosen, shaking gently to release. Slide omelet onto cutting board and let stand for 30 seconds. Using spatula, fold omelet in half. Cut omelet in half crosswise and serve immediately.

fillings

ASPARAGUS AND SMOKED SALMON FILLING

makes: ¾ cup

- 1 teaspoon extra-virgin olive oil
- 1 shallot, sliced thin
- 5 ounces asparagus, trimmed and cut on bias into ¼-inch lengths

  Pinch table salt
- 1 ounce smoked salmon, chopped
- ½ teaspoon lemon juice

Heat oil in 12-inch nonstick skillet over medium-high heat until shimmering. Add shallot and cook until softened and starting to brown, about 2 minutes. Add asparagus, salt, and pepper to taste. Cook, stirring frequently, until crisp-tender, 5 to 7 minutes. Transfer asparagus mixture to bowl and stir in salmon and lemon juice.

MUSHROOM FILLING

makes: ¾ cup

- 1 teaspoon extra-virgin olive oil
- 1 shallot, sliced thin
- 4 ounces white or cremini mushrooms, trimmed and chopped
- ⅛ teaspoon table salt
- 1 teaspoon balsamic vinegar

Heat oil in 12-inch nonstick skillet over medium-high heat until shimmering. Add shallot and cook until softened and starting to brown, about 2 minutes. Add mushrooms, salt, and pepper to taste. Cook until liquid has evaporated and mushrooms begin to brown, 6 to 8 minutes. Transfer mixture to bowl and stir in vinegar.

GALETTES COMPLÈTES

serves: 4 (Makes 4 crêpes)

total time: 1½ hours

crêpes

½ teaspoon vegetable oil

¾ cup (3⅜ ounces) buckwheat flour

¼ cup (1¼ ounces) all-purpose flour

½ teaspoon table salt

2 cups milk

3 large eggs

4 tablespoons salted butter,
   melted and cooled

filling

4 thin slices deli ham (2 ounces), divided

5½ ounces Gruyère cheese, shredded
   (1⅓ cups), divided

4 large eggs, divided

1 tablespoon salted butter, melted

4 teaspoons chopped fresh
   chives, divided

why this recipe works Brittany, France, is renowned for its crêpes, and not just the lightly sweet ones you sprinkle with sugar or smear with jam. Galettes bretonnes are dark and savory, with a distinctive earthiness. That's because they are made from rich, mineral-y buckwheat, which thrives in the cool Breton climate. This classic preparation has them partially folded around nutty Gruyère cheese and salty-sweet ham, with an egg cracked into the well. They're cooked until the eggs are set and then sprinkled with fresh herbs. Buckwheat is naturally gluten-free so you can't use only buckwheat flour, or you'll end up with brittle crêpes that tear. Blending in some all-purpose flour gives them more resilience (for more on making crêpes, see page 285). And though these crêpes are traditionally assembled individually in a skillet, arranging four on a baking sheet and sliding them into the oven lets you serve more people at once. The crêpes will give off steam as they cook, but if at any point the skillet begins to smoke, remove it from the burner and turn down the heat. Stacking the crêpes on a wire rack lets excess steam escape so that they won't stick together. The batter yields 10 crêpes, but only four are needed. You can double the filling amount to make eight filled crêpes; prep the second batch on a second baking sheet while the first batch is in the oven. Extra crêpes freeze well or you can stash them in the fridge for a couple days to use later. Salted butter is traditional, but you can substitute unsalted. If using unsalted butter, add an additional teaspoon of salt to the batter.

1 for the crêpes Adjust oven rack to middle position and heat oven to 450 degrees. Heat oil in 12-inch nonstick skillet over low heat for at least 5 minutes. While skillet heats, whisk buckwheat flour, all-purpose flour, and salt together in medium bowl. In second bowl, whisk together milk and eggs. Add half of milk mixture to flour mixture and whisk until smooth. Add melted butter and whisk until incorporated. Whisk in remaining milk mixture until smooth.

2   Using paper towel, wipe out skillet, leaving thin film of oil on bottom and sides. Increase heat to medium and let skillet heat for 1 minute. Test heat of skillet by placing 1 teaspoon batter in center and cooking for 20 seconds. If mini crêpe is golden brown on bottom, skillet is properly heated; if it is too light or too dark, adjust heat accordingly and retest.

3   Lift skillet off heat and pour ⅓ cup batter into far side of skillet; swirl gently in clockwise direction until batter evenly covers bottom of skillet, gently shaking skillet as needed. Return skillet to heat and cook crêpe, without moving it, until top surface is dry and crêpe starts to brown at edges, loosening crêpe from sides of skillet with heat-resistant rubber spatula, about 35 seconds. Gently slide spatula underneath edge of crêpe, grasp edge with your fingertips, and flip crêpe. Cook until second side is lightly spotted, about 20 seconds. Transfer crêpe to wire rack. Return skillet to heat for 10 seconds before repeating with remaining batter. As crêpes are done, stack on wire rack. (Crêpes can be wrapped tightly in plastic wrap and refrigerated for up to 3 days or stacked between sheets of parchment paper and frozen for up to 1 month. Allow frozen crêpes to thaw completely in refrigerator before using.)

4   **for the filling**   Line rimmed baking sheet with parchment paper and spray with vegetable oil spray. Arrange 4 crêpes spotty side down on prepared sheet (they will hang over edge). (Reserve remaining crêpes for another use.) Working with 1 crêpe at a time, place 1 slice of ham in center of crêpe, followed by ⅓ cup Gruyère, covering ham evenly. Make small well in center of cheese. Crack 1 egg into well. Fold in the 4 sides to make a square, pressing to adhere.

5   Brush crêpe edges with melted butter and transfer sheet to oven. Bake until egg whites are uniformly set and yolks have filmed over but are still runny, 8 to 10 minutes. Using thin metal spatula, transfer each crêpe to plate and sprinkle with 1 teaspoon chives. Serve immediately.

EGGS BENEDICT WITH FOOLPROOF HOLLANDAISE

serves: 4

total time: 40 minutes

hollandaise

- 3 large egg yolks
- 2 tablespoons lemon juice
- ¼ teaspoon table salt

  Pinch cayenne pepper, plus extra for seasoning
- 16 tablespoons unsalted butter, melted and still hot (180 degrees)

eggs benedict

- 4 English muffins, split
- 8 slices Canadian bacon
- 2 tablespoons distilled white vinegar
- 1 teaspoon table salt
- 8 large eggs

why this recipe works   Eggs Benedict has been a popular Sunday brunch choice in America since its birth at New York's Delmonico's restaurant in 1860. Today this classic brunch dish is served at bistros across the country and around the world. Thanks to our Foolproof Hollandaise (made in a blender) and easy skillet-poached eggs, it's also easy enough to make at home. And don't limit yourself to English muffins, Canadian bacon, and hollandaise. See page 267 for some other routes to a great Benedict using smoked salmon, asparagus, and more. For the best results, use the freshest eggs possible and unsalted butter.

1   **for the hollandaise**   Process egg yolks, lemon juice, salt, and cayenne in blender until frothy, about 10 seconds, scraping bottom and sides of blender jar as needed. With blender running, slowly add hot butter and process until hollandaise is emulsified, about 2 minutes. Adjust consistency with hot water as needed until sauce slowly drips from spoon. Season with salt and extra cayenne to taste.

2   **for the eggs benedict**   Adjust oven rack 6 inches from broiler element and heat broiler. Arrange English muffins split side up on rimmed baking sheet and broil until golden brown, 2 to 4 minutes. Place 1 slice bacon on each muffin half and broil until hot and beginning to brown, about 1 minute. Remove sheet from oven and tent with aluminum foil.

3   Fill 12-inch skillet nearly to rim with water. Add vinegar and salt and bring to boil over high heat. Crack 2 eggs into each of 4 cups. Carefully and simultaneously pour eggs into skillet. Cover skillet, remove from heat, and let sit until egg whites are set but yolks are still slightly runny, 4 minutes. (For firmer eggs, cook 2 to 3 minutes longer.)

4   Using slotted spoon, transfer eggs to paper towel–lined plate. Arrange 1 egg on top of each muffin half. Spoon 1 to 2 tablespoons hollandaise over each egg. Serve, passing remaining hollandaise separately.

Many Ways to Benedict

To vary flavor, update your eggs Benedict with these simple tricks:

Base: Use sourdough toast points instead of English muffins. Toast sourdough bread before topping.

Toppings: Instead of Canadian bacon, try Gravlax (page 268), store-bought smoked salmon, or Pan-Roasted Asparagus (page 229).

Sauces: We suggest topping asparagus Benedict with our Aïoli (page 17). For gravlax or smoked salmon Benedict, a mustard-dill hollandaise pairs nicely and is supereasy to make: Simply add 1 tablespoon whole-grain mustard and 1 tablespoon minced fresh dill to Foolproof Hollandaise and blend until combined but not smooth.

GRAVLAX

serves: 8 to 10 (Makes about 1½ pounds)

total time: 10 minutes, plus 72 hours curing

½ cup kosher salt

½ cup chopped fresh dill

⅓ cup packed light brown sugar

1 (1½-pound) center-cut skinless salmon fillet, about 1½ inches thick

why this recipe works Gravlax—cured salmon with Nordic roots—is delicious any which way you eat it. Cured with sugar, salt, and dill, gravlax can be enjoyed thinly sliced on bagels for breakfast or with a French omelet or Eggs Benedict (page 266) for brunch. For at-home bistro nights, gravlax makes a ridiculously simple and impressive appetizer, arranged on baguette slices with cream cheese, capers, and pickled onions. The best part is that you can make gravlax quickly and easily so it is on hand when needed. We start with a skinless, center-cut salmon fillet; its even thickness makes for more even curing. Coating the salmon in a salt mixture in a large zipper-lock bag contains the mess and makes it easy to flip. Pressing the gravlax while curing ensures that the fish has a pleasant density and firmness, and rinsing the salmon after removing it from the cure keeps it from tasting too salty. Finally, patting the gravlax dry and slicing the fillet in half lengthwise before slicing it crosswise makes it easier to create paper-thin slices. We prefer using farmed salmon here; if you choose to use wild salmon, reduce the curing time in step 2 to 36 hours, flipping the bag halfway through the curing period.

1 Combine salt, dill, and sugar in bowl. Place salmon in 1-gallon zipper-lock bag. Spread half of salt mixture evenly over top of salmon. Flip bag and spread remaining half of salt mixture over bottom of salmon (salmon should be well coated all over). Press out air and seal bag.

2 Place bag on large plate or rimmed baking sheet, making sure salmon sits flat. Place square baking dish filled with 2 large, heavy cans on top of bag. Refrigerate for 3 days, flipping bag once each day.

3 Remove gravlax from salt mixture; discard salt mixture. Rinse gravlax well with cold water and pat dry with paper towels. To serve, slice gravlax in half lengthwise, then slice crosswise on bias as thin as possible with sharp knife. (Gravlax can be wrapped tightly in plastic wrap and refrigerated for up to 3 days.)

flavoring and curing gravlax

1. Cover salmon in salt mixture in 1-gallon zipper-lock bag. The bag contains the mess and is easy to flip—an essential step for even curing.

2. Place bag on large plate or rimmed baking sheet; top it with square baking dish; and weight it with two large, heavy cans.

3. After 3 days, take gravlax out of salt mixture and rinse it off so that it is not too salty to eat. Pat it dry with paper towels before slicing.

4. Slice fillet in half lengthwise before slicing crosswise—against the grain—to make it easier to create paper-thin slices.

EGGS PIPÉRADE

serves: 6 to 8

total time: 40 minutes

5 tablespoons extra-virgin olive oil, divided

1 large onion, chopped

1 bay leaf

2 teaspoons table salt, divided

4 garlic cloves, minced

2 teaspoons paprika

1 teaspoon minced fresh thyme or ¼ teaspoon dried

¾ teaspoon red pepper flakes

3 red bell peppers, stemmed, seeded, and cut into ½-inch-wide strips

3 Cubanelle peppers, stemmed, seeded, and cut into ½-inch-wide strips

1 (14-ounce) can whole peeled tomatoes, drained with ¼ cup juice reserved, chopped

3 tablespoons minced fresh parsley, divided

2 teaspoons sherry vinegar

12 large eggs

2 tablespoons water

¼ teaspoon pepper

why this recipe works   Wondering what to serve for brunch with eggs? Try pipérade. A tangy Basque pepper and tomato sauté whose colors serendipitously match those of the red and green Basque flag, a pipérade is often paired with eggs and delivers richness, acidity, and tempered heat. While in many recipes the eggs are scrambled with the vegetables, we found the liquid from the produce caused the eggs to cook up stringy and wet. So we cook the eggs separately and simply plate the two elements together to show off their vibrant colors. The combination of fresh sweet peppers, tomatoes, and fragrant spices like paprika and bay leaf work their magic. We use canned peeled tomatoes to avoid chewy bits of tomato skin and drain the tomatoes of most of their juice to keep the dish from being watery. If you can't find Cubanelle peppers, substitute green bell peppers. You will need a 12-inch nonstick skillet with a tight-fitting lid for this recipe.

1   Heat 3 tablespoons oil in 12-inch nonstick skillet over medium heat until shimmering. Add onion, bay leaf, and ½ teaspoon salt and cook until onion is softened and lightly browned, 5 to 7 minutes. Stir in garlic, paprika, thyme, and pepper flakes and cook until fragrant, about 1 minute. Add bell peppers, Cubanelle peppers, and 1 teaspoon salt; cover and cook, stirring occasionally, until peppers begin to soften, about 10 minutes.

2   Reduce heat to medium-low. Uncover, add tomatoes and reserved juice, and cook, stirring occasionally, until mixture appears dry and peppers are tender but not mushy, 10 to 12 minutes. Off heat, discard bay leaf. Stir in 2 tablespoons parsley and vinegar and season with salt and pepper to taste. Transfer to bowl and cover to keep warm.

3   Beat eggs, water, pepper, and remaining ½ teaspoon salt with fork in bowl until thoroughly combined and mixture is pure yellow; do not overbeat.

4   Wipe skillet clean with paper towels. Heat remaining 2 tablespoons oil in now-empty skillet over medium heat until shimmering. Add egg mixture and, using rubber spatula, constantly and firmly scrape along bottom and sides of skillet until eggs begin to clump and spatula leaves trail on bottom of skillet, 1½ to 2 minutes.

5   Reduce heat to low and gently but constantly fold eggs until clumped and slightly wet, 30 to 60 seconds. Off heat, sprinkle with remaining 1 tablespoon parsley and serve immediately with pepper mixture.

CROQUE MONSIEUR

serves: 4

total time: 45 minutes

sandwiches

8 slices hearty white sandwich bread

4 tablespoons unsalted butter, melted

12 ounces thinly sliced Black Forest deli ham

¼ cup grated Parmesan cheese

4 ounces Gruyère cheese, shredded (1 cup)

Mornay sauce

2 tablespoons unsalted butter

2 tablespoons all-purpose flour

1 cup whole milk

4 ounces Gruyère cheese, shredded (1 cup)

¼ cup grated Parmesan cheese

½ teaspoon table salt

¼ teaspoon pepper

Pinch ground nutmeg

variation

CROQUE MADAME

To make a Croque Madame, simply top each cooked Croque Monsieur with a fried egg.

why this recipe works To define the croque monsieur, a popular bistro menu item, as a grilled ham-and-cheese sandwich is to vastly understate it. This favorite is a rich, runny, beautiful sight to behold. The traditional cooking method calls for griddling the sandwiches individually, topping them with cheese, and then sliding them under a broiler. To make four sandwiches at once, we turn to a baking sheet and the oven instead. Most croque monsieur recipes use a simple béchamel sauce with grated Gruyère. We combine the two to make a Mornay sauce and add Parmesan for more savoriness, and nutmeg for warmth and complexity. More cheese sauce spread over the top of and a final sprinkling of Parmesan and Gruyère before broiling creates a gorgeous, bubbly-browned top.

1 **for the sandwiches** Adjust oven rack 6 inches from broiler element and heat oven to 375 degrees. Line rimmed baking sheet with aluminum foil and spray with vegetable oil spray.

2 Brush bread on both sides with melted butter and place on prepared sheet. Bake until light golden brown on top, about 10 minutes. Remove sheet from oven and flip slices. Return to oven and bake until golden brown on second side, about 3 minutes. Reserve 4 slices for sandwich tops; evenly space remaining 4 slices on sheet.

3 **for the Mornay sauce** Melt butter in small saucepan over medium heat. Whisk in flour and cook for 1 minute. Slowly whisk in milk and bring to boil. Once boiling, remove from heat and quickly whisk in Gruyère, Parmesan, salt, pepper, and nutmeg until smooth.

4 Spread 1 tablespoon Mornay on each slice of toast on sheet. Then, folding ham slices over themselves multiple times so they bunch up, divide ham evenly among slices of toast. Spread 2 tablespoons Mornay on 1 side of each reserved slice of toast and place slices Mornay side down on top of ham.

5 Spread 2 tablespoons Mornay evenly over top of each sandwich, making sure to completely cover toast, including edges (exposed edges can burn under broiler). Sprinkle sandwiches with Parmesan, followed by Gruyère.

6 Bake until cheese on top of sandwiches is melted, about 5 minutes. Turn on broiler and broil until cheese bubbles across tops of sandwiches and edges are spotty brown, about 5 minutes. Serve.

QUICHE LORRAINE

serves: 8

total time: 2 hours, plus
2 hours cooling

crust

- ¼ cup ice water
- 4 teaspoons sour cream
- 1¼ cups (6¼ ounces) all-purpose flour
- 1½ teaspoons sugar
- ½ teaspoon table salt
- 8 tablespoons unsalted butter, cut into ¼-inch pieces and frozen for 15 minutes

filling

- 6 slices bacon, cut into ¼-inch pieces
- 1 onion, chopped fine
- 1¼ cups heavy cream, divided
- 1 tablespoon cornstarch
- 5 large eggs
- ¼ teaspoon table salt
- ¼ teaspoon pepper
- 4 ounces Gruyère cheese, shredded (1 cup)

why this recipe works When one thinks of savory French bakes, quiche lorraine often springs to mind: The buttery crust, silken egg custard, and crispy bits of bacon epitomize the elegant sumptuousness France has bequeathed to the world of food. We like making quiche for at-home bistros because a single quiche can feed eight people. Plus, our dough can be made ahead, making life simpler when it comes to putting together Sunday brunch. The day we want to serve the quiche, we prebake our shaped crust filled with pie weights to ensure that it cooks through and keeps its shape before adding the custard filling. This is vital for getting that sturdy, crisp bottom crust that is too often missing from quiche. For the egg mixture, we add cornstarch to prevent it from curdling and use sautéed onion to contribute savory, rich flavor. To make sure the bacon is fully rendered for the filling, we cook it ahead on the stovetop. Covering the quiche after adding the filling allows us to bake the custard to its optimal temperature (170 degrees), which produces a creamy texture without a burnt crust. To prevent the crust from sagging during prebaking, make sure the protruding crimped edge overhangs the edge of the pie plate slightly. Also, use plenty of pie weights (3 to 4 cups). The quiche can be served warm or at room temperature.

1 **for the crust** Combine ice water and sour cream in bowl. Process flour, sugar, and salt in food processor until combined, about 5 seconds. Scatter butter over top and pulse until butter is size of large peas, about 10 pulses. Add sour cream mixture and pulse until dough forms clumps and no dry flour remains, about 12 pulses, scraping down sides of bowl as needed.

2 Turn out dough onto sheet of plastic wrap and form into 4-inch disk. Wrap tightly in plastic and refrigerate for 1 hour. (Wrapped dough can be refrigerated for up to 2 days or frozen for up to 1 month. If frozen, let dough thaw completely on counter before rolling.)

3 Adjust oven rack to middle position and heat oven to 350 degrees. Let chilled dough sit on counter to soften slightly, about 10 minutes, before rolling. Roll dough into 12-inch circle on lightly floured counter. Loosely roll dough around rolling pin and gently unroll it onto 9-inch pie plate, letting excess dough hang over edge. Ease dough into plate by gently lifting edge of dough with your hand while pressing into plate bottom with your other hand.

4   Trim overhang to ½ inch beyond lip of plate. Tuck overhang under itself; folded edge should be flush with edge of plate. Crimp dough evenly around edge of plate using your fingers. Push protruding crimped edge so it slightly overhangs edge of plate. Wrap dough-lined plate loosely in plastic and freeze until dough is firm, about 15 minutes.

5   Place chilled pie shell on rimmed baking sheet. Line with double layer of parchment paper, covering edges to prevent burning, and fill with pie weights. Bake until edges are light golden brown, about 20 minutes. Remove parchment and weights, rotate plate, and bake until crust bottom dries out and turns light golden brown, 15 to 20 minutes. If crust begins to puff, pierce gently with tip of paring knife. Set aside. (Crust needn't cool completely before adding filling.)

6   **for the filling**   Meanwhile, cook bacon in 12-inch nonstick skillet over medium heat until crispy, 5 to 7 minutes. Using slotted spoon, transfer bacon to paper towel–lined plate. Pour off all but 1 tablespoon fat from skillet. Add onion to skillet and cook over medium heat, stirring frequently, until softened and lightly browned, 8 to 10 minutes. Set aside to cool slightly.

7   Whisk ¼ cup cream and cornstarch in large bowl until cornstarch dissolves. Whisk in eggs, salt, pepper, and remaining 1 cup cream until mixture is smooth.

8   Scatter bacon, onion, and Gruyère evenly over crust. Pour custard mixture over top. Tent quiche with lightly greased aluminum foil. Bake on baking sheet until toothpick inserted in center of quiche comes out clean and center registers 170 degrees, 50 minutes to 1 hour. Transfer to wire rack, discard foil, and let rest until cool to touch, about 2 hours. Slice and serve. (Quiche can be refrigerated for up to 3 days.)

POTATOES
LYONNAISE

serves: 4 to 6

total time: 30 minutes

4 tablespoons unsalted butter

2 pounds Yukon Gold potatoes,
   peeled and sliced ½ inch thick

1¼ teaspoons table salt, divided

½ teaspoon pepper

1 onion, halved and sliced thin

1 tablespoon minced fresh parsley

why this recipe works A hallmark dish from Lyon, one of France's premier gastronomic cities, potatoes Lyonnaise is a study in simple elegance. Although originally conceived as a dish of economy (an easy way to use up leftover boiled potatoes), it came to represent the best of classic French bistro cuisine: buttery, browned potato slices interwoven with strands of sweet, caramelized onion and fresh, grassy parsley—a simple yet complex skillet potato dish. But who wants to wait around for leftover boiled potatoes to make it? For our take on this buttery, earthy side, we jump-start the process by cooking potatoes, sliced ½ inch thick, for 15 minutes in the skillet before adding some sliced onions. We then cook the two together covered for an additional 10 minutes. We finish the dish with a sprinkling of minced fresh parsley, which adds a bright green color and freshness. Use potatoes of similar size.

1 Melt butter in 12-inch nonstick skillet over medium heat. Add potatoes and ¾ teaspoon salt and cook, covered, until just tender and golden brown, about 15 minutes, flipping potatoes occasionally to ensure even browning.

2 Reduce heat to medium-low. Add onion, pepper, and remaining ½ teaspoon salt; cover and cook until onion is tender and golden brown, about 10 minutes longer, stirring occasionally. Season with salt and pepper to taste. Transfer to serving platter and sprinkle with parsley. Serve.

OVEN-COOKED BACON

serves: 4 to 6

time: 15 minutes

If you need to cook a big batch of bacon, this oven method is for you. It cooks a pound of bacon in one shot: no fuss, no mess. The exact amount you can cook at one time will vary depending on the size of the bacon slices and the size of your baking sheet.

1 pound bacon

Adjust oven rack to middle position and heat oven to 400 degrees. Line rimmed baking sheet with aluminum foil. Arrange bacon on prepared sheet (slices can overlap slightly). Bake until brown and crispy, 10 to 15 minutes, rotating sheet halfway through baking. Transfer bacon to paper towel–lined plate to drain. Serve.

BRIOCHE
FRENCH TOAST

serves: 4

time: 45 minutes

8   large slices brioche, hearty white
    sandwich bread, or challah

1½ cups whole milk, warmed slightly

3   large egg yolks

3   tablespoons packed light brown sugar

2   tablespoons unsalted butter, melted,
    plus 2 tablespoons unsalted butter,
    divided

1   tablespoon vanilla extract

½   teaspoon ground cinnamon

¼   teaspoon table salt

The Not-So-Lost History
Of Lost Bread

People around the world soak and
cook bread and have done so for centuries, all the way back to the Romans.
Bread battering has long been a way
to transform stale bread into something new and flavorful. The French
call it pain perdu (lost bread), the
Germans have arme ritter, and in Spain
the dish is torrijas. Nineteenth-century
American cookbooks typically called
this dish arme ritter, but after World
War I the German name lost favor and
the dish went Gallic—which explains
why we call it French toast.

why this recipe works   To make French toast, we like to use
our No-Knead Brioche Sandwich Loaf (page 292) but any thick
sliced bread will work. The real secret to French toast that's crisp
on the outside and puffy and custardy, not soggy, on the inside is
not the bread but the way you quickly "stale" it by toasting in the
oven. This dries the bread out, which allows it to soak up the egg
better, while its edges stay crispy. To prevent the butter from
clumping while mixing, heat the milk in a microwave or small
saucepan until it is warm to the touch (about 80 degrees) before
adding the butter. All the pieces of soaked bread can be cooked
together on an electric griddle, but the process may take an
extra 2 to 3 minutes per side. Set the griddle temperature to
350 degrees and use the entire amount of unmelted butter to
grease the griddle. We prefer brioche but challah or white sandwich bread work almost as well. Serve with warm maple syrup.

1   Adjust oven rack to middle position and heat oven to
300 degrees. Place brioche on wire rack set in rimmed baking
sheet. Bake until brioche is almost dry throughout (center should
remain slightly moist), about 16 minutes, flipping bread halfway
through baking. Remove brioche from rack and let cool for 5 minutes. Reduce oven temperature to 200 degrees and return sheet
with wire rack to oven.

2   Whisk milk, egg yolks, sugar, melted butter, vanilla, cinnamon,
and salt together in large bowl. Transfer mixture to 13 by 9-inch
baking dish.

3   Add brioche to dish and soak until slices are saturated with
milk mixture but not falling apart, 20 seconds per side. Using firm
slotted spatula, transfer brioche to second baking sheet, allowing
excess milk mixture to drip back into dish.

4   Melt ½ tablespoon butter in 12-inch skillet over medium-low
heat. Using slotted spatula, transfer 2 slices soaked brioche to
skillet and cook until golden brown, 3 to 4 minutes. Flip and
continue to cook until second side is golden brown, 3 to 4 minutes longer. (If toast is browning too quickly, reduce temperature
slightly.) Transfer to prepared wire rack in oven to keep warm.
Wipe skillet clean with paper towels. Repeat in 3 batches with
remaining 1½ tablespoons butter and remaining 6 slices soaked
brioche. Serve warm.

MIMOSA

makes: 1 cocktail

time: 15 minutes

Champagne cocktails date back to the mid-1800s. An American brunch fave, the mimosa was invented in the 1920s at the Ritz in Paris. For our take on this festive cocktail, we begin with equal parts freshly squeezed orange juice and champagne. A little orange liqueur boosts the orange juice flavor and adds complexity; increasing the amount of sparkling wine helps ensure a more wine-forward beverage. We switched from the far more expensive champagne to prosecco (or cava), with no loss in the quality of the cocktail.

2½ ounces orange juice, plus orange twist for garnishing

¼ ounce orange liqueur

3 ounces dry sparkling wine, such as prosecco or cava, chilled

Add orange juice and liqueur to chilled wine glass or flute glass and stir to combine using bar spoon. Add wine and, using spoon, gently lift juice mixture from bottom of glass to top to combine. Garnish with orange twist and serve.

LEMON RICOTTA PANCAKES

serves: 3 to 4 (Makes twelve
4-inch pancakes)

total time: 45 minutes

⅔ cup (3⅓ ounces) all-purpose flour

½ teaspoon baking soda

½ teaspoon table salt

8 ounces (1 cup) whole-milk
   ricotta cheese

2 large eggs, separated, plus
   2 large whites

⅓ cup whole milk

1 teaspoon grated lemon zest plus
   4 teaspoons juice

½ teaspoon vanilla extract

2 tablespoons unsalted butter, melted

¼ cup (1¾ ounces) sugar

1–2 teaspoons vegetable oil

why this recipe works   At bistros across the United States,
you'll see both crêpes and pancakes on the menu. If you plan to
serve pancakes for your next brunch, give these lemon ricotta
ones a try. You'll be wowed by their exquisitely light, tender,
golden-brown goodness. You might think ricotta would make
them heavy and damp but a generous amount combined with
whipped egg whites, less flour than many pancake recipes call
for, baking soda, and lemon juice and zest makes for pillowy,
bright-tasting pancakes. An electric griddle set at 325 degrees
can also be used to cook the pancakes. We prefer the flavor
of whole-milk ricotta here, but part-skim works too; avoid non-
fat ricotta. Serve with honey, confectioners' sugar, or one of
our toppings.

1   Adjust oven rack to middle position and heat oven to
200 degrees. Spray wire rack set in rimmed baking sheet with
vegetable oil spray and place in oven. Whisk flour, baking soda,
and salt together in medium bowl and make well in center. Add
ricotta, egg yolks, milk, lemon zest and juice, and vanilla and
whisk until just combined. Gently stir in melted butter.

2   Using stand mixer fitted with whisk attachment, whip egg
whites on medium-low speed until foamy, about 1 minute. Increase
speed to medium-high and whip whites to soft, billowy mounds,
about 1 minute. Gradually add sugar and whip until glossy, soft
peaks form, 1 to 2 minutes. Transfer one-third of whipped egg
whites to batter and whisk gently until mixture is lightened. Using
rubber spatula, gently fold remaining egg whites into batter.

3   Heat 1 teaspoon oil in 12-inch nonstick skillet over medium
heat until shimmering. Using paper towels, wipe out oil, leaving
thin film on bottom and sides of pan. Using ¼-cup measure or
2-ounce ladle, portion batter into pan in 3 places, leaving 2 inches
between portions. Gently spread each portion into 4-inch round.
Cook until edges are set and first side is deep golden brown, 2 to
3 minutes. Using thin, wide spatula, flip pancakes and continue
to cook until second side is golden brown, 2 to 3 minutes longer.
Serve pancakes immediately or transfer to prepared wire rack in
preheated oven. Repeat with remaining batter, using remaining oil
as needed.

PEAR-BLACKBERRY PANCAKE TOPPING

makes: 3 cups

- 3 ripe pears, peeled, halved, cored, and cut into ¼-inch pieces
- 1 tablespoon sugar
- 1 teaspoon cornstarch
- Pinch table salt
- Pinch ground cardamom
- 5 ounces (1 cup) blackberries

Combine pears, sugar, cornstarch, salt, and cardamom in bowl and microwave, covered, until pears are softened but not mushy and juices are slightly thickened, 4 to 6 minutes, stirring once halfway through microwaving. Stir in blackberries before serving.

APPLE-CRANBERRY PANCAKE TOPPING

makes: 2½ cups

- 3 Golden Delicious apples, peeled, cored, halved, and cut into ¼-inch pieces
- ¼ cup dried cranberries
- 1 tablespoon sugar
- 1 teaspoon cornstarch
- Pinch table salt
- Pinch ground nutmeg

Combine all ingredients in bowl and microwave, covered, until apples are softened but not mushy and juices are slightly thickened, 4 to 6 minutes, stirring once halfway through microwaving. Stir before serving.

YEASTED WAFFLES

serves: 4

total time: 45 minutes, plus
12 hours rising

1¾ cups milk

8 tablespoons unsalted butter, cut into
8 pieces

2 cups (10 ounces) all-purpose flour

1 tablespoon sugar

1½ teaspoons instant or rapid-rise yeast

1 teaspoon table salt

2 large eggs

1 teaspoon vanilla extract

why this recipe works   The best place to get sweet and savory waffles in Europe, outside Belgium, is in Parisian neighborhoods like Montparnasse. French chefs sometimes use the romance of America—think chicken and waffles—to sell them. Stateside, yeasted waffles might seem old-fashioned and require some advance planning but they are well worth the effort. Crisp, tasty, and easy to prepare, waffles are a brunch stalwart. We use all-purpose flour, the right amount of yeast to provide a pleasant tang, and a full stick of melted butter for rich flavor. Refrigerating the batter overnight keeps the yeast's growth under control, producing waffles with superior flavor. While waffles can be eaten as soon as they are removed from the iron, they will have a crispier exterior if rested in a warm oven for 10 minutes. (This method also makes it possible to serve everyone at the same time.) The batter must sit in the refrigerator for at least 12 hours.

1   Heat milk and butter in small saucepan over medium-low heat until butter is melted, 3 to 5 minutes. Let mixture cool until warm to touch.

2   Whisk flour, sugar, yeast, and salt together in large bowl. In small bowl, whisk eggs and vanilla together. Gradually whisk warm milk mixture into flour mixture until smooth, then whisk in egg mixture. Scrape down bowl with rubber spatula, cover tightly with plastic wrap, and refrigerate for at least 12 hours or up to 1 day.

3   Adjust oven rack to middle position and heat oven to 200 degrees. Set wire rack in rimmed baking sheet and place in oven. Heat waffle iron according to manufacturer's instructions. Remove batter from refrigerator when waffle iron is hot (batter will be foamy and doubled in size). Whisk batter to recombine (batter will deflate).

4   Cook waffles according to manufacturer's instructions (use about ½ cup batter for 7-inch round iron and about 1 cup batter for 9-inch square iron). Serve immediately or transfer to wire rack in oven to keep warm while cooking remaining waffles.

CHOCOLATE-ORANGE CRÊPES

serves: 4

total time: 30 minutes

½ teaspoon vegetable oil

1 cup (5 ounces) all-purpose flour

1 teaspoon plus ¼ cup (1¾ ounces) sugar, divided

¼ teaspoon table salt

1½ cups whole milk

3 large eggs

2 tablespoons unsalted butter, melted and cooled

1 teaspoon finely grated orange zest

2 ounces bittersweet chocolate, grated fine

why this recipe works   Crêpes are essentially thin pancakes that can be stuffed with sweet or savory fillings, or just enjoyed with maple syrup or powdered sugar. Although crêpes have a reputation for being temperamental, the reality isn't quite so daunting. We found the batter simple; it didn't need to be made in a blender or rested as some recipes suggest. Instead, the real success of our crêpes relies on a few crucial cooking steps: heating the pan properly, using just enough batter to coat the bottom of the pan, and employing a tilt-and-shake method to distribute it. Sugared crêpes are a classic; for an elegant upgrade we flavor our sugar with orange zest and finely grated bittersweet chocolate. The crêpes will give off steam as they cook, but if the skillet begins to smoke, remove from the heat immediately and turn down the heat. Stacking cooked crêpes on a wire rack allows excess steam to escape so they won't stick together. To allow for practice, the recipe yields 10 crêpes; only eight are needed for the amount of filling.

1   Heat oil in 12-inch nonstick skillet over low heat for at least 10 minutes.

2   While oil is heating, whisk flour, 1 teaspoon sugar, and salt together in bowl. Whisk milk and eggs together in second bowl. Add half of milk mixture to flour mixture and whisk until smooth. Add melted butter and whisk until incorporated. Whisk in remaining milk mixture until smooth.

3   Using paper towel, wipe out skillet, leaving thin film of oil on bottom and sides. Increase heat to medium and let skillet heat for 1 minute. Test heat of skillet by placing 1 teaspoon batter in center and cooking for 20 seconds. If mini crêpe is golden brown on bottom, skillet is properly heated; if it is too light or too dark, adjust heat accordingly and retest.

4 Lift skillet off heat and pour ¼ cup batter into far side of skillet; swirl gently in clockwise direction until batter evenly covers bottom of skillet, gently shaking skillet as needed. Return skillet to heat and cook crêpe, without moving it, until surface is dry and crêpe starts to brown at edges, loosening crêpe from sides of skillet with heat-resistant rubber spatula, about 35 seconds. Gently slide spatula underneath edge of crêpe, grasp edge with your fingertips, and flip crêpe. Cook until second side is lightly spotted, about 30 seconds. Transfer crêpe, spotted side up, to wire rack. Return skillet to heat and heat for 10 seconds before repeating with remaining batter. As crêpes are done, stack on wire rack. in small bowl, place remaining ¼ cup sugar. Using your fingertips, rub orange zest into sugar. Stir in chocolate.

5 Transfer stack of crêpes to large plate and invert second plate over crêpes. Microwave until crêpes are warm, 30 to 45 seconds (45 to 60 seconds if crêpes have cooled completely). Remove top plate and wipe dry with paper towel. Sprinkle 1½ tablespoons sugar mixture over top half of top crêpe. Fold unsugared half over sugared half, then fold in half again. Transfer filled crêpe to second plate. Repeat with remaining crêpes. Serve immediately.

making crêpes

1. Heat oil in skillet over low heat for 10 minutes. Then wipe it out with paper towel, leaving thin film of oil on bottom and sides.

2. Increase heat to medium and heat for 1 minute. Lift skillet off heat and tilt slightly away from you. Pour ⅓ cup batter into far side of skillet.

3. Turn your wrist to rotate skillet clockwise and spread batter over entire skillet bottom. Cook without moving until top surface is dry and crêpe starts to brown at edges.
.

4. To cook second side, gently slide spatula underneath edge of crêpe, grasp edge with your fingertips, and flip crêpe.

chocolate-orange crepes
(page 284)

chocolate brioche buns
(page 288)

CHOCOLATE BRIOCHE BUNS

makes: 12 buns

total time: 2 hours, plus 4 hours rising and cooling

dough

3⅔ cups (20⅛ ounces) bread flour

2¼ teaspoons instant or rapid-rise yeast

1½ teaspoons table salt

1 cup water, room temperature

2 large eggs plus 1 large yolk

½ cup (3½ ounces) granulated sugar

12 tablespoons unsalted butter, cut into 12 pieces, softened

⅓ cup (1 ounce) unsweetened cocoa powder

filling

2 ounces bittersweet chocolate, chopped

4 tablespoons unsalted butter

3 tablespoons unsweetened cocoa powder

¼ cup (1 ounce) confectioners' sugar

1 large egg white

1 large egg, lightly beaten with 1 tablespoon water

why this recipe works Our chocolate brioche buns are beautiful to behold and buttery, rich, and tender to eat. If you're having friends or family over for brunch, these will be an indulgent treat. If your guests leave any buns uneaten, they'll make a great snack for the coming week. We use bread flour to ensure that the dough has enough structure to later fill and shape into scrolls. We add a generous ⅓ cup of cocoa powder to half of the dough, and roll the plain and chocolate doughs separately into squares, then stack them with a filling of bittersweet chocolate, cocoa powder, butter, and confectioners' sugar (made tacky with an egg white) in the middle. We refrigerate the layered doughs so that they firm up before rolling, cutting, and coiling. We also refrigerate the shaped buns to proof overnight. When kneading the dough on medium-low speed, the mixer can wobble and move on the counter. Place a towel or shelf liner underneath it to keep it in place and watch it closely.

1 **for the dough** Whisk flour, yeast, and salt together in bowl of stand mixer. Whisk water, eggs and yolk, and sugar together in 4-cup liquid measuring cup. Using dough hook on low speed, slowly add water mixture to flour mixture and mix until cohesive dough starts to form and no dry flour remains, about 2 minutes, scraping down bowl as needed.

2 Increase speed to medium-low; add butter, 1 piece at a time; and knead until butter is fully incorporated, about 4 minutes. Continue to knead until dough is smooth and elastic and clears sides of bowl, 11 to 13 minutes.

3 Transfer dough to lightly floured counter and divide in half. Knead half of dough by hand to form smooth, round ball, about 30 seconds. Place dough ball seam side down in lightly greased large bowl or container. Return remaining half of dough to mixer, add cocoa, and knead on medium-low speed until cocoa is evenly incorporated, about 2 minutes. Transfer dough to lightly floured counter and knead by hand to form smooth, round ball, about 30 seconds. Place second dough ball seam side down in second lightly greased large bowl or container. Cover bowls tightly with plastic wrap and let rise at room temperature until increased in size by half, 45 minutes to 1 hour.

4 **for the filling** Microwave chocolate, butter, and cocoa in bowl at 50 percent power, stirring occasionally, until melted and smooth, about 2 minutes. Stir in sugar until combined and let cool completely, about 30 minutes. Whisk in egg white until fully combined and mixture turns glossy.

5 Line baking sheet with parchment paper and lightly flour. Transfer plain dough seam side down to prepared sheet and press into 6-inch square. Spread filling over dough, leaving ¼-inch border around edges. Press chocolate dough into 6-inch square on lightly floured counter. Place on top of filling and press gently to adhere. Cover loosely with greased plastic and refrigerate for 30 minutes.

6 Line 2 rimmed baking sheets with parchment paper. Transfer chilled dough square to lightly floured counter. Press and roll dough into 16 by 12-inch rectangle with short side parallel to counter edge. Using sharp pizza wheel or knife, starting at 1 short side, cut dough into twelve 16 by 1-inch strips. Working with 1 dough strip at a time, tightly coil ends of strip in opposite directions to form tight S shape. Arrange buns on prepared sheets, six per sheet, spaced about 2½ inches apart. Cover loosely with greased plastic and refrigerate for at least 2 hours or up to 24 hours.

7 One hour before baking, remove buns from refrigerator and let sit at room temperature. Adjust oven racks to upper-middle and lower-middle positions and heat oven to 350 degrees. Gently brush buns egg mixture and bake until golden brown, 18 to 22 minutes, switching and rotating sheets halfway through baking. Transfer buns to wire rack and let cool completely, about 30 minutes. Serve.

layering and shaping brioche buns

1. Press and roll dough into 6-inch square with short side parallel to counter edge.

2. Spread filling over dough, leaving ¼-inch border around edges. Press chocolate dough (not shown) into 6-inch square on lightly floured counter. Place on top of filling and press gently to adhere. Refrigerate covered for 30 minutes.

3. Press and roll dough into 12 by 16-inch rectangle, with short side parallel to counter edge. Starting at 1 short side, cut dough into twelve 16 by 1-inch strips.

4. Working with 1 dough strip at a time, tightly coil ends of strip in opposite directions to form tight S shape

ALMOST
NO-KNEAD BREAD

makes: 1 loaf

total time: 11 to 11½ hours, plus
3 hours cooling

- 3 cups (15 ounces) all-purpose flour
- 1½ teaspoons table salt
- ¼ teaspoon instant or rapid-rise yeast
- ¾ cup (6 ounces) water, room temperature
- ½ cup (4 ounces) mild lager, room temperature
- 1 tablespoon distilled white vinegar

All About Autolyse

We replace kneading with a high hydration level (85 percent or 8½ ounces of water for 10 ounces of flour) and an 8- to 18-hour-long resting period called autolyse. During that time, flour hydrates and enzymes work to break up the proteins so dough needs only a brief knead to develop gluten.

why this recipe works   The three Bs of French bread might just be boule, brioche, and baguette. For a beautifully browned boule with a chewy, open interior to elevate your bistro brunch, we use our almost no-knead method. As the oven preheats, we bake the bread in the humid environment of a covered Dutch oven, which gives it an open crumb and crisp crust. When the oven reaches 425 degrees and the bread has baked for 30 minutes, we remove the Dutch oven cover and bake it for another 25 minutes, till golden brown. We add acidic tang with vinegar and a shot of yeasty flavor from beer. We prefer to use a mild American lager, such as Budweiser; strongly flavored beers will make this bread taste bitter. You will need a Dutch oven with a lid and an instant-read thermometer for this recipe.

1   Whisk flour, salt, and yeast together in large bowl. Whisk water, beer, and vinegar together in 4-cup liquid measuring cup. Using rubber spatula, gently fold water mixture into flour mixture, scraping up dry flour from bottom of bowl, until dough starts to form and no dry flour remains. Cover bowl tightly with plastic wrap and let sit at room temperature for at least 8 hours or up to 18 hours.

2   Lay 18 by 12-inch sheet of parchment paper on counter and lightly spray with vegetable oil spray. Transfer dough to lightly floured counter and knead by hand until smooth and elastic, about 1 minute. Shape dough into ball by pulling edges into middle, then transfer seam side down to center of prepared parchment.

3   Using parchment as sling, gently lower loaf into Dutch oven (let any excess parchment hang over pot edge). Cover tightly with plastic and let rise until loaf has doubled in size and dough springs back minimally when poked gently with your knuckle, 1½ to 2 hours.

4   Adjust oven rack to middle position. Using sharp paring knife or single-edge razor blade, make two 5-inch-long, ½-inch-deep slashes with swift, fluid motion along top of loaf to form cross. Cover pot and place in oven. Turn oven to 425 degrees and bake loaf for 30 minutes while oven heats. Remove lid and continue to bake until loaf is deep golden brown and registers 205 to 210 degrees, 25 to 30 minutes. Using parchment sling, remove loaf from pot and transfer to wire rack; discard parchment. Let cool completely, about 3 hours, before serving.

NO-KNEAD BRIOCHE SANDWICH LOAF

makes: 1 loaf

total time: 21 to 23 hours, plus 3 hours cooling time

1⅔ cups (9⅛ ounces) bread flour

1¼ teaspoons instant or rapid-rise yeast

¾ teaspoon table salt

3 large eggs, room temperature, plus 1 large egg, lightly beaten with 1 tablespoon water and pinch table salt

8 tablespoons (4 ounces) unsalted butter, melted

¼ cup water, room temperature

3 tablespoons sugar

why this recipe works Marie Antoinette is famously misquoted as saying, "Let them eat cake." We know now that she was likely referring to brioche. Classic brioche, an enriched bread, has the tender crumb, golden color, and buttery flavor of cake. But achieving a sumptuous result is laborious: Butter, softened to just the right temperature, is kneaded into the dough in small increments. Only after one portion is fully incorporated is the next added to ensure that the butter is completely combined. We wondered if we could simply use melted butter and our technique for Almost No-Knead Bread (page 291) instead. Happily, this works with our enriched dough, allowing us to simplify the conventional brioche method dramatically. Switching from the all-purpose flour that's used in many recipes to higher-protein bread flour helps to give the loaf sufficient structure. Some manual manipulation also builds enough strength to support an airy crumb. A folding process encourages gluten to form and ensures that the no-knead method is successful. In addition, instead of shaping the dough into a single long loaf, we divide it in two and shape each half into a ball. Placed side by side in the pan and rested before baking, the two balls merge to form a single strong loaf with a fine crumb. The test kitchen's preferred loaf pan measures 8½ by 4½ inches; if you use a 9 by 5-inch loaf pan, increase the shaped rising time by 20 to 30 minutes and start checking for doneness 10 minutes earlier than advised in the recipe. Use slices of this bread in our Brioche French Toast (page 278).

1 Whisk flour, yeast, and salt together in large bowl. Whisk 3 eggs, melted butter, water, and sugar in second bowl until sugar has dissolved. Using rubber spatula, gently fold egg mixture into flour mixture, scraping up dry flour from bottom of bowl, until cohesive dough starts to form and no dry flour remains. Cover bowl tightly with plastic wrap and let dough rest for 10 minutes.

2 Using greased bowl scraper (or your fingertips), fold dough over itself by gently lifting and folding edge of dough toward middle. Turn bowl 90 degrees and fold dough again; repeat turning bowl and folding dough 2 more times (total of 4 folds). Cover tightly with plastic and let rise for 30 minutes. Repeat folding and rising every 30 minutes, 3 more times. After fourth set of folds, cover bowl tightly with plastic and refrigerate for at least 16 hours or up to 48 hours.

3 Transfer dough to well-floured counter, divide in half, and cover loosely with greased plastic. Using your well-floured hands, press 1 piece of dough into 4-inch round (keep remaining piece covered). Working around circumference of dough, fold edges toward center until ball forms. Repeat with remaining piece of dough. Flip each dough ball seam side down and, using your

cupped hands, drag in small circles on counter until dough feels taut and round and all seams are secured on underside. (If dough sticks to your hands, lightly dust top of dough with flour.) Cover dough rounds loosely with greased plastic and let rest for 5 minutes.

4   Grease 8½ by 4½-inch loaf pan. Flip each dough ball seam side up, press into 4-inch disk, and repeat folding and rounding steps. Place rounds seam side down, side by side, into prepared pan. Press dough gently into corners. Cover loosely with greased plastic and let rise until loaf reaches ½ inch below lip of pan and dough springs back minimally when poked gently with your knuckle, 1½ to 2 hours.

5   Adjust oven rack to middle position and heat oven to 350 degrees. Gently brush loaf with egg mixture and bake until deep golden brown and loaf registers 190 to 195 degrees, 35 to 40 minutes, rotating pan halfway through baking. Let loaf cool in pan for 15 minutes. Remove loaf from pan and let cool completely on wire rack, about 3 hours, before serving.

shaping a brioche loaf

1. Using greased bowl scraper (or your fingertips), gently lift and fold edge of dough toward middle. Turn bowl 90 degrees and repeat 2 more times. Cover tightly with plastic and let rise for 30 minutes. Repeat folding and rising every 30 minutes, 3 more times. After fourth set of folds, cover bowl tightly with plastic and refrigerate for at least 16 hours or up to 48 hours.

2. Transfer dough to well-floured counter, divide in half, and cover loosely with greased plastic. Using your well-floured hands, press 1 piece of dough into 4-inch round. Working around circumference of dough, fold edges toward center until ball forms. Repeat with remaining piece of dough.

3. Grease 8½ by 4½-inch loaf pan. Flip each dough ball seam side up, press into 4-inch disk, and repeat folding and rounding steps. Flip each ball seam side down and, using your cupped hands, drag in small circles on counter until dough feels taut and round and all seams are secured on underside. Cover dough rounds loosely with greased plastic and let rest for 5 minutes.

4. Place rounds seam side down in greased 8½ by 4½-inch loaf pan, side by side. Press dough gently into corners. Cover loosely with greased plastic and let rise, 1½ to 2 hours. Gently brush loaf with egg mixture and bake until deep golden brown and loaf registers 190 to 195 degrees, 35 to 40 minutes, rotating pan halfway through baking.

AUTHENTIC BAGUETTES AT HOME

makes: four 15-inch-long baguettes

total time: 2 hours, plus 4 hours resting and 24 hours rising

¼ cup (1⅓ ounces) whole-wheat flour

3 cups (15 ounces) King Arthur all-purpose flour

1½ teaspoons salt

1 teaspoon instant or rapid-rise yeast

1 teaspoon diastatic malt powder (optional)

1½ cups (12 ounces) water

2 (16 by 12-inch) disposable aluminum roasting pans

why this recipe works   When one thinks of France, the image of a Frenchman in a beret, clasping a baguette under his arm, tends to emerge. The French do buy baguettes fresh daily, which we do not do stateside. Indeed, here a great baguette is hard to come by. Those from the supermarket or the average bakery, with their pale, soft crust and fine crumb, are no comparison to baguettes made in France. The ideal has a moist, sweet wheaty interior with just a subtle hint of tangy, complex fermented flavor. It is punctuated with irregular holes and has a deeply browned crust so crisp that it shatters into a shower of tiny shards. The darker the crust, the deeper the flavor. Even if a nearby bakery makes a great baguette, you have to buy one within hours of baking or it's rock-hard. If you want a great baguette, you should make it yourself because baguette making is not as intimidating as you might think. However excess exterior flour will dull flavor and compromise crispiness. If you can't find King Arthur all-purpose flour, substitute bread flour. We also add diastatic malt, an enzyme naturally present in flour that converts starches to sugars and ensures a caramelized, well-browned crust. Purchase diastatic malt powder, not plain malt powder or malt syrup. This recipe makes enough dough for four loaves, which can be baked anytime during the 24- to 72-hour window after placing the dough in the fridge.

1   Sift whole-wheat flour through fine-mesh strainer into bowl of stand mixer; discard bran remaining in strainer. Add all-purpose flour; salt; yeast; and malt powder, if using, to mixer bowl. Fit stand mixer with dough hook, add water, and knead on low speed until cohesive dough forms and no dry flour remains, 5 to 7 minutes. Transfer dough to lightly oiled large bowl, cover with plastic wrap, and let rest at room temperature for 30 minutes.

2   Holding edge of dough with your fingertips, fold dough over itself by gently lifting and folding edge of dough toward center. Turn bowl 45 degrees; fold again. Turn bowl and fold dough 6 more times (total of 8 folds). Cover with plastic and let rise for 30 minutes. Repeat folding and rising every 30 minutes, 3 more times. After fourth set of folds, cover bowl tightly with plastic and refrigerate for at least 24 hours or up to 72 hours.

3   Transfer dough to lightly floured counter, pat into 8-inch square (do not deflate), and divide in half. Return 1 piece of dough to container, wrap tightly with plastic, and refrigerate (dough can be shaped and baked anytime within 72-hour window). Divide remaining dough in half crosswise, transfer to lightly floured rimmed baking sheet, and cover loosely with plastic. Let rest for 45 minutes.

BAGUETTE BAKER'S KIT

Baguette-making requires a few specialty items. We've come up with some great alternatives for you too.

Couche: To proof baguettes, bakers use a heavy linen couche. It maintains the loaves' shape and wicks away moisture. The fabric easily releases the dough, too. Our favorite is the San Francisco Baking Institute Linen Canvas (Couche) ($9 for a 36 by 18-inch couche). Alternatively, use a double layer of 100 percent linen tea towels at least 16 inches long and 12 inches wide.

Flipping Board: To move baguettes from the couche to the oven, professional bakers use a flipping board. A homemade substitute, made by taping two 16 by 4-inch pieces of heavy cardboard together with packaging tape, works equally well.

Lame: For the proper almond-shaped slashes, with one edge that bakes up into a crispy ridge, you must cut the loaf at a low angle, something much more easily done with the curved blade of a lame. Alternatively, a sharp paring knife or unused box cutter blade will work.

Diastatic Malt Powder: During the long proofing time, nearly all the sugars in this dough are consumed by the yeast. Since sugars are responsible for browning and caramelization, this will leave the crust pale and dull-tasting. Adding diastatic malt powder guarantees a supply of sugar at baking time and thus a crust that browns and caramelizes.

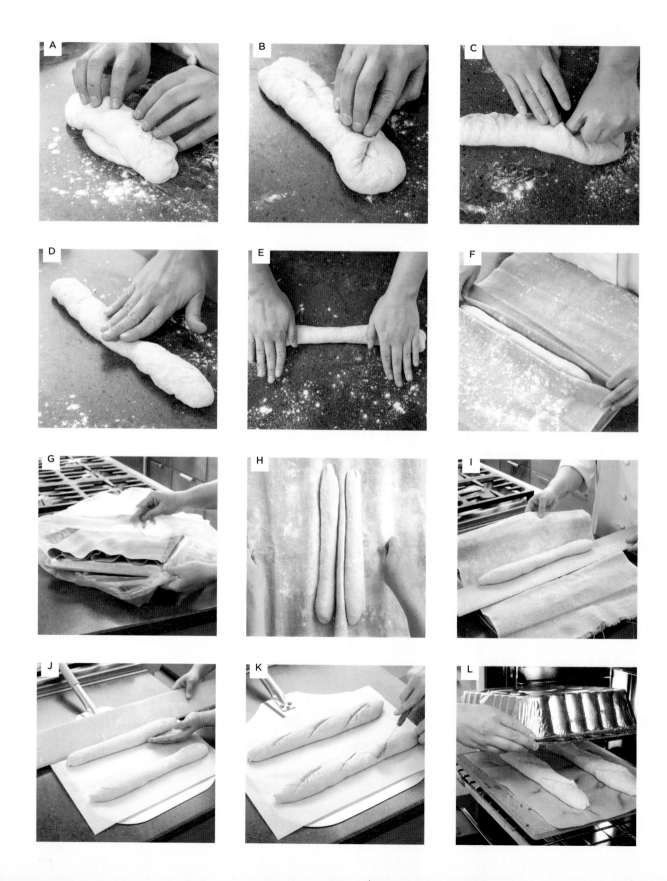

4   (A) On lightly floured counter, roll each piece of dough into loose 3- to 4-inch-long cylinder; return to floured baking sheet and cover with plastic. Let rest at room temperature for 30 minutes.

5   Lightly mist underside of couche with water, drape over inverted baking sheet, and dust with flour. Gently press 1 piece of dough into 6 by 4-inch rectangle on lightly floured counter, with long edge facing you. Fold upper quarter of dough toward center and press gently to seal. (B) Rotate dough 180 degrees and repeat folding step to form 8 by 2-inch rectangle.

6   (C) Fold dough in half toward you, using thumb of your other hand to create crease along center of dough, sealing with heel of your hand as you work your way along the loaf. Without pressing down on loaf, use heel of your hand to reinforce seal (do not seal ends of loaf).

7   (D) Hold your hand over center of dough and roll dough back and forth gently to tighten (it should form dog-bone shape).

8   Starting at center of dough and working toward ends, gently and evenly roll and stretch dough until it measures 15 inches long by 1¼ inches wide. (E) Moving your hands in opposite directions, use back-and-forth motion to roll ends of loaf under your palms to form sharp points.

9   Transfer dough to floured couche, seam side up. (F) On either side of loaf, pinch edges of couche into pleat, then cover loosely with large plastic garbage bag.

10   Repeat steps 4 through 9 with second piece of dough and place on opposite side of pleat. (G) Fold edges of couche over loaves to cover completely, then carefully place sheet inside bag, and tie or fold under to enclose.

11   (H) Let stand until loaves have nearly doubled in size and dough springs back minimally when poked gently with your fingertip, 45 to 60 minutes. While bread rises, adjust oven rack to middle position, place baking stone on rack, and heat oven to 500 degrees.

12   Line pizza peel with 16 by 12-inch piece of parchment paper with long edge perpendicular to handle. Unfold couche, pulling from ends to remove pleats. Gently pushing with side of flipping board, roll 1 loaf over, away from other loaf, so it is seam side down. Using your hand, hold long edge of flipping board between loaf and couche at 45-degree angle. (I) Then lift couche with your other hand and flip loaf seam side up onto board.

13   (J) Invert loaf onto parchment-lined peel, seam side down, about 2 inches from long edge of parchment, then use flipping board to straighten loaf. Repeat with remaining loaf, leaving at least 3 inches between loaves.

14   (K) Holding lame concave side up at 30-degree angle to loaf, make series of three 4-inch-long, ½-inch-deep slashes along length of loaf, using swift, fluid motion, overlapping each slash slightly. Repeat with second loaf.

15   (L) Transfer loaves, on parchment, to baking stone, cover with stacked inverted disposable pans, and bake for 5 minutes. Carefully remove pans and bake until loaves are evenly browned, 12 to 15 minutes longer, rotating parchment halfway through baking. Transfer to cooling rack and let cool for at least 20 minutes before serving. Consume within 4 hours.

chapter ten

desserts

———————

RECIPE EXTRAS

CHOCOLATE POTS DE CRÈME

serves: 8

total time: 25 minutes, plus
4 hours chilling

10 ounces bittersweet chocolate, chopped fine

5 large egg yolks

5 tablespoons (2¼ ounces) sugar

¼ teaspoon table salt

1½ cups heavy cream

¾ cup half-and-half

1 tablespoon vanilla extract

½ teaspoon instant espresso powder mixed with 1 tablespoon water

Whipped Cream (page 301)

Cocoa, for dusting (optional)

Chocolate shavings, for sprinkling (optional)

why this recipe works "Pot de crème" literally means "pot of cream" but it is also the name of an indulgent bistro classic. This baked custard can be finicky and laborious to make, needing a hot water bath in the oven to keep the air moist so the custard doesn't crack. Unfortunately, the bath threatens to splash the custards whenever the pan is moved. Also, individual custards don't bake at the same rate. For a user-friendly recipe that delivers silky texture, we cook the custard on the stovetop instead, before pouring it into ramekins to set. For richness and body, we use a combination of heavy cream and half-and-half with egg yolks, then combine it with bittersweet chocolate. We like using bittersweet chocolate with 60 percent cacao, but you can use 70 percent bittersweet chocolate; just be sure to reduce the quantity of chocolate to 8 ounces. A tablespoon of strong brewed coffee may be substituted for the instant espresso and water. Use an instant-read thermometer to judge when the custard has reached the proper temperature. You can also judge the progress of the custard by its thickness. Dip a wooden spoon into it and run your finger across the back. The custard is ready when it coats the spoon and a line drawn maintains neat edges. Serve with Whipped Cream (page 301), cocoa, and chocolate shavings, if desired.

1 Place chocolate in medium heatproof bowl; set fine-mesh strainer over bowl and set aside.

2 Whisk egg yolks, sugar, and salt in medium bowl until combined, then whisk in heavy cream and half-and-half. Transfer mixture to medium saucepan. Cook mixture over medium-low heat, stirring constantly and scraping bottom of pot with wooden spoon, until thickened and silky and registers 175 to 180 degrees, 8 to 12 minutes. (Do not let custard overcook or simmer.)

3 Immediately pour custard through strainer over chocolate. Let mixture stand about 5 minutes. Whisk gently until smooth, then whisk in vanilla and dissolved espresso. Divide mixture evenly among eight 5-ounce ramekins. Gently tap ramekins against counter to remove any air bubbles.

4 Cool pots de crème to room temperature, then cover with plastic wrap and refrigerate until chilled, at least 4 hours or up to 3 days. Before serving, let pots de crème stand at room temperature for 20 to 30 minutes.

5 Dollop each pot de crème with about 2 tablespoons of whipped cream and garnish with cocoa and/or chocolate shavings, if using. Serve.

WHIPPED CREAM

makes: about 1 cup

total time: 10 minutes

- ½ **cup heavy cream, chilled**
- 2 **teaspoons sugar**
- ½ **teaspoon vanilla extract**

1 Using stand mixer fitted with whisk attachment, whip cream, sugar, and vanilla on medium-low speed until small bubbles form, about 30 seconds.

2 Increase speed to medium-high and continue to whip until mixture thickens and forms stiff peaks, about 1 minute.

CHOCOLATE-CARDAMOM CAKE WITH ROASTED PEARS

serves: 8

total time: 2 hours, plus 1½ hours cooling

pears

1 tablespoon unsalted butter

3 ripe but firm Bartlett or Bosc pears (6 to 8 ounces each), peeled, halved, and cored

cake

½ cup (2½ ounces) all-purpose flour

¼ cup (¾ ounce) unsweetened cocoa powder

1 teaspoon ground cardamom

¼ teaspoon baking powder

¼ teaspoon table salt

¾ cup (5¼ ounces) granulated sugar

2 large eggs, room temperature

8 tablespoons unsalted butter, melted and cooled

1 teaspoon vanilla extract

2 ounces semisweet chocolate, chopped fine

Confectioners' sugar

why this recipe works Chocolate, pears, and cardamom might not be the first ingredients you imagine combining for a cake. But they marry successfully in this simple, elegant dessert that transports you to the City of Love with every bite. Pears on their own can be quite mild; caramelization is the key to bringing out their floral quality. Before adding them to our cake, we roast the pears in a 450-degree oven until they are caramelized and tender. For a cake with a crumb that's sturdy enough to hold up the pears so they sit pretty on top, we use cocoa powder rather than melted chocolate. This makes a thick—almost brownie-like—batter that bakes up tender and moist with the pears. Ground cardamom complements the pears' spice notes, and chopped chocolate adds surprise gooey pockets. Fanning the thinly sliced roasted pears over the batter gives this balanced cake a gorgeous Parisian presentation. Cakes are often baked at 350 degrees, but we found that 325 works better for slow, even baking from edge to center. When baked at higher temperatures, this cake had hard edges. If you would like some whipped cream on the side, turn to page 301.

1   **for the pears** Adjust oven rack to middle position and heat oven to 450 degrees. Melt butter in 12-inch ovensafe skillet over medium-high heat. Arrange pears cut side down in skillet and cook, without moving pears, until just beginning to brown on first side, 3 to 5 minutes. Transfer skillet to oven and roast for 10 minutes. Flip pears and continue to roast until fork easily pierces fruit, 8 to 12 minutes. Remove skillet from oven (skillet handle will be hot) and transfer pears cut side down to paper towel–lined plate. Reduce oven temperature to 325 degrees.

2   **for the cake** Grease 9-inch springform pan. Whisk flour, cocoa, cardamom, baking powder, and salt together in bowl. Whisk granulated sugar and eggs in large bowl until pale yellow, about 1 minute. Whisk in melted butter and vanilla until combined. Using rubber spatula, fold in flour mixture until few streaks remain. Fold in chocolate until just combined (don't overmix).

3   Transfer batter to prepared pan and smooth into even layer. Cut 1 pear half crosswise into ¼-inch-thick slices; leave pear intact on cutting board. Discard first 4 slices from narrow end of sliced pear. Slide small offset spatula under pear and gently press pear to fan slices toward narrow end. Slide fanned pear onto batter with narrow end facing center and wide end almost touching edge of pan. Do not press pear into batter. Repeat slicing, fanning, and placing remaining 5 pear halves evenly around pan. Bake until toothpick inserted in center comes out with few moist crumbs attached, 45 to 55 minutes, rotating pan halfway through baking.

4   Let cake cool in pan on wire rack for 20 minutes. Remove sides of pan and let cake cool completely, about 1½ hours. To unmold cake, slide thin metal spatula between cake bottom and pan bottom to loosen, then slide cake onto serving platter. Dust with confectioners' sugar before serving.

WHITE CHOCOLATE MOUSSE WITH RASPBERRY SAUCE

serves: 4 (makes about 3 cups)

total time: 35 minutes, plus
8 hours chilling

12   ounces white chocolate, chopped fine

3   large egg yolks

1   cup heavy cream, chilled

5   ounces (1 cup) frozen raspberries

4   teaspoons sugar

4   teaspoons lime juice

why this recipe works   The word "mousse" immediately brings France to mind and evokes rich, dark chocolate. But if you think of Paris in the springtime, a white chocolate mousse with a stunning raspberry sauce may be more apropos. White chocolate is prone to scorching, so we melt it gently in a double boiler with egg yolks and water. Conventional wisdom says you shouldn't combine water and chocolate, as small amounts of water cause chocolate to seize, or form grainy lumps. But by melting white chocolate with enough water, we create a smooth liquid that's easy to combine with whipped cream. Folding in cream whipped to soft peaks makes for a fluffy, luscious mousse. Refrigerating the mousse for at least 8 hours gives it the right amount of structure: It melts in the mouth but holds its shape on a spoon. A sweet-tart raspberry sauce balances the mousse's richness and adds lovely color contrast. Garnish with pistachios for crunch, if desired. We prefer bar chocolate from brands such as Ghirardelli or Callebaut for this recipe. We use a glass bowl for the double boiler because glass conducts heat more evenly and gently than metal.

1   Stir chocolate, egg yolks, and 2 tablespoons water together in medium glass bowl with rubber spatula. Set bowl over large saucepan of barely simmering water (water should not touch bottom of bowl) and cook, stirring and scraping sides of bowl constantly, until chocolate is just melted. (Once chocolate begins to melt, remove bowl from heat every 10 to 15 seconds so yolks don't overcook.)

2   Using stand mixer fitted with whisk attachment, whip cream on medium-low speed until foamy, about 1 minute. Increase speed to high and whip until soft peaks form, 1 to 2 minutes.

3   Gently whisk one-third of whipped cream into chocolate mixture until fully combined. Gently fold in remaining whipped cream with rubber spatula, making sure to scrape up any chocolate mixture from bottom of bowl, until no streaks remain.

4   Distribute mousse evenly among four 6-ounce ramekins or serving glasses. Cover with plastic wrap and refrigerate for at least 8 hours or up to 2 days.

5   About 1 hour before serving, combine raspberries, sugar, and lime juice in bowl. Let sit at room temperature until raspberries defrost; stir periodically to combine. (Raspberry sauce can be made simultaneously with mousse and allowed to thaw in refrigerator.)

6   Spoon raspberry sauce over mousse. Serve.

PROFITEROLES WITH CHOCOLATE SAUCE

makes: 24 puffs

total time: 2½ hours

cream puffs

2 large eggs plus 1 large white

5 tablespoons unsalted butter, cut into 10 pieces

6 tablespoons water

2 tablespoons whole milk

1½ teaspoons sugar

¼ teaspoon table salt

½ cup (2½ ounces) all-purpose flour, sifted

chocolate sauce

¾ cup heavy cream

3 tablespoons light corn syrup

3 tablespoons unsalted butter, cut into 3 pieces

Pinch table salt

6 ounces bittersweet chocolate, chopped fine

1 quart vanilla or coffee ice cream

why this recipe works Who doesn't love the indulgence of a profiterole, a choux pastry stuffed with ice cream and topped with dark, luxurious chocolate sauce? It's a treat to eat profiteroles at a bistro but you can easily make them at home, too. For crisp, tender, and airy pastry, we use water and milk in the dough. Incorporating the eggs all at once using the high speed of a food processor rather than laboriously hand-beating them in one at a time also helps us achieve airier pastry. A really hot oven causes the water in the dough to turn to steam, which expands and inflates the puffs nicely. The initial blast of heat jump-starts browning; we then lower the heat to let the interiors cook through. So that the puffs remain crisp, immediately following baking they must be slit to release steam and returned to a turned-off, propped-open oven to dry out. Prescooping the ice cream makes serving quick and neat.

1 **for the cream puffs** Adjust oven rack to middle position and heat oven to 425 degrees. Spray rimmed baking sheet with vegetable oil spray and line with parchment paper; set aside. Beat eggs and white in measuring cup. (You should have about ½ cup; discard excess.)

2 Bring butter, water, milk, sugar, and salt to boil in small saucepan over medium heat. When mixture reaches full boil (butter should be fully melted), immediately remove saucepan from heat and stir in flour with spatula until combined and mixture clears sides of pan. Return saucepan to low heat and cook, stirring constantly, using smearing motion, for 3 minutes, until mixture is slightly shiny with wet-sand appearance and tiny beads of fat appear on bottom of saucepan (temperature should register 175 to 180 degrees).

3 Immediately transfer mixture to food processor and process with feed tube open for 10 seconds to cool slightly. With machine running, gradually add eggs in steady stream. When all eggs have been added, scrape down sides of bowl, then process for 30 seconds until smooth, sticky paste forms. (If not using immediately, transfer paste to bowl, press sheet of plastic wrap sprayed with oil spray directly on surface, and store at room temperature for up to 2 hours.)

4A   to portion using pastry bag   Fold down top 3 or 4 inches of 14- or 16-inch pastry bag fitted with ½-inch plain tip to form a cuff. Hold bag open with your hand in cuff and fill bag with paste. Unfold cuff, lay bag on work surface, and, using your hands or bench scraper, push paste into lower portion of pastry bag. Twist top of bag and pipe paste into 1½-inch mounds on prepared baking sheet, spacing them 1 to 1¼ inches apart (you should be able to fit all 24 mounds on baking sheet).

4B   to portion using spoons   Scoop 1 level tablespoon of dough. Using second small spoon, scrape dough onto prepared sheet into 1½-inch mound. Repeat, spacing mounds 1 to 1¼ inches apart (you should be able to fit all 24 mounds on baking sheet).

5   Use back of teaspoon dipped in bowl of cold water to smooth shape and surface of piped mounds. Bake for 15 minutes (do not open oven door), then reduce oven temperature to 375 degrees and continue to bake until puffs are golden brown and fairly firm (puffs should not be soft and squishy), 8 to 10 minutes longer. Remove baking sheet from oven. With paring knife, cut ¾-inch slit into side of each puff to release steam; return puffs to oven, turn off oven, and prop oven door open with handle of wooden spoon. Dry puffs in turned-off oven until centers are just moist (not wet) and puffs are crisp, about 45 minutes. Transfer puffs to wire rack to cool. (Cooled puffs can be stored in airtight container at room temperature for up to 24 hours or frozen in zip-per-lock bag for up to 1 month. Before serving, crisp room temperature puffs in 300-degree oven for 5 to 8 minutes, or 8 to 10 minutes for frozen puffs.)

6   for the chocolate sauce   Bring cream, corn syrup, butter, and salt to boil in small saucepan over medium-high heat. Off heat, add chocolate while gently swirling saucepan. Cover pan and let stand until chocolate is melted, about 5 minutes. Uncover and whisk gently until combined. (Sauce can be cooled to room temperature, placed in airtight container, and refrigerated for up to 3 weeks. To reheat, transfer sauce to heatproof bowl set over saucepan of simmering water. Alternatively, micro-wave at 50 percent power, stirring once or twice, for 1 to 3 minutes.)

7   Line baking sheet with parchment paper; freeze until cold, about 20 minutes. Using 2-inch ice cream scoop (about same diameter as puffs), scoop ice cream onto cold sheet and freeze until firm, then cover with plastic wrap; keep frozen until ready to serve. (Ice cream can be scooped and frozen for up to 1 week.)

8   When ready to serve, use paring knife to split open puffs about ⅜ inch from bottom; set 3 or 4 bottoms on each dessert plate. Place scoop of ice cream on each bottom and gently press tops into ice cream. Pour sauce over profiteroles and serve immediately.

profiteroles (and gougeres) start to finish

1. Cook dough over low heat, stirring constantly using smearing motion, until mixture has wet-sand appearance (for profiteroles) or forms ball that pulls away from pan (for gougères, see page 31).

2. Using food processor, process dough briefly to cool slightly. Add eggs in steady stream, processing to smooth, sticky paste.

3A. To pipe puffs: Fold down top of pastry bag to form cuff and fill bag with dough. Unfold cuff, lay bag on counter, and, using your hands or bench scraper, push dough into lower portion of bag. Twist top of bag and pipe paste into 1½-inch mounds on baking sheet.

3B. To spoon puffs: Scoop 1 level tablespoon of dough and, using second spoon, scrape dough onto sheet into 1½-inch mounds.

4. For profiteroles, use back of teaspoon dipped in water to smooth pastry mounds (for gougères, see page 31).

5. If stuffing: Cut slit into side of each baked puff to release steam. Return puffs to turned-off oven to dry.

CRÈME BRÛLÉE

serves: 6

total time: 1 hour, plus 4 hours chilling

1 vanilla bean

3 cups heavy cream, divided

½ cup (3½ ounces) granulated sugar

Pinch table salt

9 large egg yolks

9 teaspoons turbinado sugar or
Demerara sugar

why this recipe works   The translation of "crème brûlée" in English is "burnt cream," which does not quite express the delicacies and contrasts of this exquisite dessert, often served at bistros. Crème brûlée is rightly beloved because of the dramatic contrast it offers between its crisp sugar crust and the silky vanilla-scented baked custard underneath. Luckily it is not difficult to put together at home and makes a lovely final course for a special evening. In case you are looking for varied flavor, we offer a version with orange blossom water, which lends an elegant floral, citrus taste to the custard. While we prefer turbinado or Demerara sugar for the caramelized sugar crust, regular granulated sugar will also work, but remember to use only 1 teaspoon for each ramekin. Once the sugar on top is brûléed, serve within 30 minutes or the sugar crust will soften. You will need six 4- to 5-ounce ramekins (or shallow fluted dishes or jars) for this recipe as well as a torch to caramelize the sugar coating on the custard.

1   Adjust oven rack to lower-middle position and heat oven to 300 degrees. Cut vanilla bean in half lengthwise. Using tip of paring knife or spoon, scrape out vanilla seeds. Combine vanilla bean pod and seeds, 2 cups cream, granulated sugar, and salt in medium saucepan. Bring mixture to boil over medium heat, stirring occasionally to dissolve sugar. Off heat, cover and let steep for 15 minutes.

2   Stir remaining 1 cup cream into cream mixture. Whisk egg yolks in large bowl until uniform. Whisk about 1 cup cream mixture into yolks, then repeat with 1 cup more cream mixture. Whisk in remaining cream mixture until thoroughly combined. Strain mixture through fine-mesh strainer into 8-cup liquid measuring cup, discarding solids.

3   Meanwhile, place dish towel in bottom of large baking dish or roasting pan. Set six 4- or 5-ounce ramekins (or shallow fluted dishes) on towel. Bring kettle of water to boil.

4   Divide cream mixture evenly among ramekins. Set baking dish on oven rack. Taking care not to splash water into ramekins, pour enough boiling water into dish to reach two-thirds up sides of ramekins. Bake until centers of custards are just barely set and register 170 to 175 degrees, 25 to 35 minutes depending on ramekin type, checking temperature 5 minutes early.

5   Transfer ramekins to wire rack and let custards cool completely, about 2 hours. Set ramekins on rimmed baking sheet, cover tightly with plastic wrap, and refrigerate until cold, about 4 hours.

6   Uncover ramekins and gently blot tops dry with paper towels. Sprinkle each custard with 1 to 1½ teaspoons turbinado sugar (depending on ramekin type). Tilt and tap each ramekin to distribute sugar evenly, then dump out excess sugar and wipe rims of ramekins clean. Caramelize sugar with torch until deep golden brown, continually sweeping flame about 2 inches above ramekin. Serve.

variation

CRÈME BRÛLÉE WITH ORANGE BLOSSOM

Add 2 teaspoons orange blossom water to strained custard before portioning into ramekins.

the "brûlée" in crème brûlée

Sprinkle each container with 1 to 1½ teaspoons turbinado sugar. Tilt and tap each container to distribute sugar evenly. Carefully ignite torch and lower it until end of flame is about 2 inches from sprinkled sugar. Hold flame in place until you see sugar melt and caramelize to deep golden brown. Continually sweep flame until entire custard has a golden crust.

GÂTEAU BRETON WITH APRICOT FILLING

serves: 8

total time: 2 hours, plus 30 minutes cooling

filling

⅔ cup water

½ cup dried California apricots, chopped

⅓ cup (2⅓ ounces) sugar

1 tablespoon lemon juice

cake

16 tablespoons (2 sticks) unsalted butter, softened

¾ cup plus 2 tablespoons (6⅛ ounces) sugar

6 large egg yolks (1 lightly beaten with 1 teaspoon water)

2 tablespoons dark rum

1 teaspoon vanilla extract

2 cups (10 ounces) all-purpose flour

½ teaspoon table salt

why this recipe works   As its name implies, this cake hails from the Brittany region of France, which lies on the western edge of the country, abutting the Atlantic Ocean. It's a simple yet pretty cake, rich in butter, with a dense, tender crumb that falls somewhere between shortbread cookies and pound cake. In some versions, the cake camouflages a thin layer of jam or fruit filling baked into its center, which delivers a vein of sweet acidity that balances the cake's richness. The cake's firm structure allows it to be cut into thin wedges for nibbling with tea or coffee. To avoid introducing too much air into the batter of this French butter cake, which would lead to a fluffy, airy texture, we cream the butter and sugar for only 3 minutes before adding the egg yolks and flour. Briefly freezing a layer of the batter in the cake pan helps us when we spread a bright homemade apricot filling onto it. The pan then goes back into the freezer to firm so that the top layer of batter also can be easily added. All that is left to do is pretty up the cake with an egg wash and diamond-patterned design. We prefer the flavor of California apricots in the filling. Mediterranean (or Turkish) apricots can be used, but increase the amount of lemon juice to 2 tablespoons. This cake is traditionally served plain but can be dressed up with fresh berries, Crème Anglaise (page 313), or Crème Fraîche (page 16), if desired.

1   **for the filling**   Process water and apricots in blender until uniformly pureed, about 2 minutes. Transfer puree to 10-inch nonstick skillet and stir in sugar. Set skillet over medium heat and cook, stirring frequently, until puree has darkened slightly and heatproof rubber spatula leaves distinct trail when dragged across bottom of pan, 10 to 12 minutes. Transfer filling to bowl and stir in lemon juice. Refrigerate filling until cool to touch, about 15 minutes.

2   **for the cake**   Adjust oven rack to lower-middle position and heat oven to 350 degrees. Grease 9-inch round cake pan.

3   Using stand mixer fitted with paddle, beat butter on medium-high speed until smooth and lightened in color, 1 to 2 minutes. Add sugar and continue to beat until pale and fluffy, about 3 minutes longer. Add 5 egg yolks, one at a time, and beat until combined. Scrape down bowl, add rum and vanilla, and mix until incorporated, about 1 minute. Reduce speed to low, add flour and salt, and mix until flour is just incorporated, about 30 seconds. Give batter final stir by hand.

4   Spoon half of batter into bottom of prepared pan. Using small offset spatula, spread batter into even layer. Freeze for 10 minutes.

5   Spread ½ cup filling in even layer over chilled batter, leaving ¾-inch border around edge (reserve remaining filling for another use). Freeze for 10 minutes.

6   Gently spread remaining batter over filling. Using offset spatula, carefully smooth top of batter. Brush with egg yolk wash. Using tines of fork, make light scores in surface of cake, spaced about 1½ inches apart, in diamond pattern, being careful not to score all the way to sides of pan. Bake until top is golden brown and edges of cake start to pull away from sides of pan, 45 to 50 minutes. Let cake cool in pan on wire rack for 30 minutes. Run paring knife between cake and sides of pan, remove cake from pan, and let cool completely on rack, about 1 hour. Cut into wedges and serve.

CRÈME ANGLAISE

makes: about 1½ cups (serves 6)

total time: 45 minutes, plus 45 minutes cooling

Crème anglaise, a velvety pourable custard, is one of the gold standards of custard sauces thickened with egg yolks. It makes a great accompaniment to baked pies and tarts, cakes, or a bowl of fresh fruit. We use half a vanilla bean for this sauce, but 1 teaspoon of vanilla extract can be used instead; if using vanilla extract, skip the steeping stage in step 1 and stir the extract into the sauce after straining it in step 3.

  ½   vanilla bean

 1½   cups whole milk

      Pinch table salt

  4   large egg yolks

  ¼   cup (1¾ ounces) sugar

1   Cut vanilla bean in half lengthwise. Using tip of paring knife, scrape out seeds. Bring vanilla bean and seeds, milk, and salt to simmer in medium saucepan over medium-high heat, stirring occasionally. Remove from heat, cover, and let steep for 20 minutes.

2   Whisk egg yolks and sugar in large bowl until smooth. Whisking constantly, very slowly add hot milk mixture to yolk mixture to temper. Return milk-yolk mixture to saucepan and cook over low heat, stirring constantly with heatproof rubber spatula, until sauce thickens slightly and registers 175 to 180 degrees, 5 to 7 minutes.

3   Strain sauce through fine-mesh strainer set over clean bowl; discard vanilla bean. Cover and refrigerate until cool, about 45 minutes. (Sauce can be refrigerated, with plastic wrap pressed directly on surface, for up to 3 days.)

variation

ORANGE CRÈME ANGLAISE

Substitute 2 (3-inch) strips orange zest for vanilla bean. Stir 1 tablespoon Grand Marnier into finished sauce after straining.

gâteau breton with apricot filling (page 312)

Grand Marnier soufflé
(page 316)

GRAND MARNIER SOUFFLÉ

serves: 6 to 8

total time: 1 hour

soufflé dish preparation

- 1 tablespoon unsalted butter, softened
- ¼ cup sugar
- 2 teaspoons sifted cocoa powder

soufflé

- 5 tablespoons (1½ ounces) all-purpose flour
- ½ cup (3½ ounces) sugar, divided
- ¼ teaspoon table salt
- 1 cup whole milk
- 2 tablespoons unsalted butter, at room temperature
- 5 large eggs, separated
- 1 tablespoon grated zest from 1 orange
- 3 tablespoons Grand Marnier
- ⅛ teaspoon cream of tartar

why this recipe works A soufflé, beloved French restaurant dessert, is prepared only once it has been ordered because it must be served straight from the oven, hot and risen. Though soufflés have a reputation for being temperamental, they are relatively easy to make at home. The best ones have a crusty top layer above the rim of the dish and a contrasting rich, creamy, almost-fluid center, so we wanted to produce height without making the entire dish foamy. An equal number of egg whites and yolks is the right proportion for rise versus richness. For the base, we begin with a bouillie—a paste of flour and milk. Butter keeps the egginess at bay, and increasing the usual amount of flour prevents the frothiness we want to avoid. Adding a little sugar and some cream of tartar to the whites while we whip them stabilizes them so that they hold their structure. The sugar must be added gradually partway through the beating process, not at the beginning, or the soufflé will not rise properly and will taste too sweet. Make the soufflé base and immediately begin beating the whites before the base cools too much. Once the whites have reached the proper consistency, they must be used at once. Do not open the oven door during the first 15 minutes of baking time; as the soufflé nears the end of baking, you may check its progress by opening the oven door slightly. (Be careful here; if your oven runs hot, the top of the soufflé may burn.) Remove the soufflé from the oven while the center is still loose and moist to prevent overcooking. Confectioners' sugar or Crème Anglaise (page 313) is a nice finishing touch, but a soufflé waits for no one, so be ready to serve it immediately.

1 **to prepare the soufflé dish** Adjust oven rack to upper-middle position and heat oven to 400 degrees. Grease 1½-quart porcelain soufflé dish with butter, making sure to coat all interior surfaces. Stir sugar and cocoa together in small bowl; pour into buttered soufflé dish and shake to coat bottom and sides with thick, even coating. Tap out excess and set dish aside.

2 **for the soufflé** Whisk flour, ¼ cup sugar, and salt in small saucepan. Gradually whisk in milk, whisking until smooth and no lumps remain. Bring mixture to boil over high heat, whisking constantly, until thickened and mixture pulls away from sides of pan, about 3 minutes. Scrape mixture into medium bowl; whisk in butter until combined. Whisk in yolks until incorporated; stir in orange zest and Grand Marnier.

3   Using stand mixer fitted with whisk attachment, whip egg whites, cream of tartar, and 1 teaspoon more sugar on medium-low speed until combined, about 10 seconds. Increase speed to medium- high and whip until frothy and no longer translucent, about 2 minutes. With mixer running, sprinkle in half of remaining sugar; continue whipping until whites form soft, billowy peaks, about 30 seconds. With mixer still running, sprinkle in remaining sugar and whip until just combined and soft peaks form, about 10 seconds.

4   Using rubber spatula, immediately stir one-quarter of beaten whites into soufflé base to lighten until almost no white streaks remain. Scrape remaining whites into base and fold in whites with balloon whisk until mixture is just combined, gently flicking whisk after scraping up sides of bowl to free any mixture caught in whisk. Gently pour mixture into prepared dish and run your index finger through mixture, tracing circumference about ½ inch from side of dish, to help soufflé rise properly. Bake until surface of soufflé is deep golden brown, it has risen 2 to 2½ inches above rim of dish, and interior registers 170 degrees, 20 to 25 minutes. Serve immediately.

making and baking a soufflé

1. Grease soufflé dish and coat it evenly with cocoa mixture.

2. Gently pour soufflé batter into prepared dish, leaving 1 inch headroom so batter can set before it rises above top of dish.

3. Bake soufflé until surface is deep golden brown and it has risen 2 to 2½ inches above rim of dish.

4. To test for doneness, use instant-read thermometer to check that interior registers 170 degrees.

APPLE TARTE TATIN

serves: 6 to 8

total time: 1¾ hours, plus
20 minutes cooling

4 tablespoons unsalted butter, cut into
   1-tablespoon pieces, divided

5 Gala or Golden Delicious apples
   (6 to 7 ounces each), peeled,
   quartered, and cored

¼ teaspoon table salt

¾ cup (5¼ ounces) sugar

¼ cup water

2 tablespoons light corn syrup

1 recipe All-Butter Pie Dough, rolled and
   chilled (page 321)

why this recipe works   The most famous example of an upside down tart may be a tarte Tatin, for which apples are cooked in caramel in a skillet; topped with pastry; baked; and inverted so that the pastry base wears a gleaming, deeply bronzed apple crown. It's a treat that can't help but impress. We make ours supereasy and foolproof by parcooking the apples on the stovetop to drive off moisture and prevent the finished tart from being too liquid-y. The first step is making our easy All-Butter Pie Dough, which we roll out immediately and then let rest in the fridge for at least 2 hours. We also use a separate saucepan to cook the caramel instead of making it the traditional way in the skillet with the apples. This gives us greater control over the final color of the caramel and the texture of the apples. A little of the sugar is replaced with corn syrup to help prevent the caramel from crystallizing. We pour the amber caramel over the softened apples, top with chilled pastry, and bake until the crust turns golden brown and the caramel filling is thick and syrupy. After cooling the tarte Tatin, we flip it out of the skillet safely and easily to reveal a gorgeous spiral of caramelized apples atop the flaky crust. We like Gala or Golden Delicious apples here because they retain their shape and provide mild sweetness. If your apples are large, you may have one or two pieces that won't fit. Serve with vanilla ice cream, if desired.

1   Adjust oven rack to middle position and heat oven to 350 degrees. Melt 1 tablespoon butter in 10-inch ovensafe nonstick skillet over medium-low heat. Off heat, arrange apple quarters on their sides in melted butter in circular pattern around edge of skillet, nestling fruit snugly. Tuck remaining apples into center (it is not necessary to maintain circular pattern in center). Sprinkle salt over apples.

2   Cover and cook over medium-low heat until apples have released enough juice to cover bottom of skillet and juice just begins to reduce, 10 to 15 minutes. Uncover and continue to cook until liquid has mostly evaporated, 3 to 5 minutes longer (apples may brown on undersides). Remove skillet from heat and set aside.

3   Bring sugar, water, and corn syrup to boil in large heavy-bottomed saucepan over medium-high heat. Cook, without stirring, until mixture begins to turn straw-colored around edge of saucepan, 4 to 8 minutes. Reduce heat to medium-low and continue to cook, swirling saucepan occasionally, until mixture is light amber–colored and registers 355 to 360 degrees, 2 to 5 minutes longer. (To take temperature, remove saucepan from heat and tilt to 1 side; stir with thermometer to equalize hotter and cooler spots, avoiding bottom of saucepan.)

4   Off heat, carefully stir in remaining 3 tablespoons butter (mixture will bubble and steam). Working quickly, pour caramel over apples (caramel will not completely cover apples). Carefully slide prepared dough over apples.

5   Bake tart until thick, syrupy bubbles form around edge and crust is golden brown, 50 minutes to 1 hour. Transfer skillet to wire rack and let sit until cool enough to handle, 20 to 30 minutes.

6   Run thin rubber spatula or plastic knife around edge of skillet to loosen tart. Invert large serving platter over skillet (make sure platter is larger than skillet and has sloped sides to catch excess caramel). Swiftly and carefully invert tart onto platter (if apples shift or stick to skillet, rearrange with spoon). Cut into wedges and serve warm or at room temperature.

A Tart Slice of History

Tarte Tatin was created by sisters Stéphanie and Caroline Tatin at their hotel in Lamotte-Beuvron, France, in the 1880s. Legend has it that Stéphanie created the tart by accident. Maybe the apples got too dark, the tart was assembled upside down, or it was dropped. Whatever it was, patrons enjoyed the upside down tart. The sisters never formally put the dessert on their menu nor published the recipe. We know the dish because it was popularized in the 1930s at Maxim's in Paris, where it is still served to this day.

PEACH TARTE TATIN

serves: 8

total time: 1¼ hours, plus
40 minutes cooling

- 3 tablespoons unsalted butter, softened

- ½ cup (3½ ounces) plus 2 tablespoons
  sugar, divided

- ¼ teaspoon table salt

- 2 pounds ripe but firm peaches, peeled,
  pitted, and quartered

- 1 recipe All-Butter Pie Dough, rolled and
  chilled (page 321)

- 1 tablespoon bourbon (optional)

why this recipe works   To make peach tarte Tatin, simply swapping fruits produces a cloying tart awash in juice. Peaches have less pectin than apples and don't retain their juices as well. So after baking the tart, we pour off excess liquid. First we cook butter, sugar, salt, and peaches until the peach juice is deeply browned. Then we cover the fruit with pastry and bake till the crust is browned and crisp. We cool the tart, pour off excess juice, reduce it with bourbon, and brush it over the inverted peaches. Firm fruit is easier to peel and retains its shape when cooked. Yellow peaches are preferable to white peaches. When pouring off liquid, the peaches may shift; shaking the skillet will help redistribute them.

1   Adjust oven rack to middle position and heat oven to 400 degrees. Smear butter over bottom of 10-inch ovensafe skillet. Sprinkle ½ cup sugar over butter and shake skillet to distribute sugar in even layer. Sprinkle salt over sugar. Arrange peaches in circular pattern around edge of skillet, nestling fruit snugly. Tuck remaining peaches into center, squeezing in as much fruit as possible (it is not necessary to maintain circular pattern in center).

2   Place skillet over high heat and cook, without stirring fruit, until juice is released and turns from pink to deep amber, 8 to 12 minutes. (If necessary, adjust skillet's placement on burner to even out hot spots and encourage even browning.) Remove skillet from heat. Carefully slide prepared dough over peaches, making sure dough is centered and does not touch edge of skillet. Brush dough lightly with water and sprinkle with remaining 2 tablespoons sugar. Bake until crust is very well browned, 30 to 35 minutes. Transfer skillet to wire rack set in rimmed baking sheet and let sit until cool enough to handle, 20 to 30 minutes.

3   Place inverted platter on top of crust. With your hand firmly securing platter, carefully tip skillet over bowl to drain juice (skillet handle may still be hot). When all juice has been transferred to bowl, return skillet to wire rack, remove platter, and shake skillet firmly to redistribute peaches. Carefully invert tart onto platter, then slide tart onto wire rack. (If peaches have shifted during unmolding, gently nudge them back into place with spoon.)

4   Pour juice into now-empty skillet (handle may be hot). Stir in bourbon, if using, and cook over high heat, stirring constantly, until mixture is dark and thick and starting to smoke, 2 to 3 minutes. Return mixture to bowl and let cool until mixture is consistency of honey, 2 to 3 minutes. Brush mixture over peaches. Let tart cool for at least 20 minutes. Cut into wedges and serve.

ALL-BUTTER PIE DOUGH

makes: 1 nine-inch pie crust

total time: 15 minutes, plus
2 hours chilling

Use this easy dough to make tender,
flaky crusts for Apple Tarte Tatin
(page 318) and Peach Tarte Tatin
(page 320).

- 1 **cup (5 ounces) all-purpose flour**
- 2 **teaspoons sugar**
- ½ **teaspoon table salt**
- 8 **tablespoons unsalted butter, cut
  into ½-inch pieces and chilled**
- ¼ **cup ice water**

1 Line large, flat plate with parchment paper. Process flour, sugar, and
salt in food processor until combined,
about 3 seconds. Scatter butter over
top and pulse until irregular, large
chunks of butter form with some small
pieces throughout, about 5 pulses.
Add ice water and process until little
balls of dough form and almost no
dry flour remains, about 10 seconds,
scraping down sides of bowl after
5 seconds.

2 Turn out dough onto clean counter
and gather into ball. Sprinkle dough
and counter generously with flour and
shape dough into 5-inch disk, pressing
any cracked edges back together. Roll
dough into 9-inch circle, reflouring
counter and dough as needed. Loosely
roll dough around rolling pin and gently unroll it onto prepared plate. Cut
three 2-inch slits in center of dough.
Cover dough loosely with plastic wrap
and refrigerate until dough is very
firm, at least 2 hours or up to 2 days.

nutritional information for our recipes

To calculate the nutritional values of our recipes per serving, we used The Food Processor SQL by ESHA research. When using this program, we entered all the ingredients, using weights wherever possible. We also used our preferred brands in these analyses. Any ingredient listed as "optional" was excluded from the analyses. If there is a range in the serving size, we used the highest number of servings to calculate nutritional values. We did not include additional salt or pepper for food that's seasoned to taste.

	CALORIES	TOTAL FAT (G)	SAT FAT (G)	CHOL (MG)	SODIUM (MG)	TOTAL CARB (G)	DIETARY FIBER (G)	TOTAL SUGARS (G)	PROTEIN (G)
CHAPTER 1: BUTTER, SAUCES, & SEASONINGS									
Cultured Butter	103	11	7	41	31	1	0	1	1
Compound Butter	100	11	7	30	0	0	0	0	0
Chive-Lemon-Miso	100	11	7	30	0	0	0	0	0
Parsley-Caper	100	11	7	30	35	0	0	0	0
Parsley-Lemon	100	11	7	30	0	0	0	0	0
Tarragon-Lime	100	11	7	30	0	1	0	0	0
Crème Fraîche	52	6	4	21	10	1	0	1	1
Make-Ahead Homemade Mayonnaise	129	15	1	16	43	0	0	0	0
Aïoli	137	15	1	8	43	0	0	0	0
Saffron Rouille	135	15	2	13	25	2	0	0	1
Red Pepper Rouille	75	7	1	0	23	2	0	0	0
Foolproof Hollandaise	180	20	12	104	72	0	0	0	1
Foolproof Saffron Hollandaise	180	20	12	104	72	0	0	0	1
Mint Persillade	140	14	2	0	180	2	0	0	2
Chermoula	120	14	2	0	100	2	0	0	0
Green Zhoug	200	21	3	0	150	1	0	0	0
Caramelized Onion Jam	94	6	0	0	150	12	2	8	0
Herbes de Provence	5	0	0	0	0	1	1	0	0
CHAPTER 2: SNACKS & SMALL PLATES									
Baguette with Radishes, Butter, and Herbs	194	13	8	31	194	17	1	2	4
Lillet Tonique	222	0	0	0	50	54	1	51	0
Gruyère, Mustard, and Caraway Cheese Coins	258	18	12	48	222	18	0	0	12
Baked Brie with Honeyed Apricots	218	15	9	46	293	10	0	9	11
Gougères	88	6	4	46	82	4	0	0	4
Gochujang and Cheddar Pinwheels	170	11	5	30	170	13	0	1	5
French Kiss	35	0	0	0	2	1	0	0	0
Pissaladière	470	13	2	5	900	73	5	8	14

	CALORIES	TOTAL FAT (G)	SAT FAT (G)	CHOL (MG)	SODIUM (MG)	TOTAL CARB (G)	DIETARY FIBER (G)	TOTAL SUGARS (G)	PROTEIN (G)
CHAPTER 2: SNACKS & SMALL PLATES (CONT.)									
Socca with Sautéed Onions and Rosemary	245	15	2	0	325	20	4	5	7
Fennel, Olive, and Goat Cheese Tart	331	26	11	26	417	8	2	2	12
Chicken Liver Pâté	160	11	6	180	210	3	0	2	8
Marinated Olives	170	18	2	0	510	3	1	0	0
Pink Pickled Turnips	5	0	0	0	42	1	0	1	0
Pork Rillettes	390	32	17	110	550	4	1	1	16
Anchoïade	427	39	4	12	547	13	4	6	12
Oysters on the Half Shell	162	5	1	100	230	10	0	0	19
Lime-and-Soy-Marinated Scallions	4	0	0	0	110	1	0	0	0
Red Wine Vinegar Mignonette Granité	6	0	0	0	2	1	0	0	0
Roasted Oysters on the Half Shell with Mustard Butter	249	14	7	125	243	10	0	0	19
Salt Cod Fritters	170	10	4	65	1290	9	1	1	12
Broiled Shrimp Cocktail with Creamy Tarragon Sauce	202	17	7	111	434	2	0	0	11
CHAPTER 3: SALADS & SOUPS									
Herb Salad	107	8	1	0	98	11	6	0	2
Apple-Fennel Rémoulade	78	6	1	3	192	7	2	4	1
Creole Potato Salad	423	30	5	84	615	33	5	3	6
Bibb and Frisée Salad with Grapes and Celery	220	18	6	19	317	9	1	7	7
Bibb and Frisée Salad with Radicchio and Hazelnuts	150	14	2	0	125	6	4	1	3
Salade Niçoise	560	39	7	205	460	27	5	7	26
Easy-Peel Hard Cooked Eggs	72	5	2	186	71	0	0	0	6
Salade Lyonnaise	449	36	10	581	677	6	3	1	25
Perfect Poached Eggs	145	10	3	372	251	1	0	0	13
Crispy Lentil and Herb Salad	213	19	3	6	185	8	0	6	4
Carrot and Smoked Salmon Salad	221	11	2	9	682	23	6	12	9
Cauliflower Salad with Moroccan Chermoula	231	16	2	0	514	22	5	12	5
Wilted Spinach and Shrimp Salad with Bacon-Pecan Vinaigrette	450	31	7	170	1420	17	6	8	24
Brussels Sprout Salad with Mustard Vinaigrette	233	15	1	0	441	21	7	7	7
Artichoke Soup à la Barigoule	269	15	6	29	1108	28	8	5	9
Creamy Cauliflower Soup with Hawaij	270	24	4	0	740	12	4	4	4
French Onion Soup	604	31	15	68	1762	50	6	17	28
Soupe au Pistou	329	18	4	8	1067	31	7	4	13
Provençal Fish Soup	230	9	3	65	920	5	2	2	26
Lobster Bisque	628	33	18	373	2001	16	2	4	51

	CALORIES	TOTAL FAT (G)	SAT FAT (G)	CHOL (MG)	SODIUM (MG)	TOTAL CARB (G)	DIETARY FIBER (G)	TOTAL SUGARS (G)	PROTEIN (G)
CHAPTER 4: POULTRY									
Chicken Salad with Quick Pickled Fennel and Watercress	300	17	3	97	596	5	2	2	32
Seared Duck Breast with Orange and Blackberry Salad	290	8	2	85	980	31	6	22	25
Orange-Ginger Vinaigrette	70	4	1	0	150	9	0	7	1
Brie-Stuffed Turkey Burgers with Red Pepper Relish	676	31	13	161	967	54	3	32	45
Chicken Paillard	755	58	8	160	814	11	1	8	45
Leek and White Wine Pan Sauce	20	1	1	5	45	0	0	0	0
Dill and Orange Pan Sauce	90	8	5	25	130	3	0	2	1
Coq au Vin	1430	91	29	385	1440	20	1	8	93
Coq au Riesling	709	41	12	185	1507	20	4	5	49
Poulet au Vinaigre	469	33	10	167	697	6	1	2	28
Chicken with 40 Cloves of Garlic	734	53	18	274	1081	16	1	2	43
Chicken Provençal with Saffron, Orange, and Basil	677	46	12	234	1442	13	4	5	43
Chicken Bouillabaisse with Saffron Rouille	1109	70	12	176	1563	54	6	11	59
Croutons	130	3	0	0	290	23	0	0	3
Herbes de Provence Roast Chicken with Fennel	792	50	13	333	1243	15	7	7	72
Whole Roast Duck with Cherry Sauce	1999	185	62	357	1743	26	1	22	55
Duck Confit	330	22	6	145	690	0	0	0	32
Duck Confit Banh Mi	530	33	6	80	1610	37	2	10	22
Turkey Thigh Confit with Citrus- Mustard Sauce	964	74	24	220	1032	30	3	19	46
CHAPTER 5: BEEF, PORK & LAMB									
French Onion Burgers	923	59	28	246	1309	23	1	4	73
Grind-Your-Own Sirloin Burger Blend	599	45	20	207	408	0	0	0	45
Bistro Burgers with Pâté, Figs, and Watercress	705	37	14	318	896	39	3	15	54
Pan-Seared Steak with Brandy–Pink Peppercorn Sauce	723	55	24	171	181	6	1	2	44
Miso-Butter Pan Sauce	140	12	7	30	710	4	0	3	3
Creamy Black Pepper–Tarragon Pan Sauce	220	19	12	60	140	4	0	2	2
Steak au Poivre with Brandied Cream Sauce	768	57	27	239	988	5	1	2	47
Steak Frites	1644	139	40	179	1449	58	5	2	47
Pan-Roasted Filets Mignons with Garlic-Herb Butter	721	57	26	210	1061	11	6	5	44
Daube Provençale	910	63	23	220	1280	19	3	6	48
Pot Au Feu	1199	105	10	130	1200	20	5	5	41
Carbonnade à la Flamande	696	40	12	164	844	28	4	10	51

	CALORIES	TOTAL FAT (G)	SAT FAT (G)	CHOL (MG)	SODIUM (MG)	TOTAL CARB (G)	DIETARY FIBER (G)	TOTAL SUGARS (G)	PROTEIN (G)
CHAPTER 5: BEEF, PORK & LAMB (CONT.)									
Beef Burgundy	763	47	20	168	1389	23	3	6	48
Choucroute Garnie	732	62	22	133	1864	10	4	3	29
Braised Lamb Shanks with Bell Peppers and Harissa	676	41	18	175	1513	20	4	10	54
Cassoulet	940	41	14	155	1910	77	18	9	59
Pork and White Bean Casserole	650	38	12	85	1350	43	17	5	29
Enchaud Périgourdin	502	33	11	129	669	9	2	5	39
Enchaud Périgourdin with Port and Figs	534	33	12	130	637	18	3	11	41
French-Style Pork Stew	531	28	9	124	1025	25	4	6	44
Leg of Lamb en Cocotte	550	30	13	255	180	1	0	0	69
CHAPTER 6: SEAFOOD									
Oven-Steamed Mussels	526	19	6	142	1303	20	1	1	54
Oven-Steamed Mussels With Hard Cider and Bacon	622	31	10	167	1499	21	0	1	58
Oven-Steamed Mussels with Leeks and Pernod	645	23	5	134	1473	34	2	5	56
Scallops with Fennel and Bibb Salad	427	30	4	41	920	17	5	5	25
Sole Meunière	380	27	12	120	800	11	0	0	23
Pan-Seared Trout with Brussels Sprouts and Bacon	570	35	7	127	845	19	5	4	45
Seared Tuna Steaks with Wilted Frisée and Mushroom Salad	477	22	3	77	1213	17	5	6	55
Crispy Pan-Seared Sea Bass with Ramp Pistou	370	23	4	70	1270	4	1	2	34
Baked Scallops with Couscous, Leeks, and Orange Vinaigrette	524	18	3	41	964	58	5	5	28
Cod en Papillote with Leeks and Carrots	300	12	7	105	710	12	2	4	32
Halibut en Cocotte with Roasted Garlic and Cherry Tomatoes	326	16	3	100	721	5	1	2	39
Pomegranate-Roasted Salmon with Lentils and Swiss Chard	473	33	6	95	1000	42	10	10	47
Roasted Salmon with Orange Beurre Blanc	491	38	15	122	461	5	2	1	30
Monkfish Tagine	178	7	1	28	529	8	2	3	20
Bouillabaisse	570	21	3	90	1880	48	4	10	31
Garlic-Rubbed Croutons	270	9	1	0	456	40	2	4	8
CHAPTER 7: VEGETABLE MAINS									
Savory Fennel-Apple Tarte Tatin	740	46	19	5	600	76	6	23	16
Upside Down Tomato Tart	98	4	2	5	310	15	2	10	2
Nettle and Mushroom Galette	490	33	16	90	660	36	3	3	11
Mushroom Bourguignon	341	15	2	1	1351	28	6	9	13

	CALORIES	TOTAL FAT (G)	SAT FAT (G)	CHOL (MG)	SODIUM (MG)	TOTAL CARB (G)	DIETARY FIBER (G)	TOTAL SUGARS (G)	PROTEIN (G)
CHAPTER 7: VEGETABLE MAINS (CONT.)									
Walkaway Ratatouille	178	11	2	0	752	19	6	9	3
Campanelle with Porcinis and Cream	470	17	10	45	280	63	5	4	17
Gnocchi à la Parisienne with Pistou	741	63	25	228	611	23	1	1	23
Foolproof Cheese Fondue	767	38	22	120	888	49	2	5	42
Tartiflette	649	42	21	110	924	41	5	5	22
Grown-Up Grilled Cheese Sandwiches with Comté and Cornichon	487	31	18	88	719	29	2	4	21
Grown-Up Grilled Cheese Sandwiches with Gruyère and Chives	491	31	18	92	753	29	2	4	24
Grown-Up Grilled Cheese Sandwiches with Cheddar and Shallot	489	31	18	88	719	30	2	4	21
Grown-Up Stovetop Macaroni and Cheese	520	23	12	55	679	52	2	5	25
Individual Cheese Soufflés with Frisée and Strawberry Salad	420	32	14	245	690	12	2	6	20
CHAPTER 8: VEGETABLE SIDES									
Pan-Roasted Asparagus	105	6	3	7.5	563	10.5	4.5	4.5	4.5
Blanched Green Beans with Mustard Vinaigrette	170	14	2	0	240	8	3	3	2
Modern Cauliflower Gratin	199	14	9	35	493	12	4	4	9
Celery Root Purée	156	9	6	28	396	17	3	3	3
Bacon, Garlic, and Parsley Topping	42	4	1	7	65	1	0	0	1
Fennel Confit	747	81	11	0	400	7	3	4	1
Leeks Vinaigrette	196	14	3	3	243	14	2	3	4
Roasted King Trumpet Mushrooms	140	11	7	30	300	7	0	5	3
Red Wine–Miso Sauce	100	3	2	10	430	7	0	4	1
Brown Butter–Lemon Vinaigrette	110	11	7	30	180	2	0	1	0
Lemony Roasted Radicchio, Fennel, and Root Vegetables	242	7	1	0	369	42	9	13	6
Sautéed Radishes with Vadouvan and Almonds	106	8	4	15	305	7	3	3	2
Vadouvan Curry Powder	60	3	0	0	11	9	3	1	3
Easier French Fries	599	43	8	2	759	50	6	2	6
Chive and Black Pepper Dipping Sauce	143	16	3	12	108	1	0	0	0
Thick-Cut Sweet Potato Fries	655	47	8	6	721	55	7	9	4
Potato Galette	177	7	5	19	300	26	3	1	3
Duck Fat–Roasted Potatoes	319	13	4	13	649	47	6	2	5
Pommes Purée	367	30	19	80	441	22	2	3	4
CHAPTER 9: BRUNCH & BREAD									
Omelet with Cheddar and Chives	380	30	14	602	435	2	0	1	26
Ham, Pear, and Brie Omelet	533	40	19	650	982	9	1	4	34
Kale, Feta, and Sundried Tomato Omelet	424	34	17	616	520	6	1	2	24

	CALORIES	TOTAL FAT (G)	SAT FAT (G)	CHOL (MG)	SODIUM (MG)	TOTAL CARB (G)	DIETARY FIBER (G)	TOTAL SUGARS (G)	PROTEIN (G)
CHAPTER 9: BRUNCH & BREAD (CONT.)									
Fluffy Omelet	386	27	13	413	660	8	1	3	28
Asparagus and Smoked Salmon Filling	60	3	0	5	170	5	2	3	5
Mushroom Filling	45	2	0	0	151	5	1	3	2
Galettes Complètes	616	41	22	424	725	31	3	7	32
Eggs Benedict with Foolproof Hollandaise	900	80	40	665	1320	18	0	2	26
Gravlax	170	9	2	37	176	7	0	7	14
Eggs Pipérade	412	31	6	372	1034	20	7	11	16
Croque Monsieur	794	51	28	172	1937	38	4	7	46
Croque Madame	906	60	31	363	2008	39	4	7	52
CHAPTER 9: BRUNCH & BREAD (CONT.)									
Potatoes Lyonnaise	285	12	7	31	601	42	5	2	5
Oven-Cooked Bacon	315	30	10	50	500	1	0	1	10
Brioche French Toast	480	20	10	175	490	59	0	21	11
Mimosa	135	0	0	0	6	14	0	10	1
Lemon Ricotta Pancakes	117	6	3	46	117	11	0	5	4
Pear-Blackberry Pancake Topping	223	1	0	0	79	55	7	42	1
Apple-Cranberry Pancake Topping	219	1	0	0	77	57	12	37	2
Yeasted Waffles	333	17	10	94	315	36	1	5	8
Chocolate-Orange Crêpes	415	17	9	164	241	54	2	26	12
Chocolate Brioche Buns	401	19	11	87	282	51	3	13	9
Almost-No Knead Bread	250	0	0	0	580	52	0	0	7
No-Knead Brioche Sandwich Loaf	170	3	1	95	250	29	1	5	8
Authentic Baguettes at Home	130	0	0	0	290	28	0	0	4
CHAPTER 10: DESSERTS									
Chocolate Pots de Crème	440	36	21	175	105	30	2	10	6
Whipped Cream	60	5	3.5	15	0	1	0	1	0
Chocolate-Cardamom Cake with Roasted Pears	310	16	10	80	105	42	2	29	4
White Chocolate Mousse with Raspberry Sauce	741	53	31	238	106	61	2	58	9
Profiteroles with Chocolate Sauce	403	24	15	44	77	49	3	42	5
Crème Brûlée	567	49	29	382	104	28	0	27	6
Crème Brûlée with Orange Blossom	570	49	29	382	104	27	0	27	6
Gâteau Breton with Apricot Filling	577	27	16	199	157	78	1	50	6
Crème Anglaise	110	5	2	130	55	12	0	11	4
Orange Crème Anglaise	110	5	2	130	55	13	0	12	4
Grand Marnier Soufflé	206	8	4	131	131	25	0	20	6
Apple Tarte Tatin	368	18	11	46	227	52	3	34	2
Peach Tarte Tatin	310	15	10	40	220	40	2	26	3
All-Butter Pie Dough	170	11	7	30	150	14	0	1	2

conversions & equivalents

Some say cooking is a science and an art. We would say that geography has a hand in it, too. Flours and sugars manufactured in the United Kingdom and elsewhere will feel and taste different from those manufactured in the United States. So we cannot promise that the loaf of bread you bake in Canada or England will taste the same as a loaf baked in the States, but we can offer guidelines for converting weights and measures. We also recommend that you rely on your instincts when making our recipes. Refer to the visual cues provided. If the dough hasn't "come together in a ball" as described, you may need to add more flour—even if the recipe doesn't tell you to. You be the judge.

The recipes in this book were developed using standard U.S. measures following U.S. government guidelines. The charts below offer equivalents for U.S. and metric measures. All conversions are approximate and have been rounded up or down to the nearest whole number.

EXAMPLE:

1 teaspoon = 4.9292 milliliters, rounded up to 5 milliliters
1 ounce = 28.3495 grams, rounded down to 28 grams

VOLUME CONVERSIONS:

U.S.	Metric
1 teaspoon	5 milliliters
2 teaspoons	10 milliliters
1 tablespoon	15 milliliters
2 tablespoons	30 milliliters
¼ cup	59 milliliters
⅓ cup	79 milliliters
½ cup	118 milliliters
¾ cup	177 milliliters
1 cup	237 milliliters
1¼ cups	296 milliliters
1½ cups	355 milliliters
2 cups (1 pint)	473 milliliters
2½ cups	591 milliliters
3 cups	710 milliliters
4 cups (1 quart)	0.946 liter
1.06 quarts	1 liter
4 quarts (1 gallon)	3.8 liters

WEIGHT CONVERSIONS:

Ounces	Grams
½	14
¾	21
1	28
1½	43
2	57
2½	71
3	85
3½	99
4	113
4½	128
5	142
6	170
7	198
8	227
9	255
10	283
12	340
16 (1 pound)	454

CONVERSIONS FOR COMMON BAKING INGREDIENTS:

Baking is an exacting science. Because measuring by weight is far more accurate than measuring by volume, and thus more likely to produce reliable results, in our recipes we provide ounce measures in addition to cup measures for many ingredients. Refer to the chart below to convert these measures into grams.

Ingredient	Ounces	Grams
Flour		
1 cup all-purpose flour*	5	142
1 cup cake flour	4	113
1 cup whole-wheat flour	5½	156
Sugar		
1 cup granulated (white) sugar	7	198
1 cup packed brown sugar (light or dark)	7	198
1 cup confectioners' sugar	4	113
Cocoa Powder		
1 cup cocoa powder	3	85
Butter†		
4 tablespoons (½ stick or ¼ cup)	2	57
8 tablespoons (1 stick or ½ cup)	4	113
16 tablespoons (2 sticks or 1 cup)	8	227

* *U.S. all-purpose flour, the most frequently used flour in this book, does not contain leaveners, as some European flours do. These leavened flours are called self-rising or self-raising. If you are using self-rising flour, take this into consideration before adding leaveners to a recipe.*

† *In the United States, butter is sold both salted and unsalted. We generally recommend unsalted butter. If you are using salted butter, take this into consideration before adding salt to a recipe.*

OVEN TEMPERATURES:

Fahrenheit	Celsius	Gas Mark
225	105	¼
250	120	½
275	135	1
300	150	2
325	165	3
350	180	4
375	190	5
400	200	6
425	220	7
450	230	8
475	245	9

CONVERTING TEMPERATURES FROM AN INSTANT-READ THERMOMETER:

We include doneness temperatures in many of the recipes in this book. We recommend an instant-read thermometer for the job. Refer to the table above to convert Fahrenheit degrees to Celsius. Or, for temperatures not represented in the chart, use this simple formula:

Subtract 32 degrees from the Fahrenheit reading, then divide the result by 1.8 to find the Celsius reading.

EXAMPLE:

"Roast chicken until thighs register 175 degrees."

To convert:

175°F – 32 = 143°

143° ÷ 1.8 = 79.44°C, rounded down to 79°C

seared duck breast with
orange and blackberry salad
(page 96)

index

Note: Page references in italics indicate photographs.

fennel confit
(page 236)